DESTINATION
UNKNOWN

An Evacuee's Story

GAY M. GRANT
and
Pat North

DESTINATION UNKNOWN
An Evacuee's Story

©2014 Gay M. Grant

ISBN: 978-1-63381-014-3

Goodnight Children Everywhere
Words and Music by Harry Arthur Phillips and Gabriel Rogers
Copyright (c) 1939 J. NORRIS MUSIC PUBLISHING CO.
Copyright Renewed
All Rights Administered by UNIVERSAL MUSIC CORP.
All Rights Reserved Used by Permission
Reprinted by Permission of Hal Leonard Corporation

Designed and produced by
Maine Authors Publishing
558 Main Street, Rockland, Maine 04841
www.maineauthorspublishing.com

Manufactured in the United States of America

This book is dedicated to the memory of
Peter Reginald North, 1928–2000
&
Gail Shirley Parker, 1952–2012

CONTENTS

ACKNOWLEDGMENTS

Having taken nearly two decades to finish, this book would not have been written without the help of many individuals, and I deeply apologize to anyone I may have forgotten to include here. First, heartfelt thanks go to Pat for her friendship, and for placing her trust in me to write her story and write it the way it needed to be written. The book's dedication to Peter cannot contain the gratitude I feel toward him for his help in the research, in taking me back in time and making the history of the war period come alive in my imagination. The friendship the three of us shared as we delved together into their past transcended an ocean and a generation that separated us. I will be forever grateful. Peter didn't live to see the book finished, but in many ways the writing of this story immortalizes him for me in a way nothing else ever could.

To Clare Hadwell, I owe thanks for making any of this possible in the first place. Had she not insisted that I come to England in the fall of 1979, I would have missed so much, including the lifelong friendship between us that stands to this day. Her parents, Jean and Charles Hadwell, also have my gratitude for their years of friendship and hospitality, and for their help with this project from the start. They arranged interviews with former evacuees and former host families in the Abberley area so that I could gain insight and perspective into how Pat's evacuation experience compared with those of others who lived during this pivotal time in history. Accordingly, I thank former evacuees Warren Grimes and Ray Bolwell, and the former host families of Mrs. Jones and Mrs. Beaman for sharing their stories. I also thank the Norths' former next-door neighbor and evacuee George Rovai for sharing his memories of being an inner-city London kid transported overnight to the verdant Hampshire countryside.

No one researches history without the invaluable help of librarians and museum curators—and most of this work was done in pre-Internet days! First and foremost, thanks to Hazel Morey, a dear friend of the Norths, and at the time I began this research, she was recently retired as reference librarian for the Hampshire County libraries. I also wish to thank Phillipa Stevens of Hampshire County Library in Winchester and Alan King of the Portsmouth Central Library. Additionally, museum curators and research assistants at the Imperial War Museum in London and the Royal Marines Regimental Museum in Portsmouth have my sincere appreciation.

I also wish to thank friends and family who gave feedback on earlier drafts. These include Cathy Sears, Spencer Sears, Rinaldo Colby, Melissa Orth, and Logan Johnston. My sister, Bonny Saxon, was a reader and also transcribed all of my interview tapes, a truly Herculean feat. My writing group, Sister Elizabeth Wagner and Annabelle Baldwin, provided much-needed editorial comment and encouragement. To Genie Dailey of Fine Points Editorial Services, friend and editor extraordinaire, I trusted you with my words and you made them mind their "P's and Q's." Thank you to Dorcas Miller, my friend and writing colleague at the Write Way, for your wise counsel and encouragement that helped me to finish this last leg of a long writing marathon.

During the early drafts, when the book was intended for a young adult audience, Debora Marceau, an eighth-grade teacher at the Gardiner (Maine) Regional Middle School, allowed me to share the manuscript with a group of students who gave me feedback to make the book stronger for young adult readers. I promised those students that when the book was published, their names would be in the Acknowledgments, and though they are now adults, a promise is a promise, so thanks to Marcello Genovese, Erica Wysocki, Alecia Lorance, Lauren Sirois, and Haley Williams.

Sisters Bernadette and Elizabeth at Transfiguration Hermitage have my gratitude for the peaceful hospitality of their Retreat Center where this book was finally finished. Our dear friend, the late Gail Parker, is also remembered in the Dedication of this book because she and her husband, Al, became part of the North/Grant family through their love and friendship. Our trip together in 2006 to visit so many of the places in this story provided me with inspiration and memories I shall always cherish. Soon Gail's memory will be honored with the Hermit-age's permanent chapel. It is all so woven together!

My children, Aaron Grant and Melody Grant Santos, are part of this story too; they literally grew up with this book project! I know that for them having Pat as their "English grandmother" has been a great gift. Melody did an amazing job editing this final manuscript. I would not have finished without her work and her encouragement. She is a writer of great skill and I look forward to doing the same for her someday. I also thank my mother Sylvia Harriman Myshrall for her encouragement of my writing, for helping me get to England that first time, and for teaching me to believe that I can accomplish anything I set my mind to.

To my husband Ron I owe my deepest gratitude. It takes a special man to welcome a stranger into his family, embracing this friendship with Pat as much as me, and even building an addition on our house! He supported all the trips to England, the years of writing and rewriting, and kept me going when I was ready to throw in the towel. His years of reading books about the Second World War also made him my most valuable reader, ensuring that my military references were correct. He is part of it all, and truly is 'the wind beneath my wings.'

"All wars, just or unjust . . . are waged against the child."

—EGLANTYNE JEBB
Founder of British Save the Children Fund, 1919
(From the Children in War exhibit, Imperial War Museum, London)

PROLOGUE:
How It All Began

This book is about healing and the power of friendship. Though it starts with the Second World War, seen through the eyes of a child, it is also the story of a unique, three-thousand-mile friendship that formed a generation later. The project began eighteen years ago as a book for young people about the wartime memories of Patricia Phillips North, a British war evacuee. It has evolved into a memoir of an unlikely friendship between Pat and me. Our friendship helped Pat find within herself the courage to delve into painful memories of a childhood and adolescence forged in wartime. Before the book was even written, this friendship would set both Pat and me on new journeys, some of which we would travel together.

Whenever Pat North from Winchester, England, visits my family and me here in Maine, people ask how we met. What they really want to know is this: How can two women, separated by a generation, from two different countries and widely different lives, be such close friends? It's a curious thing, to be sure, but for us, it feels completely natural.

This journey began in 1978. When I was a sophomore at the University of Southern Maine, I befriended an English exchange student named Clare Hadwell. Clare spent the better part of two months trying to convince me that I *had* to go to England the next year on exchange to her school, King Alfred's College in Winchester. I was the oldest of five children from a working-class family and the first to go to college. I had no money that I could spare from my education expenses. Not to mention I'd never traveled outside of New England.

One day, Clare showed up in my dorm room with application

forms for the British exchange program.

"Here, fill these out," she said.

"You are nothing if not persistent," I said. "I'll fill them out to shut you up, but I won't be coming to King Alfred's College in September. I'll be lucky to get back here for another semester. I won't be able to come up with that kind of money."

"You only need a plane ticket, and whatever travel money you can get," she responded. "You pay the same tuition and room and board as if you're coming here again because you just literally change places with a KAC student. You'll never regret it. Coming to America has been the best thing I've ever done. It will change your life."

I did fill out the forms, and I was accepted to the program. Unexpectedly, I had the opportunity for a full-time office job over that summer, in addition to my numerous housecleaning jobs. The trip began to look possible after all. My family members all pitched in when I held a giant lawn sale to raise cash for travel. So it was that on September 3, 1979, at the age of 19, I left the U.S. for the first time in my life, aboard a plane for London. That trip did change my life. And it wasn't until I was working on this book and reread my journal from that time that I noticed the date I left America for the first time was September 3rd. It's also Pat's birthday, and the date the Second World War had started.

On the morning of September 4, 1979, twenty-four of us from the University of Southern Maine and the University of California at Long Beach arrived in Winchester. We were welcomed to Denstone House, a large three-story stone house a few minutes' walk from the King Alfred's College campus. We were introduced to three English ladies who would be looking after us during the first three weeks of our stay, two called Pat and one called Nora. One of the Pats was Pat North. The three women were friendly and motherly and immediately began to help us get acclimated to our new surroundings and to "translating" English words. The old saying "two great nations divided by a common language" took on a whole new meaning for us.

The fall school term at King Alfred's wouldn't begin for three weeks. All of us American students planned to travel during this time, some to Europe and others to destinations within Britain. I'd saved enough to buy an unlimited-mileage Eurail Pass, but otherwise had no idea where I was going or with whom I would travel. I didn't know any of the other American students, but I figured I would hook up with others going abroad and we would get a plan together. I titled my journal for that period "Innocent Abroad," paraphrasing the title of the Mark Twain novel, and looking back I see how true that was.

On the day my fellow exchange student Nancy Champagne and I headed out with our backpacks, intending to catch the train from Winchester to Dover, then the ferry to Calais, France, we were full of expectations and ideas, but we didn't even know how to get to the local train station! Pat North was horrified that we were taking off to parts unknown with no idea how to look after ourselves. She tried to convince us to stay in Winchester and explore the region from there, but we would not be dissuaded. Exasperated, she finally took us to the station in her tiny car, imparting all the motherly advice she could possibly cram into that short drive. Thankfully, we had a wonderful three weeks traveling in France and Switzerland, and came back safe and sound to Winchester in time for the school term.

After that initial three weeks, we lived among the English students in other houses. I lived in Christchurch House and had an American roommate, Anne Harrison (now Anne Jordan, who is still one of my dearest friends). I traveled across Britain on the weekends, and spent lots of time with Clare, of course. During that time, we cemented our life-long friendship, and her parents, Charles and Jean Hadwell, graciously took Anne and me on a three-day "culture soak" of their native stomping grounds, the West Midlands, around Worcestershire.

I didn't see Pat North again that fall until all of us American students were moved back to Denstone House for the remaining two weeks between end of term and our departure for home. It was in this brief period just before Christmas in 1979 that I struck up my friendship with Pat. She told me all about her husband, Peter, who was a policeman, just like my own father, and all about her four children. The only one still living at home was her youngest son, Patrick.

Pat also told me of her plans to someday come to America. "You'll have to come visit me," I said, as people do in that situation. The day before we left, I remember Patrick sitting on my suitcases to help me close them. He happily took my "real American jeans" so I could make space for the Christmas presents I was bringing back to my family and friends! I didn't meet any of the other Norths, and frankly never expected to see any of them—or the other students—again.

After I was married in 1980, my husband, Ron, and I saved for a year for a honeymoon in England in 1981, staying with the Hadwells on Hayling Island, off the coast of Portsmouth. We drove through Winchester, but didn't stop to see the Norths. In 1986, Ron and I were living in our hometown, in our first house, with our three-year-old son, Aaron, and our year-old daughter, Melody. I'd regularly received cards, letters, and parcels from Pat with hand-knit sweaters for my children, but I figured after seven years the idea of her actually coming to America had really been just a fantasy. Then she called and said, "I'm finally coming to America. Will it still be all right to visit you?" Peter didn't want to travel—he never did—but since she would be traveling on her own, he wanted her to have a home base in the States.

"What do you want to see while you're here?" I asked.

"The Statue of Liberty, Niagara Falls, the Grand Canyon, Florida, and the Pacific Ocean." she said.

"How long do you plan to stay?"

"About six weeks," she said.

I thought, What on earth am I going to do with a 54-year old English housewife I barely know for six weeks in this small town in Maine with two little kids and just one car that my husband has to take to work?

But what I said was, "Of course you can come." We'd work out the details later.

From that first day, in July of 1986, Pat fit right in with our whole family. We managed to arrange visits for her with friends and family across the country so she could see a lot of that ambitious list of hers during that first visit. Among the first to be checked off were the Statue of Liberty, the Grand Canyon, and Niagara Falls. After that, Pat made pretty much annual visits, splitting the six weeks between visiting with us and traveling across the U.S. She very quickly became part of our large extended family and made many friends here who looked forward to her annual visits as much as we did.

On one of those visits, during the winter of 1992, the First Gulf War was in full swing in the deserts of Kuwait. One evening, Ron, Pat, and I were watching the television news. Our children, then ages eight and six, were sitting on the floor coloring. From the TV, as an Iraqi Scud missile hit Tel Aviv, the eerie sound of an air-raid siren filled our living room. Pat suddenly stopped knitting and sat motionless, her eyes fixed on some distant point in the room.

"Pat, are you all right?" I asked, concerned.

When I spoke to her, she shivered a bit, put down her knitting, and, looking at my children, she said, "I was about their age when I was taken away from my mother and was evacuated during the war. War was declared on my seventh birthday. September third, 1939."

Though I had studied British history in college, I knew very little about the evacuations of children.

"What do you mean, 'taken away from your mother?'" I said.

"Do you remember the C. S. Lewis *Narnia* series, when the children are leaving London and going to live with the old gentleman in the big house? They were evacuees, and so was I," she said. "And there's that Disney movie with Angela Lansbury, *Bedknobs and Broomsticks*. Those children were evacuees, too."

"I thought it was just kids from London who were moved during the Blitz," I said.

"No. Cities like Portsmouth, where I lived, were also bombed. I haven't thought about it for years, not until I heard that air-raid siren. You never forget that sound."

"Do you want to talk about it?"

"Not really," she said. "Maybe sometime."

Though the writer in me sensed a story, I let the subject drop. I thought that perhaps such a deep and long-buried wound might be too painful to reopen, and I decided not to revisit the topic unless she brought it up.

It was another three years before Pat began to talk to me about her wartime and evacuation experiences. In May of 1995, a series of events and celebrations took place all across Britain to mark the 50th anniversary of Victory in Europe Day, followed by Victory in Japan Day in August. That milestone celebration saw many folks of that generation begin to tell their own wartime stories to family, friends, and historians. That winter of 1996, when Pat made her annual visit, she began to talk to me about her childhood experiences during the war, and I began to take down some notes.

In October of 1996, I made the first of three research trips to England. Ron and I had taken the children to visit Pat and Peter and their family in the fall of 1992, but this was my first solo trip since 1979. I focused my research on Pat's experience, and on gathering background information about the British government's evacuation program. Not surprisingly, I had found very little on the subject here in the United States, as this was prior to the ease of research on the Internet. I sent Pat a list of the books I wanted to read but couldn't find in America, and their friend Hazel Morey, a research librarian for Hampshire County, found all of them, and they were waiting for me the day I arrived. This saved me many hours and gave me a solid grounding for the subject as we began to delve into Pat's experiences in more detail.

Peter drove us all across Hampshire County, where Pat has lived her entire life. Most importantly, we went back to the house to which Pat had been evacuated. She had not been back since shortly after leaving her host family. Pat and I also went up to London to the Imperial War Museum for background information.

With the assistance of Charles and Jean Hadwell, who by this time had moved back to Worcestershire, I was also able to interview two other former evacuees and two host parents. I made additional research trips in 1997 and 1998, until I had developed a draft manuscript. My goal then was to write a book for young adults about the evacuation, focused on Pat's experiences and the experiences of the others I had interviewed on that trip. During those intensely focused visits, going back in time over their war memories and the history of their courtship, I became very close friends with both Peter and Pat.

Pat took copies of the early manuscript to share with the teachers at the local schools when they invited her to speak to their classes about her evacuation experiences as part of their "War on the Home Front" curricula. These teachers found my research invaluable as they tried to bring this period of British history alive for their students. U.S. publishers showed no interest in the manuscript, and I had no idea how to go about publishing the book in the UK. Self-publishing, then called "vanity press," was prohibitively expensive. However, I continued to polish and market the manuscript as a labor of love and respect for Pat.

Being the witness to Pat and Peter's history took our friendship to a whole different place. Somehow I went from an observer and recorder to a participant in their story. Those events three thousand miles away, a generation before I was born, changed the trajectory of my own life, and the life of my family. Our stories are now intertwined.

Pat's friendship has been one the most treasured gifts of my life. She is such an integral part of our family that we cannot imagine her not being with us. Though the book was originally intended as a narrative history for young people, after seventeen years of rewrites and format changes, I present here the original manuscript, along with what dozens of friends have called the perhaps more interesting "story of the story," as I journeyed with Pat and Peter back to the days that changed the world, their lives, and mine forever.

Transfiguration Hermitage, Windsor, Maine
December 12, 2013

INTRODUCTION

On a September morning in 1940, eight-year-old Patricia Phillips and her thirteen-year-old brother, John, became "evacuees," leaving their native city of Portsmouth to settle in the country village of Bramdean. During World War II, nearly four million people across Britain—one quarter of the nation's population—left their homes in cities and coastal areas for safer places in the countryside. Some fled Britain altogether, going to Canada, New Zealand, Australia, the United States, and other countries far from home. Families who had the means to leave or send their children away did so on their own. Those who could not afford to leave on their own, or who did not have friends or families outside the country to sponsor them, depended on the government to move them to safety. Roughly two million mothers and children, the sick, elderly, and disabled were moved from their homes under the British government's evacuation scheme. This first mass movement of people from London, Portsmouth, Birmingham, and other large cities took place over a period of several days before war was officially declared on September 3, 1939.

A year later, Portsmouth and other large British cities endured a month of particularly heavy air attacks by the German Air Force (the Luftwaffe), and this important seaport and military city was bombed beyond recognition. Throughout the summer of 1940, there were rumors of a German invasion. After the British Channel Islands came under Nazi occupation, invasion was felt to be an imminent threat. The Phillips family and thousands of others living along the vulnerable south coast of England were faced with a life-or-death choice whether to evacuate their children as the government was exhorting them to do. Should they continue to risk the death or injury of their children in the bombing, or send them away to live with complete strangers? This was a terrible choice to make, and Pat's mother and father wrestled with it for more than a year before deciding there was no longer any choice at all if they wanted their children to survive.

Like millions of her fellow evacuees, Patricia Phillips North kept her evacuation experiences to herself for most of her life. Though Pat and John became very close during their stay with the Barter family in Bramdean, and John took very seriously his mother's charge to look after his little sister, the two never discussed their experiences later, as adults. John never spoke of those years with his wife, Joan, or his three daughters. Pat reflected many years later on why this was so. There were too many painful memories, she told me, and by the end of the war, after six long years of uncertainty and loss, everyone was anxious to move on and rebuild what they could of their lives.

In 1995, when the world celebrated the 50th anniversary of the end of the war, many people like Pat, who had endured the hardships of World War II looked back on those years and began to share their stories with their children, grandchildren, and anyone interested in knowing what it was like to live through the most destructive war the world has ever known. British schools now regularly invite former evacuees to visit their classrooms and share their war experiences with students as part of their history lessons.

Naturally, after so many years, events and dialogue presented in this book have had to be reconstructed from Pat's childhood memories. In the years since my first draft, the use of "invented dialogue" in non-fiction, particularly for young people, has gone in and out of fashion. When Pat read this manuscript she said simply, "It's like you were there. I can hear their voices!" I don't know how much more authentic I could make it. I present it here in the way that feels most immediate and present to me. Today it's called "creative nonfiction."

The names of the teachers, with the exception of Miss Carpenter, are fictitious, since Pat no longer remembers their actual names. The essence of her experience is related here as she remembers it. The evacuation came at a formative time for her. Pat hopes that her experiences will shed light on this unique time in history before stories like hers are lost with her generation. Her story shows the resilience of the human spirit, and that the most awful circumstances can bring unexpected blessings.

—Gay M. Grant

Chapter One

The Gathering Storm

Six-year-old Patricia Phillips slid out of bed and set her favorite doll, Topsy, on the chair next to her bed. The little doll sat rigidly on the neatly pressed Sunday clothes Pat's mother, Nora, had set out the night before. Topsy had dark brown skin and three tufts of black yarn for hair, one over each ear and one poking straight up from the middle of her head. The doll's eyes opened when she was upright and closed when she was laid down, and Pat took her everywhere she went. It was the last Sunday of August 1939, and Pat's birthday was just a week away.

"Next Sunday, I'll be seven," she told the little doll. Pat liked the sound of saying "seven" out loud. "I wonder what my present will be?" she asked the doll. "Mum has been sewing my school dresses. Perhaps she's made you some new clothes to match."

Pat carefully made her bed so there would be no wrinkles in the bedclothes. Her mother had taught her how to tuck in the corners so there were no creases. She kissed Topsy and placed the doll on the bed in front of the pillow, and put on her dressing gown and slippers. "I'll come get you when we're ready to go to Sunday school."

In the kitchen, Pat's 12-year-old brother, John, was sitting at the table finishing his breakfast. Her father, Arthur, and her mother, Nora, were having their tea at the kitchen table reading the newspaper. Arthur looked up when Pat came in.

"Good morning, Pat, how are you this lovely morning?"

"Fine, Dad, thanks," she said.

She hugged her father, said good morning to her mother and brother, and sat down to her breakfast. The family ate in their usual, companionable silence. After breakfast, her mother told her to hurry along and get ready for Sunday school. As Pat was leaving the kitchen, she heard her father say to her mother, "Churchill was right. The Germans have rearmed and no one's stopping them. The paper says the Prime Minister has signed an agreement with Poland. If the Germans try to take over Poland like they did Austria, we'll be going to war again. I don't know who's going to come to our assistance."

"What will that mean for you?" Nora asked.

"I haven't had any new orders yet, but something's coming; they're calling up the reservists," Arthur said.

"The schools aren't opening for the fall term," Nora said. "They've been evacuating the kids by schools—in the care of just the teachers, mind you—out into the country somewhere."

"Then let's go down to Clarence Pier today," Arthur said. "The way things are going, who knows when we'll get another chance. Besides, Pat's birthday's next week."

Pat went upstairs to dress in her Sunday clothes. She wondered what her father meant by another war. She wanted to ask what *evacuating* meant, but she didn't want her mother to know she'd been eavesdropping. Her mother always said children didn't ask questions about grown-up matters. Pat wondered what her mother meant about there being no school, but the prospect of going to the seafront pushed all other unpleasant thoughts away.

Pat's father was in the Royal Marines, stationed with the Portsmouth Division at Eastney, and he served aboard His Majesty's Ship *Victory*. Corporal Arthur William John Phillips had joined the marines at the age of 14, in February 1918, as a member of the Boy's Brigade. Now he was 36, a bugler in the Marine Band, and also played the drums. His red hair and freckles had earned him the nickname "Ginger" from his shipmates. He had told Pat and John all about training new recruits out at Whale Island in the "gun run." He described how the men took apart the big cannons and reassembled them under time drills and in competitions.

Arthur had gone up to London once on the King's birthday for a parade at the Centograph at Whitehall. He told the family how the bands played and paraded before the royal viewing box, where the King and Queen watched. Arthur often told stories of his sea adventures to Pat and John, usually when they were all working in the garden together.

He spent hours polishing the brass buttons on his uniform, and his boots were polished to such a sheen that Pat could practically see her reflection in them. She loved to sit on the floor beside him; the smell of the shoe polish and the sound of his brush buffing his boots formed a backdrop for his stories of the faraway places he'd been —Gibraltar, Malta, Tripoli, and other exotic-sounding ports of call.

Pat knew the names of all the ships her father had served on: the *Tiger*, the *Cairo*, the *St. Vincent*, and the *Dolphin*. Now he served aboard the *Victory*, made famous by Admiral Lord Nelson. He'd earned medals, too. In 1922, he received the British War Medal. When Pat was very young, her father was sometimes away at sea for months at a time, as the marine bands played for special occasions all over the Commonwealth. When he came home, he told the family colorful stories of the big parades and official occasions for which the Marine Band had played. He was a wonderful storyteller, and could always see the humorous side of any situation. Despite his frequent absences, Pat was very close to her dad. She especially liked to help him in the garden.

Whenever Arthur was going to sea again, he would tell John, "You're the man of the house now, so help your mother and look after your sister." For John, keeping an eye on his little sister was one of his main responsibilities. Today, as on every Sunday, John would walk Pat to the church a few blocks from their house.

"Come on, Pat, or we're going to be late, as usual," John called up the stairs. Pat hurried down and followed John out the front door, clutching Topsy in her arms.

As the pair turned out of 41 Highgate Road, they walked along the row of terraced houses lining the streets of their neighborhood. Pat liked to sneak a look into the front windows of the other houses as they passed, though she was careful not to appear to be snooping. She liked to see how each front room was arranged. All the houses in the neighborhood had the same style bow-front windows in their front rooms. People rarely used their front rooms except for holidays or for entertaining special guests. Nora's piano and her Chinese tea set held pride of place in the Phillipses' front room. Arthur had brought the tea set home for his wife when he returned from one of his longer sea trips, before Pat was born. It was real Chinese porcelain, delicately hand-painted with exotic Asian scenes. Pat had never seen her mother actually use the tea set.

Pat held John's hand as they walked the streets toward the church. That was one of their mother's strictest rules. They walked "properly," without running or skipping, because it was Sunday, and that is how they were taught to behave on Sundays.

According to Nora, "nice children" did not play on the street on Sundays. There were other rules for what they could and could not do. Nora was a stickler for all sorts of rules. Pat loved Sunday because it was family day and only the most necessary chores were done. In the evening, or if the weather was foul, they played family games indoors. Charades and Hide-the-Thimble were typical, but Patricia's favorites were Ludo, Snakes and Ladders, and "Shove Ha'penny."

Occasionally, the family would go across the city to visit their Grandfather Thompson, Nora's father. They didn't visit him often, but whenever they did, he would give Pat and John a shilling for pocket money. Grandfather Thompson was a large, jolly man who loved to tease and tell jokes. This was funny to Pat because her mother seemed so serious most of the time. Grandfather Thompson worked for a moving company called Humphries, along Commercial Road.

Nora often said with evident pride that her father was so well thought of at Humphries that he was given the trickiest moving jobs, like pianos out of second-story windows. "He can move anything out of anywhere, no matter what the size of the furniture, or how small the doors and windows," she might say. Grandmother Thompson had died when Pat was a baby.

By far, Pat's favorite outing was a walk along the seafront, and on this particular Sunday she could hardly concentrate on her coloring at Sunday school for thinking about going there. The class seemed to drag before the teacher assembled them for final hymns, the recitation of the "Our Father," and dismissal. Pat practically skipped all the way home, and the only reason she didn't run was because John wouldn't allow her to.

That day, the family took a bus to the seafront to "promenade" and have a picnic. Portsmouth was a bustling place, with the marine barracks at Eastney, where her father worked, the Royal Naval Barracks across from grand Victoria Park, and the Royal Dockyard at Portsea, where naval ships were built and repaired. The city's busy docks were full of vessels of all sizes, bringing people and cargo from all around the world.

Arthur told his children that Britain's very lifeblood depended upon the thousands of merchant ships that carried goods in and out from all over the world. It was the job of the Royal Navy and Marines, he said, to make sure the shipping routes were safe. Portsmouth was also a busy spot for tourists during the summer, with its beaches and grand hotels lining Southsea Common and the ever-popular Clarence Pier.

As they got off the bus, Pat felt in her coat pocket the pennies she'd been saving for the penny arcade. John had his pennies, too, and she could hear them jingling in his pocket as she held his hand on the way to the arcade. They were delighted to meet their close family friends George and Lillian Parker in front of the arcade. Pat was always glad to see the Parkers, whom she and John called Uncle George and Aunt Lil. The adults talked while Pat and John waited impatiently to be given permission to go into the arcade to play the coin-operated games.

"Are you going to evacuate your kids?" Uncle George asked.

"No, we're going to wait and see what happens," her dad replied. "It's voluntary, at least for now."

"Most of the schools aren't going to open for the autumn term. How will you keep them occupied, Nora?" asked Aunt Lil. "The newspaper and wireless are full of it, where the kids are to meet up with their classes and teachers and what they're to bring. Most of our other friends with children are sending them out. They're terrified of what might happen if they don't."

"You know well enough that my children have been taught to be useful, and I have the name of a woman over in Copnor Road who is a retired teacher offering to conduct lessons for some of the children who aren't going out. I will make arrangements and keep them at home until I see exactly what is going to happen," Pat's mother said.

"If you ask me, Hitler's not going to keep any of the promises he made to Prime Minister Chamberlain. All that talk about 'peace in our time' is a load of rubbish," Uncle George said. "Especially now Hitler's signed a deal with Stalin in Russia."

Pat didn't want to hear any more. She didn't understand any of it. She walked to the window of a shop on the pier and looked at the trinkets and postcards in the crowded little window. She was confused by all of this talk about war. She looked up at the "Fish & Chips" sign above the next window. The shop was closed, as were most of the shops on Sunday. The adults said their goodbyes, and in a few minutes, Pat's father came up beside her as she continued peering into the shop window.

"How about an ice cream cone?" he said.

Arthur bought them each a cone at the little pushcart on the promenade, and the family stood together by the bandstand in the late afternoon sunshine to enjoy their treat. The salty taste of the sea air mingled with the sweet ice cream on Pat's tongue. She relished every lick and tried to make it last as long as she could before it began melting down her hand. She knew her mother would be cross if she got ice cream on her Sunday clothes. After they had finished their ice cream, Pat and John spent their pennies in the arcade, and the family walked to the bus stop near Clarence Pier to begin the journey home.

The following week passed quietly, and Pat counted the days until her birthday. Meanwhile, she helped her father pick the vegetables in their allotment garden each evening. Every day, her mother was busy preserving the vegetables and fruit they'd grown. The allotment gardens were communal public gardens for growing food, and their father's garden was not too far from their house, beyond the Southern Railway lines. There was a footbridge over the railroad tracks at Saltern's Crossing, near the Sports Ground. To get to the allotment, they walked, rode bikes, or, if they needed to, pulled a wagon. Beyond the allotment were the clay pits and the brick works.

Mr. Marchant, their next-door neighbor and friend, also had an allotment garden. When Arthur was out to sea, Mr. Marchant tended both allotments, and the two families shared their produce. Mr. Marchant was a quiet man, tall and thin, and he wore very thick glasses. He worked at the Royal Dockyard. Mrs. Marchant was a short, plump lady with thick, sturdy legs. She was friendly, laughed a lot, and loved to talk. She and Nora often chatted over the garden wall while they pegged out their washing or tended their flowerbeds. Occasionally the two ladies went inside one of their kitchens for a cup of tea. Mrs. Marchant was the only friend Pat saw her mother spend any time with, apart from their Aunt Lil. The Marchants had two children, Alan, 12, and Nora, seven.

That Friday, her mother and Mrs. Marchant stood and chatted by the low brick wall that separated their two gardens. Pat and little Nora had their dolls spread out on a blanket nearby.

"What do you think, Nora, about this evacuation scheme?" Mrs.

Marchant asked.

Pat pretended not to be, but she was listening to their conversation.

"We're not going to do anything until we see what happens," her mother said. "The war hasn't even started yet, and they're already evacuating the children. I'm not going to have strangers take care of my children. There's no telling what kind of people they might end up with," she said, pegging a shirt on the line and pausing to make sure the children weren't listening. Pat's eyes were on her doll, but her ears were glued to what her mother was saying. "My kids will be safer at home with us."

"If we wait and the Germans start dropping bombs, like everyone says they will, what'll we do with the children then? Where will they go to school if the war lasts longer than a few weeks? Will they still be able to find places for them in the country later if we wait?" Mrs. Marchant sounded very worried.

"Pat, please go into the house and bring me some more pegs," her mother said.

When Pat came back with the pegs, the train was just coming. She and young Nora ran to the back of the garden to sit on the garden wall and wave to the conductor as the train passed. The conductor always blew the horn and waved if he spotted them.

This time the train was full of children looking out the windows as if they were on a school trip or going on a holiday. A few children waved when Pat and Nora waved to them, and Pat thought she recognized some of the older girls from her school. All the children were wearing paper tags on their coats.

"Where are they going?" little Nora asked.

"I don't know. John says it's an e-vac-u-a-tion," Pat said, sounding out the word as she said it. "He said most of the kids are going away because of the war." She felt grown-up and quite superior because she knew things Nora didn't know.

"What's a war?" Nora asked.

But Pat didn't really know what to tell Nora about that, so she said, "Let's not talk about it anymore. Let's go see if your mother has any biscuits so we can have a tea party with Topsy and the other dolls."

"Okay," Nora said, and they went inside to gather the things for their tea party.

The next morning was Saturday—just one more day and it would be Pat's birthday. After she had done her chores, she and little Nora went out front to play hopscotch.

"Are you going to the Fun Fair for your birthday tomorrow?" Nora asked, sounding as if she would like to be invited along.

"No. Mum and Dad want to be home for something on the wireless at eleven o'clock. We might play games, too." Pat tried not to sound too disappointed about the Fun Fair. "We went to the seafront last week, anyway," she added.

"Do you know why we can't go to school?" Nora asked.

"Something about the Germans and a war," Pat said. "Mum said she found a lady who's going to give us lessons at her house until school opens again, but it won't be at the school. Are you and Alan coming with us?"

"Yes," said Nora. "I like being able to play all day, after chores. It's better than going to school."

Mrs. Marchant came out to their front door and called Nora in for lunch.

Pat rode her three-wheeled bicycle up and down the pavement, between the three lampposts that served as her boundary markers. She wished her mother would let her ride farther. The other girls her age in the neighborhood could ride the whole length of Highgate Road, but Pat's mother said she couldn't go past the third lamppost.

As she rode, she wondered, now that she was about to turn seven, if perhaps her mother would let her ride to the end of Highgate Road. She knew better than to argue with her mother. She would ask, but she would wait for a moment when her dad was home—her mother was more likely to say yes when her dad was there. He always told them "ask your mother" if they asked him directly.

As she reached the third lamppost at the corner of Seafield Road, Pat saw John and Alan coming home from their cricket game. They and the other neighborhood boys had been playing at the far end of the road, where it backed onto the tall brick wall surrounding the school ground. Sometimes the boys went up to the cricket pitch at the Sports Ground, but mostly they used the end of the road where there was little traffic. Few people in their neighborhood owned cars anyway. The boys used chalk to mark out where the wickets would be on the road.

Pat wished she were allowed to go wherever John went. She rode her bicycle up to meet them, but they kept walking and talking, taking little notice of her.

"I bet your dad will be going off again, when the war starts," Alan said. "My dad says it can't be far off now, since the Germans marched into Poland yesterday."

"I wish I was old enough to join up for the army," John said.

"Me too," Alan said. "I don't miss school much, though, do you?"

"Not really," John said, "but it's kind of boring with nothing to do."

"My mum seems to find me plenty to do. Yours is even worse," Alan said. "But I suppose that's because your dad is down at the barracks so much."

"Everyone's talking about the evacuation and all the kids going out to the Isle of Wight. In the newspaper, it said thousands went out from Pompey and Gosport to the Isle of Wight, Chichester, Droxford, Winchester, and Eastleigh. One story said they were all singing as the bus pulled out of the station, like it was some holiday caper."

"I've never been to the Isle of Wight, have you?"

"No," John said. "Mum told Dad she thought they'd all be home in a week. I still think it would have been fun to go."

Pat parked her bike in their front garden, closed the gate behind her, and followed John in for lunch.

"Let's go down to Woolworth's and the Land Port Drapery this afternoon," her father said as the family ate their Saturday lunch. He finished work at midday on Saturdays. "Both Pat and John need new coats for winter, and we can look to see what's there," he added, putting down his newspaper.

"I have a few nice pieces of cloth already, but there are a few other items on my shopping list we can take care of," her mother said.

Pat liked to go to the shops, though she did not like riding the bus very much. After lunch, the family walked the few blocks to the bus stop and rode to busy Commercial Road. Many of the city's largest department stores were located there, such as Woolworth's, C & A, and Timothy White's. The Land Port Drapery Bazaar was the star attraction.

A large family department store, the Land Port Drapery's long row of front windows always featured colorful displays of the very latest merchandise. Pat and John looked at the toy displays while their parents carefully examined the clothing and household goods. People were busily coming in and out of the shops, laden with packages as the Phillips family stood outside, window-shopping. It seemed to Pat that everyone did their shopping on Saturday, there were so many people bustling about.

She rarely saw her parents actually buy any of the things they saw in the shop windows. They made whatever they could themselves—both of her parents could knit and sew. Her father could also carve or build practically anything out of wood. They had taught John and Pat to knit and sew, and Pat made hats and scarves for her dolls and was learning to make dishcloths.

"That style coat would suit Pat," her mother said to her father as they examined the winter coat display in the window of the Land Port Drapery. "I've taken apart that green coat your sister gave me. The lining material was in perfect shape, too, so we have the material we need, even the buttons."

"That will work," her father said. Neither of them asked Pat what she thought, but she looked longingly at the bright red coat in the shop window.

"I have a length of navy blue that will do for John. That color doesn't show the dirt," her mother said.

Arthur sketched a picture with a tiny stub of a pencil on the little notepad he always carried in his pocket. First he drew the coat on the little girl mannequin, and then he sketched the one Nora had pointed out on the boy mannequin. Pat knew what would happen when they got home. Her dad would take his notes and make a sketch on a bigger piece of paper. Next, he'd measure her and then John, and then he and her mother would make paper patterns out of pieces of old newspaper taped together. The newspaper pattern would then be carefully laid out on whatever piece of fabric her mother had found on a sale or from some other garment she had carefully taken apart. Arthur would do the cutting and Nora would sew on the machine in the kitchen that also served as their living room. The end product wouldn't always be the same as the displays in the shop windows. Sometimes it was even better.

Because of their careful money management, her parents had been able to buy their house, not rent as most of their neighbors did.

They were very proud of this fact, and told their children often, "Waste not, want not." Pat's father told them that when you owned your own house, it was yours and no one could take it away from you.

When Arthur was a boy, his father fell out of a boat while drunk and drowned off Horsea Island. Arthur's mother and sisters had to go into the workhouse. Arthur was sent into the Marines' Boy's Brigade, and the little money he made was sent back to his mother so the family could pay their debts and get out of the workhouse. Pat had never seen the workhouse, but she could tell it was a very horrible place. Her dad assured her that no such thing would ever happen to them. That was why he and Nora worked hard and took good care of their money, and why he never drank alcohol. He often said, "Drinking is a waste of money and leads to no good."

When Arthur was at sea, during his off-duty hours he would knit, carve, or sew gifts to bring home. Most of the gifts he brought back were handmade and something they needed, or a clever toy he'd seen in one of his ports of call and copied for them. Once, someone's cast-off fur coat became Teddy bears for Pat and John. She still had hers and loved its soft brown fur. Arthur saved his chocolate rations to bring home, too. The marines were also given a rum ration, but Arthur traded his for more chocolate to bring home to his children.

After supper and chores that evening, the family played Hide-the-Thimble until their favorite programs came on the wireless. The news on the wireless was all about the German army's march into Poland and the Prime Minister's speech that was expected the next day. There were evacuee kids sending greetings to their parents, telling how wonderfully they were doing in their new foster homes in the country. Pat was waiting for the good programs to come on. She saw her parents look at each other, but they didn't say anything, and that made her stomach feel all jumpy, though she didn't know why. She tried to think about her birthday the next day instead.

* * * *

"There's the birthday girl," her dad said when Pat came into the kitchen for breakfast on Sunday morning. She had already taken a peek at the lovely birthday cake on the china plate on the table in the front room. She hugged her father and sat down to the table. Her mother and brother both wished her "happy birthday and many happy returns of the day," and they ate their breakfast as usual.

"I made cucumber and watercress sandwiches," her mother said, "and we can eat our lunch out in the garden today." She seemed to be making an effort to act cheerful this morning.

"We'll have to listen to the Prime Minister's speech on the wireless before lunch, then," her father said.

"You don't have to go to Sunday school this morning," her mother said. "You and John can go out into the garden after breakfast if you want."

After the breakfast dishes were done, Pat and John took their toys outside. John took his lead army men and Pat put Topsy in her little doll's pram.

"Why is everybody so nervous about the Prime Minister's speech?" she asked John.

"There's going to be a war with Germany. There's nothing for it now. The Germans marched into Poland and the Prime Minister gave them an ultimatum to get out or we'd fight to help the Poles," John said. "But you're too young to understand any of this."

"I understand some," she said. "But what's an ultimatum?"

"If I tell you 'do this or else I'm going to sock you one,' then that's an ultimatum," he said. He began to arrange his lead army men in battle formations on the little hill of dirt near the flower border.

Pat thought for a minute about what John had said. "Why do the Germans want to march into Poland if it's not their country?" she asked.

"Because there's a bad man named Adolph Hitler running Germany now, and he thinks he can just push everybody around and take over all of Europe. Friday, he marched his Nazi troops into Poland. We promised the Poles we'd help them, so if the Nazis don't march back out the way they came, we've got no other choice. You have to stand up with your friends," he said.

"Will Dad have to go away, like Alan said?" Pat asked.

"Maybe," John said. "Dad said he thinks he'll be helping to train the new recruits out at Whale Island at the Gunnery School, so we might see him at night like we do now. But you're too little to worry about that stuff. Anyway, I'll look after you."

"I'm not little! I'm seven today!" Pat protested.

Their parents came out to the garden and Arthur organized a game. At a few minutes before eleven o'clock, her father stopped the game and they all went inside to listen to Chamberlain's speech on the wireless. Pat watched her father's face as the voice came from the wireless, but his face was without expression. Her mother sat motionless as the Prime Minister's voice crackled into the room from London, and Pat thought that his voice sounded very sad and tired.

> This morning, the British ambassador in Berlin handed the German government a final note, stating that unless we heard from them by eleven o'clock that they were prepared at once to withdraw their troops from Poland, a state of war would exist between us. I have to tell you now that no such undertaking has been received, and that consequently, this country is at war with Germany...

Following Prime Minister Chamberlain's words was the long wail of an air-raid siren. Pat's father reached over and switched off the wireless. He didn't say a word, just looked at her mother.

"Let's have our lunch out in the garden, then," her mother said.

When Pat went out to the garden, she heard church bells ringing all over the city. Her parents and John came out behind her, carrying the picnic. The sound reminded Pat of the bells ringing on New Year's Eve at the stroke of midnight. Her parents had let her stay up this year to hear them. Today, the bells made her shiver a little. She didn't get that happy feeling listening to the bells ring now, as she had on New Year's.

"Why are the bells ringing?" she asked her father. He looked at her mother a moment before answering her.

"They won't ring again until the end of the war, unless the Germans invade. Don't worry about that. The Germans will never touch foot on British soil. Life is going to change for a while, though. You have to promise me that you'll help your mother all you can. All of us will have to do our bit, even you children."

As Pat walked Topsy down the path to the back of the garden, she heard her parents talking.

"It's begun," her father said. "People say it will be over by Christmas, but I don't think so."

"Let's talk about it later," her mother said.

That day, the family did all of the usual birthday rituals. They played games, ate cake, and sipped lemonade, and Pat opened her gifts. But she could feel that something had changed. It no longer felt like the celebration she'd so looked forward to. She had no idea what a war was. She only knew the war had spoiled her seventh birthday.

Chapter Two

The Country Prepares for War

As soon as war was declared, Pat's family and people all across Britain prepared for war as best they could. Her father needed to get things done at home quickly, so there was a frenzy of activity, and Pat found herself getting more and more anxious.

"There is one bit of good news," she heard her father tell her mother a few days after her birthday. "Churchill's back as First Lord of the Admiralty. The signal came across the wires, 'Winston's back,' and all the men at the barracks cheered. Churchill never trusted the Germans after Hitler came to power. If they'd listened to him, we wouldn't be in the state we are now." Her father tossed the paper on the table and reached for his tea.

"How bad is it, Arthur?" her mother asked quietly.

"They've got about twice as many planes, their U-boats are fast and deadly, and our ships are sitting ducks. It'll take some doing to catch up. Meanwhile, the Americans are reminding everyone they are still neutral and aren't getting into this European conflict. The French aren't going to be much help. It's like we've all been asleep," he said, running his hands through his now slightly graying red hair.

"The poor Poles were on horseback when the Nazis rolled into Warsaw in armored tanks," he added quietly.

"We'll catch up, we've got to," her mother said. "Meanwhile, I can take care of things here. You worry about your work."

"They're coming around with bomb shelters soon, and I'll get that dug in, then you'll have to carry on from there. You've got John to help. If things get bad, I trust you'll use your judgment about this evacuation scheme."

"For now, I'm staying and the kids are staying. I need to be here for you, and I'm not prepared to send them to God-knows-where."

"It may not come to that; we'll have to wait and see," her father said.

A few days later, John helped their mother put sticky tape on all the windows. Nora showed John on the kitchen window how to place a taped X across each windowpane, and Pat was told to help him.

"Why are we putting tape on all the windows?" she asked as she handed him the strips of tape to put on her own bedroom window.

"If a German bomb lands nearby and shatters the window, the tape will keep the broken glass from blowing all through the room," he said. "Hand me those scissors, will you?"

"Why do the Germans want to bomb us?" she asked. She really didn't know what a bomb was, but it sounded pretty awful.

"I don't think we'll have to worry about them bombing our house," he said. "They've got bigger targets, and they'll have to get through the RAF first."

"What's the RAF?" she asked.

"The Royal Air Force," he said. "I saw some Spitfires overhead the other day."

When they'd finished taping all of the windows, they went down-stairs to see if lunch was ready. Their mother was at the sewing machine, surrounded by yards and yards of heavy black fabric making curtains. These "blackout curtains" would have to be tightly closed each night before the lights could be turned on, their mother told them.

"Not a single ray of light can escape to the outside," she warned, "or a warden will come around and we'll have to pay a fine."

When Pat was alone with John again, she asked, "Why can't we let any light out?"

"Because the Germans, if they get this far, will see the light and use it for a target for their bombs," he said.

A few nights later, men in boiler suits wearing tin hats with "W's" taped on the visors came around their neighborhood with clipboards and pencils in their hands. Pat was coming down the stairs and stood there staring when her mother opened the door to the man who came to their house.

"We're from the ARP, that's Air Raid Precautions, ma'am. We're seeing that everyone has blackout curtains up. Your windows look very good indeed," the man said, tipping his steel helmet.

"Thank you," her mother said.

"I wish I could say the same for everyone in the neighborhood. People don't seem to realize that we're in a war here. A German pilot hundreds of feet overhead can see a single lighted match. People will take it seriously when they get slapped with a five-hundred-pound fine or two years in prison," the ARP Warden said. "Have a nice evening." He tipped his helmet again as he left, headed to the next house on the street.

Every night as Pat lay in bed in the total darkness, she heard the wardens patrolling the neighborhood. "Put that light out!" she heard them shout. She wondered how a lighted match could be seen from so high up in the sky. All the changes around her made her uneasy. Sometimes when she overheard people talking about the war, she felt sick to her stomach with fear. Still she had to listen because she was curious, even though she often wished afterward that she hadn't heard.

She especially hated the dark; she wasn't used to it. Before the war, lights glowed all over the city and shined through the thin net curtains that had hung in her bedroom. She never remembered it being so dark before. So she hugged Topsy all the more tightly as she lay in her bed at night. In the early days, her mother let her put a torch next to her bed. As batteries became more expensive and scarce, though, Pat had to do without the light. Her mother said she'd just have to get used to the dark.

Cars and lorries had to have metal covers screwed over the headlamps, with just three or four slits angled toward the street. They didn't provide much light at all, so the running boards on the sides of vehicles were painted white to make them more visible to other drivers and pedestrians. Pat overheard her mother tell Mrs. Marchant that more people would be killed in road accidents than by German bombs.

Everyone was issued a gas mask, and all were required to carry it with them wherever they went. The masks fit inside boxes with string handles. Little children's gas masks were made to look like Mickey Mouse, with ears and goofy eyes, so they wouldn't be afraid to put them on. Pat's was a smaller version of the adult gas mask.

"Dad, what do I have to wear this for?" she asked her father as he was showing her how to put it on.

"In the last war, the Germans put bad things in the bombs—a gas you can't see but will make you very sick if you breathe it. If they drop bombs with gas here, you'll need this. If you're told to put this on, do not ask questions, just do it," he said.

"Yes, Dad," Pat said. She knew this was serious. She put her gas mask on and her father put on his, but when they looked at each other, they couldn't help laughing.

"You look like a big housefly," Pat said.

"You see, it's nothing to be afraid of," her father said, taking his mask off.

Pat was glad to take hers off. It was very hot with it on, and her face had started to sweat. Both of their faces had red marks where the rubber had been pressed to their faces.

"I hope we never have to wear them," she said.

"We probably won't use them at all, so don't worry. But it's best to be prepared."

Soon big lorries came around the neighborhood unloading large pieces of ribbed metal. When bolted together at the top, these parts formed a U-shaped dome about the size of a small garden shed.

"What's this?" John asked his father as the family looked at the huge monstrosity sitting in their garden.

"It's called an Anderson shelter, named after the Home Secretary, Sir John Anderson. He heads the part of the government in charge of health and education and home front plans. It's pretty clever, and very simple. We're going to dig a hole over there, at the side of the garden, put this frame over it, and pack sandbags on top. If this area is ever bombed by the Germans, this will keep you safe."

John helped his father dig a hole about eight feet square and three feet deep for the Anderson shelter. It was at the end of the garden path, just a few feet from the garden wall. Arthur put boards on the bottom of the hole for a floor, and John helped him fit the metal shelter over the floor, like a domed tent with metal ribs. Arthur dug steps down into the shelter from the lawn and put a thick blanket over the entry to serve as the door. He said he would replace the blanket with a proper door later, to help keep out the noise and weather and to make it safer.

Over the roof of the shelter, their father and John placed large sacks filled with the dirt that had been dug from the holes. Pat held the bags while her mother scooped shovels full of dirt into them. Over this layer of sandbags, the men packed the remainder of the dirt. Later, her father even planted flowers on the top—a "rockery," he called it.

"Why are we planting flowers on top of the shelter?" Pat asked as she handed him the plants to set in the dirt.

"No sense it being more of an eyesore than it has to be," he said. The shelter in their neighbors' yards looked just like mounds of earth. "It can either look like that," he said, pointing to the shelter mound next door, "or it can look like this."

When they were finished, her father stood up, brushed the dirt from his hands and said, "That's it, then, all 'ship-shape and Bristol fashion.'"

Pat thought it looked like a playhouse with a garden for a roof. At the bottom of the shelter's steps, most adults had to bend down a little to go inside, but her father had dug the hole deep enough so that he and her mother could stand up inside. Neither of them was very tall anyway. Her father and John built a small set of bunk beds along one wall. Next to them they placed a small table and a chair.

Pat helped her mother carry in blankets, candles, torches, bottles of water, and tins and jars of food and other supplies. Inside the house, her mother had fitted out the cupboard under the stairs as a bomb shelter, as well.

"This cupboard will do in a pinch, if we haven't time to get out to the Anderson shelter," she explained, as they filled the cupboard with a few essential supplies.

One day, Pat's mother and Mrs. Marchant were pegging out their wash on the clotheslines and chatting over the garden wall while Pat and little Nora played nearby. Naturally, Pat's ears were tuned in to their conversation.

"They won't take my husband in the services because of his bad eyes," Mrs. Marchant said. "He feels terrible, of course, wants to do his duty same as everyone else. But I can't help being relieved. But once the bombing starts, which they keep saying could happen any day, the dockyard will be a target anyway."

"There are signs all over town telling men and women to sign up for the services. I'm not sure where my Arthur will be yet, but they're keeping some marines in port to protect the dockyard and in case of invasion. He's training new recruits now," her mother said.

"There are a lot of women going to work in the factories, working at farms as 'Land Girls,' so the men can enlist. They're calling it the Women's Land Army. Women are enlisting in the services, too," Mrs. Marchant continued.

"The Queen was on the wireless saying we women have to do our part on the home front, too," Pat's mother said. "If the bombs start falling, there won't be much difference between the front and the home front. I don't know who would look after my kids and keep my house going if I tried to do that, but I have signed up for Red Cross work while the kids are having their lessons."

"I'm glad you found that teacher for the kids. I was worried about them falling behind," said Mrs. Marchant. "I'll be joining you with the Red Cross. Say, your Arthur's done a real nice job on your Anderson shelter. Ours isn't so fancy, but it will serve if it has to."

"Let's hope we don't have to use them at all," her mother said, as she pegged up the last piece of clothing in her wash basket.

"It's been quiet so far, hasn't it?" Mrs. Marchant commented, shaking out a towel to peg on her line. "It's eerie, just watching and wondering when and if something's going to happen. The Lord Mayor in the paper said he was concerned to see so many kids in the city not evacuated, but I heard someone at the shop saying some of the evacuees are coming back home, seeing as no bombs have dropped on the city."

"I heard the same thing," her mother said. "The kids were homesick and wetting the beds every night, so people say. I'm not surprised. What does the Lord Mayor know about children?"

After the two women went back into their houses, Pat and little Nora pushed their dolls up and down the garden path in Pat's doll pram. They heard the train coming and ran to the garden wall to watch it pass. Pat wondered how her schoolmates were doing out in the country, wherever that was. She was glad she didn't have to go away, but she missed her favorite teachers from school.

Every day, she and John, little Nora, and Alan walked to Mrs. Q's house for their school lessons. They used the sitting room and were joined by some other children from their neighborhood who hadn't been evacuated. They did a bit of reading and some arithmetic, but mostly they just drew pictures and colored. Mrs. Q had a piano in her front parlor and she played patriotic songs they all sang together, like "God Save the King" and "Rule Britannia," and some hymns from a dilapidated hymnbook borrowed from the nearby Copnor Road Church. When Pat finished her work, she was allowed to play with a little farmyard set, so she hurried through her assignments so she'd have more time to play. It was certainly not like the work they'd done in real school.

Even at Mrs. Q's, the children had to do gas-mask and air-raid drills. Since she lived on her own, Mrs. Q didn't have her own air-raid shelter, so they practiced walking quickly to the nearest bomb shelter, which was on the street corner. There were street shelters all across town now, and piles of sandbags started to appear on every street. Mrs. Q's husband was an officer in the marines, and her son was in the marines, too. Her daughter had joined the "Wrens," the Women's Royal Naval Service, she explained.

After their school lessons in the morning, Pat and John came home for lunch and spent the remainder of the day helping their mother with household chores. During their free time, Pat and the other girls in her neighborhood who hadn't been evacuated played hopscotch and jumped rope as they had done before the war.

Sometimes Pat rode her three-wheeled bike as far as she was allowed to on the pavement in front of their house. Since the war had started, it seemed to her that her mother was even more anxious to keep her and John close to home. She was allowed to play at Nora Marchant's or with girls across the street, but otherwise she had to be with John at lessons or Sunday school or at Miss Cannoway's for her dance classes. John walked her everywhere.

In the evenings, the family sat and listened to the wireless. Each night, there was bad news from Europe. German U-boats were attacking merchant ships trying to bring goods to Britain. Pat's mother explained that it was absolutely vital to keep the shipping lanes around Britain clear, but it was getting harder to do. Though her father was stationed at Portsmouth, more and more nights he stayed at the barracks, resting between training and coast watches. He went out on ships in the Channel, as well.

Defense of the coastline became critical, and people grew even more nervous after a disaster in Scapa Flow, off the coast of Northern Scotland near the Orkney Islands. On Saturday, the fourteenth of October, a German U-boat sneaked past heavy defenses at Britain's massive northern naval base. Pat had never seen her father as upset as he was after that terrible attack.

"A torpedo pierced the outer shell of the battleship *Royal Oak* as it lay at anchor. More than eight hundred men went down with the ship. Fewer than half the crew survived," Arthur said, his voice shaking. "Right in Scapa Flow. No one saw that U-boat coming and no one thought that a single torpedo could rip through the hull of a heavily armored battleship."

John was very upset listening to his father. He and his friends hardly talked of anything but the war, and he desperately wanted to do something more to help defeat the Germans. Pat often heard him say he wished he were old enough to join the service. That night, with his father so upset about the *Royal Oak*, he took his chance.

"Can I join the Local Defense Volunteers, Dad?" he asked.

"No, son, you're not old enough yet. Your mother needs you here, as I will soon be going out to sea again. Right now, the Defense Volunteers are mostly older men who served in the Great War or men who have other reasons they can't join the services. I'm hoping this war will be over before you're old enough to enlist or be conscripted."

John protested, "I'm almost thirteen. I could help patrol the seafront. My eyes are probably better than the old fellows they have down there now. Some of my friends who are Boys Scouts are training to be stretcher carriers or help with the fire department."

Pat had seldom heard her brother argue with either of their parents before, and she listened wide-eyed.

"I need your help here, John" their mother said. "I know you want to be doing other things, but I'll soon need your help even more."

Something in the tone of her voice made John stop, and the conversation was ended. Pat soon found out what had made her mother so firm about needing more help: she would be having a new baby sometime in February.

The cold, wet days of late autumn settled into short November days. Pat's mother had finished making the dull pea-green coat Pat was to wear for the winter, and unless she grew too much, the next winter, as well. She asked her mother if she couldn't at least have pretty red buttons on the coat. "The very idea!" her mother said dismissively. "You'd look like a Christmas tree and stick out like a sore thumb. At least you've got a coat, which is more than we can say for those poor London kids evacuated out to the country in nothing but the clothes they stood up in."

Pat didn't say another word about the pea-green coat, but she hated wearing it and felt guilty for feeling that way, especially when she heard her parents talking about what her father had read in the newspapers.

"Some of those kids from London and Birmingham went out to the country without anything to keep them warm for the winter. It said in the paper the government had to give the host families fifteen-pound vouchers to buy coats and hats and boots," her father said.

"Mrs. Marchant was saying the other day about the poor kids no one would even take, troubled kids or ones with wheelchairs and so forth. They've built a bunch of special camps, 'hostels,' they call them, to house them in. Imagine what the parents think of that!" her mother said.

"For some of those kids, it's probably better than they had at home," her father observed. "Still, members of Parliament are getting complaint mail by the sack-full, it said in the paper the other day. The foster families are complaining because all these kids have been dumped on them without proper clothes, and heads full of lice, and the parents are in the cities missing their kids and want them back. It's a right mess, if you ask me."

"I'm not getting our kids mixed up with that scheme," her mother said firmly, and that was a big relief for Pat.

As Christmas approached, her father was gone much of the time, and the family was never sure when they would see him. Despite the grim news on the wireless, her mother tried hard to maintain their normal family life. When their jobs were finished and the evening meal had been cleared away, they still sat in the kitchen-living room and played games together as they had always done. Pat hardly noticed the time pass when she was involved in their games.

At other times, they sat and listened to their favorite programs on the wireless, and their mother would help Pat and John with their sewing or knitting projects. Nora was knitting wool socks for the Red Cross, and Pat helped her wind the yarn into balls. Before the lights could come on, all the blackout curtains had to be drawn and tucked into place.

John and Pat and their classmates at Mrs. Q's spent a lot of time making Christmas decorations out of scraps of paper and string, and added Christmas carols to their daily singing of patriotic songs. They learned a bit about geography, with a big map spread out on the table. The older boys liked to line their lead toy army men on the map and mark out the latest battles of the war. Mrs. Q assured the children that Britain would win the war.

With Christmas just a few days away, everyone seemed to need a reason to be cheerful. Pat and John decorated the house with the paper chains and decorations they'd made at Mrs. Q's. Nora was busy finishing her sewing and knitting projects and getting ready for the new baby. She'd sent John up to the loft to get their old baby clothes out of storage, and she'd washed and ironed them and put them in the dresser in the front room. An old baby cot had been placed in the front room, too, and a small crib placed upstairs in Nora and Arthur's bedroom. Pat's father worked more late hours at the training ground. Still, their mother reminded them, they were lucky to have their dad home for Christmas this year, or at least for part of it. That was more than many families could say.

Christmas Eve was on Sunday, so on that Saturday, Arthur came home at midday and took Pat and John to the Charlotte Street Market to help him carry home the Christmas feast. At about four o'clock, just an hour before the stalls lining each side of the street were due to close for the day, the prices came down and the sellers were anxious to get rid of their perishable foods. Arthur found a lovely fat turkey for their Christmas dinner because the man at the stall was selling it cheap. It was fun for Pat to listen as her father haggled over the price with the man at the poultry stall.

The stalls along Charlotte Street sold every imaginable thing from vegetables to teapots. Market days were usually Wednesdays and Saturdays, but this Saturday was special because it was the day before Christmas Eve. Despite the war, there was a festive mood among both sellers and buyers. The people behind the stalls called out as customers came by, "Come get your fresh turkey," and "Practically giving away these lovely cabbages." Their father made the necessary purchases for the Christmas feast and for Boxing Day, and soon their bags were full and the stalls were being cleared away. The last stop was the baker's stall, and as a treat, their father bought them each a hot Cornish pasty to eat before they got back on the bus with all their bags.

Christmas day, the family sat by the Christmas tree in the front sitting room and opened their few gifts. They feasted on turkey and roasted potatoes, and Nora had made a Christmas cake with marzipan icing. They had their Christmas stockings from Father Christmas, each with an orange, some nuts, and some chocolates. John also had a comic book and some new toy army men for his collection, and Pat had a feeding set for her baby doll, and her mother had made some new clothes for the baby doll and for Topsy. They each had new mittens and scarves, and Pat had a new balaclava hat with tassels on the ties.

That evening, the family sat in the living room and listened to the King's annual Christmas speech on the wireless. There were several kids who had been evacuated out of London sending "Happy Christmas" messages home to their parents, and saying how well they were doing. According to the news, hundreds of children and teenagers who had been evacuated in August and September had come home to be with their families for Christmas, if their families could afford to bring them home. John had talked to several of his friends who had gone out of Portsmouth and come home for the holidays.

"Some of my friends said they aren't going back out to their foster families again, no matter how many bombs fall on the city," John told the family. "Others are having the time of their lives and can't wait to go back."

After the wireless switched to music, the family played a few games of Hide-the- Thimble, and then had a light tea with cold turkey sandwiches and cake. The Marchants came over, and the two families gathered in the front sitting room to sing Christmas carols. Pat's mother played the piano and everyone sang along. There was a toast to peace and a moment of silence before the two families parted and the children went to bed.

The next day was Monday, but it was Boxing Day, and while their father had to get back to Whale Island, Grandfather Thompson and their mother were taking Pat and John to the pantomime show at the Princess Theatre. It was a wonderful play with a princess and a wolf, and Pat sat mesmerized throughout the show. She clapped and shouted with the entire audience when, on cue, they all chanted "He's behind you!" as the wolf was sneaking up on the prince with the axe.

Grandfather Thompson gave them each a little sack of sweets, and Pat was thrilled to have a whole bag of gobstoppers and anise-seed balls. Despite the war, the bells not ringing, and their father having to work on Boxing Day, it had been a nice Christmas. The war, however, had not been "over by Christmas," as so many back in September had said it would be.

Chapter Three

Portsmouth Under Fire

After the New Year, Nora began to plan in earnest for the birth of her new baby. She tired easily and often had to sit down and put her feet up. John and Pat helped her every day after their lessons at Mrs. Q's. Nora sat a lot and knitted, and they helped her with the cooking and with keeping the house clean. While her mother finished knitting sweaters and caps and socks for the baby, Pat made simple things of the scraps for Topsy. She washed dishes and swept floors.

John kept the coal bucket full and the fire in the kitchen-living room going. He could also cook fairly well and made many of their meals. He helped with anything that was heavy to lift or move.

Their father was often down at the barracks for days at a time. In January, the mandatory service age was extended to men aged 20 to 27, and he was busy training new "ratings," along with round-the-clock coast watches. The family never knew when he would be home—he would just appear at the door.

In the New Year, 1940, rationing began, starting with butter, bacon, and ham, very soon followed by sugar and all meats. Pat's mother explained that rationing was to make sure that everyone got their fair share—and no more—of other precious goods, as well as certain foods. These items were in short supply because they had to be brought in by merchant ships, or they were important for the war effort. Everyone was issued "ration books" containing coupons, and these had to be presented with their money to buy goods that were on a special list. They also had to register with their local store and had to buy their rationed items only from that shop. Still, the shops often ran out of things.

On the way home from the local shop one day, Pat and John saw an old man putting posters up on the wall of a bomb shelter at the end of the street. Pat examined one sign that featured a smiling, winking pig. She was trying to read the sign to see what the pig was saying, but she was struggling with a few of the words.

"What does that say?" she asked John.

"'We want your kitchen waste,'" he read. "You know the swill cart comes around the neighborhood to collect food scraps from everyone's kitchen. They feed it to the pigs on the farms."

Pat knew that her mother kept a covered pail under the sink for vegetable peelings, but she didn't know it was to feed pigs. There were other posters on the wall, and John told her that everyone had to be careful of wasting things like cloth and paper because they were needed for the war effort. Fuel for the cars and lorries was rationed, he said, so you had to have special coupons to buy it, along with your money. Their family didn't own a car, so that didn't affect them except that it made the bus fares go up.

"Our parents have never wasted anything in their lives," John said, looking at the posters as they continued walking. One of the colorful posters featured a horse with a saddle shaped like a leather lace-up shoe. "'Go by Shank's Pony,'" John read aloud as they walked by. "'Walk short distances and leave room for those who have longer journeys.' I guess that means walk instead of taking the bus or train. We do that anyway," he said.

"What's a shank?" Pat asked him.

"I read somewhere it's an old word for legs," John said. "So let's move our shanks so we can get home instead of stopping and gawking at posters."

On the wireless and in the newspapers, people were being encouraged not to waste anything. Pat was most interested in the cartoons featuring a housewife named "Mrs. Sew-and-Sew," who was dressed in a striped pinafore and was usually shown sewing a patch onto a piece of clothing. Pictures of Mrs. Sew-and-Sew popped up everywhere, giving housewives tips on how to mend things, remake old clothing into new clothes, or make garments using as little fabric as possible—like making coats and pants without pockets. Pat thought her mother could teach Mrs. Sew-and-Sew a few tricks, since she'd always sewed that way, never wasting buttons or thread or fabric even before the war came, and without posters, the wireless, or newspapers telling her how.

Nora did her best to maintain a normal family life despite the war, the rationing, and the shortages. Like most service wives, she was used to her husband being away and used to filling the role of both mother and father to her children, and she always knew exactly where her children were. With all of the uncertainty of wartime, and the threat of attack literally hanging over their heads, she was nervous about having another baby. John was a great help and comfort to her.

However, with no bombs falling, people began to call it a "phony" war. More evacuees had stayed with their families after Christmas than had gone back to their evacuation homes in the country. A few schools in the city had to be reopened to accommodate them, but Pat and John's schools remained closed because there were not enough teachers, many of them having evacuated with their students or enlisted in the military or support services.

As February began and the baby's arrival drew closer, John helped his father move his parents' bed downstairs to the front parlor, which was temporarily converted to their bedroom so they would be closer to the air-raid shelter in case of an attack.

Since the hospital where John and Pat had been born was now reserved for wounded soldiers and air-raid victims, a midwife came to assist with the delivery of Nora's baby. One night, quite late, John was sent next door to fetch Mrs. Marchant, who came over right away, and the midwife came shortly after. The front sitting room door was closed. A little while later, Mrs. Marchant came out and found Pat and John waiting on the stairs in the hallway near the closed door.

"John, take your sister upstairs and help her get settled into bed. Don't either of you come downstairs or into the parlor. We have everything under control, and in a few hours you'll have a new baby brother or sister," Mrs. Marchant said.

So John and Pat reluctantly went upstairs, and John tucked Pat into bed the way her mother usually did.

"John, how are babies born?" she asked.

John's face turned red, as if she had somehow embarrassed him with her question.

"You'll have to ask Mum when she's feeling better. That's her job," he told her. "Anyway, you don't have to know tonight. All you need to know is that it just happens and it's all right," he said.

Pat had no idea why her question had made John so nervous, and she didn't think she would ask her mother at all. She was curious, though, and as soon as she heard John's door close and things had quieted down, she lay there waiting and wondering. She must have dozed off for a while, because it was much later when she heard voices and movement downstairs.

She quietly got out of bed, put on her slippers, and crept to the landing at the top of the stairs, crouching down so she could see the door to the sitting room open and close as the midwife or Mrs. Marchant went in or out. She tried to see what was going on. All at once, she heard her mother cry out as if in great pain, and then the soothing voices of the women in the room with her. Frightened, Pat jumped up and ran back to her bed, covered her head with her blankets, and hugged Topsy until she fell back into a fitful sleep.

The next morning, the twentieth of February, Pat woke to the sounds of a baby's cry. John came into her room and sat down on the edge of her bed. "Well, we have a baby sister, and Mum's called her Diane," he said. "I've seen her—she's all pink and wrinkly looking, with downy hair, but Mum's okay. Want to come down and see for yourself?"

Pat wasn't sure she really wanted to see the new baby, but she got up and followed John downstairs anyway. The sitting-room door was open and her mother was holding a tiny bundle wrapped snugly in a blanket. Nora was soothing the infant and singing softly to her. She looked up and saw Pat at the door. "Good morning, Patricia. Come see your new baby sister—her name's Diane."

There were dark circles under her mother's eyes, and Pat couldn't recall the last time she'd seen her mother sitting in her nightdress in bed. John brought his mother a cup of tea and set it on the table beside her. Pat came a little farther into the room, but very slowly.

"Thanks, John," her mother said, as she took the tea.

Pat inched toward the bed and stood next to her brother. Together they looked down at the baby, and John touched the tiny hand poking out from the blanket. Pat came closer and John helped her sit up on the edge of the bed so she could see the baby. She had never seen a baby so tiny before. The baby's eyes were open and she looked right at Pat.

"You were this tiny once," her mother said.

"I was?"

"You had lots of ginger hair when you were born."

Mrs. Marchant came back into the room and said, "I'll take the children to my house and see to their breakfast, Nora. You need your rest. I'll pop in from time to time to see if you need anything."

Mrs. Marchant came to the bed and Nora gave her the baby, and she laid the child in the little cot next to the bed. Pat looked in and watched the baby's eyes close. Both of her tiny hands were poking out of the blanket, and Pat thought she looked like a doll.

"Come along," Mrs. Marchant said. "Get dressed and make your beds, and I'll have your breakfast ready in a few minutes."

For some reason she couldn't explain, Pat yearned to climb up into the bed with her mother and be cuddled. Instead, she did as she was told and followed John to the kitchen.

Later in the day, their father came home to see his new baby daughter and to check on their mother. He soon appeared at the Marchants' kitchen door, and Pat ran and threw herself into his arms. She had not seen him for several days. He thanked Mrs. Marchant for all her help, and Pat and John gathered up the games they'd been playing and went home with him.

Pat soon got used to the sounds of the baby's crying. It seemed that all babies did was sleep and cry. A lady with a white uniform and cap came in every day to look in on the baby and Nora, and Arthur came home as often as he could. John helped with the cooking, and Pat helped whenever she was asked to, but was mostly left to amuse herself.

As the days passed, the baby was awake more and more, and Pat couldn't help but be fascinated with her. She was also jealous when she saw her father making a fuss over the baby. Sometimes she just wanted someone to pay attention to *her*, but at least she still had John.

She and John still went to Mrs. Q's for lessons, walked to Sunday school together, and went to the shops for their mother. Each evening, the family gathered in the living room to listen to their usual wireless programs and the news. One of Pat's favorite programs was *The Archers*, about a farmer and his family. She'd never been to the country or visited a farm, and she found the Archer family fascinating.

In March came the news that the British Fleet at Scapa Flow had been bombed by the Luftwaffe, and the first British civilian was killed in that air raid. John had to explain some of the news to Pat because she always wanted to know what was going on, but couldn't understand the news on the wireless. She knew Scapa Flow was way up in Scotland and it was important—she remembered the way her father had talked when the *Royal Oak* was sunk. Her mother told her not to worry about her father, that he would be all right. Yet she always knew her mother kept things from her, and even John began to be careful of how much he said to her.

"You're only seven," he'd say, "you wouldn't understand these things."

At their school lessons, the older boys and girls went over to the map and Mrs. Q pointed to the countries they'd heard about on the wireless the night before. In May, the Germans invaded Belgium, Holland, and Luxembourg, along with parts of France. It seemed the Germans were unstoppable. Now the threat of invasion along the British coast sent fear through everyone in Portsmouth. Children from London and other cities who had been evacuated to the Isle of Wight and other coastal areas had to be moved again, to Wales and the Midlands.

On May 10, 1940, the wireless announced the news everyone had been dreading since war was declared: the first air attacks on British civilians. Two villages near Canterbury in Kent were hit. No one was hurt and no damage was done, but the war no longer felt so far away. Their mother would no longer let John go to the sports field with his friends, saying he needed to stay close to home "just in case I need you for something."

The family listened to the wireless the night Prime Minister Chamberlain announced his resignation. Again, Pat thought his voice sounded sad and tired, even more so than on the day the war began. Mr. Chamberlain asked everyone to support the new Prime Minister, Winston Churchill.

"That's good," her father said. "Churchill will not give in to the Germans. Now we've got a real leader." It was the first time in quite a while that Pat had seen her father look more optimistic

Two weeks later, on May 26th, British troops and their French allies were trapped at Dunkirk, on the coast of France. Arthur did not come home for several nights. The rest of the family listened as the news broadcaster called for British civilians with boats of any type to come help bring the stranded men of the British Expeditionary Force back to England. People with boats of every size and description heeded the call. Volunteers in boats that barely floated under the load of men dodged relentless attacks from the German Luftwaffe overhead. The disaster at Dunkirk stunned the whole nation.

"The war in Europe has now come home," Pat heard people say. Their own shores were now the front lines. The family gathered around the wireless as Churchill warned them all of what lay in store now that the Germans had overrun France:

> The Battle of France is over. The Battle of Britain is about to be-
> gin....The whole fury and might of the enemy must very soon be
> turned on us. Hitler knows that he will have to break us in this
> island or lose the war. If we can stand up to him, all Europe may
> be freed....Let us therefore brace ourselves to our duty. So bear
> ourselves that if the British Empire and its Commonwealths last for
> a thousand years, men will say this was their finest hour.

Pat had seen Mr. Churchill's picture in the newspapers. He was thickly built and solid-looking, often wearing a workman's boiler suit and a bowler hat. In one hand he always seemed to be holding a cigar, while the other often held up the sign that soon became his trademark—the V for victory. Yet it was his voice, thick and booming, that filled her with confidence.

The room was silent for a moment after her mother switched off the wireless, then Pat asked her what the Prime Minister had meant. Nora explained that everyone would have to be brave and do his part so that Britain could win the war. It was exactly what her father had told her the day war was declared. Pat wondered when it would all be over and life would go back to normal.

The next day, when Pat and John went to the corner shop to pick up some items for their mother, they overheard other adults talking about how "it's just us now...the French are done...if you bring down morale, you could get into trouble..." Pat didn't understand all of it and she wasn't sure John did either, so she didn't even ask him to explain.

The summer weather had finally turned warm. Pat looked for-ward to the Sunday school picnic, but it wouldn't be held up at Portsdown Hill as it usually was: the hills around the city were now covered with antiaircraft guns. Instead, the picnic would be held in the church, so it would not really be a picnic at all.

The eleventh of July brought the first air raids on Portsmouth, in the Kingston Cross district. Eighteen people were killed and 80 were injured. The German bombing attacks continued and intensified throughout that summer. Pat quickly learned that the sound of air-raid sirens would be immediately followed by her mother's shout to get to the Anderson shelter. Pat's reaction, at first total panic, became a numb sort of trancelike response. Often she'd find herself in the shelter, curled up on the bunk with Topsy, but with no memory of how she got there.

Her father's absences became longer. In addition to their other duties, the marines were also clearing debris and helping to locate victims in the rubble of bombed-out buildings. John wanted to join the groups of Boy Scouts who were helping with the war effort, but his mother forbade it.

"There's so much more I could be doing to help, not just around here," he said in frustration one day.

Pat was sure he'd be scolded for talking back, but it didn't happen.

"I've told you before, with your father away, I need you here to look after Pat. We need to stay together and I need to always know where you are," their mother said as she warmed the baby's bottle.

"But the Scouts are carrying messages between command posts. They're carrying stretchers with wounded people and helping fight fires. I can't just sit here!" John argued.

"Right now, your father is preoccupied with his work, protecting the country. You're old enough to know that the threat of a German invasion is real. Your father needs to know his family is safe so he doesn't have to worry about us, too. I'll not have you running among burning buildings and be worried about you as well as your father. This discussion is closed. You may continue to help with the paper drives," Nora said.

John said no more to his mother on the subject, and Pat was relieved. She didn't like to hear him argue or speak up to their mother. He'd never done so before. She felt he was growing up and away from her, and it hurt, almost more than her father being away all the time.

She worried about her father, too. The wireless and the newspapers and the talk all around them was of the great sea battles between the British Navy and the Germans, especially the dreaded U-boats. John and Alan were discussing the U-boats one day as Pat walked behind them on their way home from Mrs. Q's.

"I can't believe these German U-boats," Alan said. "They attack our ship convoys in 'wolf packs'—more like sharks, if you ask me."

"Yeah, they gang up under cover of darkness, and come up to the surface and attack a ship from all directions at full speed. I've heard my dad talk about it with Uncle George," John said.

"It's just us against the Germans now."

"I just wish I could be doing something more to help."

"Me too," Alan replied.

On the twenty-fourth of August, when the streets of Portsmouth's commercial district were full of Saturday shoppers, the sky above grew suddenly dark with German planes dropping scores of bombs on the city. The next day, as word came of the terrible destruction, Pat's mother sat for a long time without saying a word. On that one day, more than a hundred people had been killed and many more were injured. A direct hit to the Princess Theatre, where just last year they had gone to the pictures and the pantomime show, killed eight people.

A full-scale German invasion of the southern coast had been feared for some months, and Nora began to wonder if they'd made the right decision in not evacuating John and Pat. It had been so important to keep the family together, and for them all to be there when Arthur was able to get home. Now she wondered if she should send her older children to safety so that at least two members of the family would survive if the worst came to pass.

City officials tried to convince parents to send their children out of harm's way. They made constant appeals through the wireless, and notices were posted around the city and in the newspaper.

"I just don't know what to do about the kids," said Mrs. Marchant one day. "Should we send them out or not?"

"I don't know," Nora said.

Pat had never seen her mother look so tired, or so worried. The baby in her pram started to cry.

"Pat, please push baby Diane up and down the garden to quiet her," Nora said, and Pat obeyed.

Mrs. Marchant said, "If it gets worse, as they say it will, there won't be much choice left."

* * * *

Wherever Pat and John walked to their lessons or to Sunday school, they saw burned-out shells of buildings silhouetted against the sky. One house had the side completely missing and the insides were open to view. It looked to Pat like a giant doll's house. The entire outside wall of the house was a pile of rubble spilling out into the street. The table and chairs and all the other furniture were still in place, and even the flowers in a vase on the table hadn't moved. Everything was coated with a thick layer of dust. John hurried her past such scenes, but each day, Pat saw more damaged houses and pavements and roads pockmarked with bomb craters. Familiar landmarks around the city were completely obliterated.

The parks where they had once had picnics were now occupied by antiaircraft guns and other artillery. Portsdown Hill was lined with big guns, which bravely shot back at the German planes attacking the city. The big guns made an "ack-ack" kind of barking sound, so that's what people called them—Ack-Acks—and they started calling the hills around the city "Tin Pan Alley."

Soon huge balloons the size of lorries were seen floating above the city.

"What are those?" Pat asked her brother, pointing to the sky.

"They're called barrage balloons, and they're filled with helium."

To Pat, they looked like schools of fat fish swimming in the sky.

"What are they for?" she asked.

"At night, those steel cables holding them to the ground can't be seen from the air. The idea is that the German planes will run into the balloons or get tangled up in the cables," John said.

As they walked by another huge hole where the middle of the street used to be, they saw a warning sign: "Danger: UXB!" A policeman directed them to detour up another street. "You can't come this way, kids. Unexploded bomb down there," the policeman said. "Move along quickly, please."

John told Pat about the teams of volunteers who came to defuse these bombs. "The Germans set them with delay timers to go off after everything is quiet and you think it's safe. You wouldn't get me down in those holes with ticking time bombs," he said. "Some of those men and women figure out how to defuse thirty or forty of them before their luck runs out. Bloody Germans booby-trap them and make them trigger all different ways."

Getting through the city was an adventure, and it seemed a new route had to be taken every day. Roads, railway lines, and pavements were closed for blocks at a stretch and traffic was snarled up all over the city.

The Germans were hitting London hard by day and night. Grand-mother Phillips and Aunt Winnie, who lived in London, wrote to say that people there were sleeping in the Underground stations because they made the best shelters. People just left their beds and belongings in the tunnels, went above ground to work during the day, and came back to the Underground to sleep at night.

Soon the sound of air-raid sirens threw Pat into a complete panic. Whenever they blared, she would grab Topsy, run out the back door, through the tiny, windowed conservatory, and throw herself headlong into the shelter, not bothering with the stairs at all. She never felt anything until afterward, when bruises and scrapes appeared all over her arms and legs.

Because the bombs fell every night, the family no longer slept in their beds, but slept in the Anderson shelter. Nora read to them, and they played games and listened to the wireless. In early September, air raids continued day and night. From inside the shelter, Pat could hear the sounds of the planes, the Ack-Acks returning fire, the explosions of bombs as they hit somewhere in the city. The ground shook if a bomb fell nearby. The damp smell of the earth surrounded them. She tried not to think about what was going on outside, and listened to her mother's voice trying to soothe her. She even welcomed the baby's crying because it drowned out the awful sounds above them.

Every day, the local newspaper's front page carried the night's bombing damage inflicted by the Royal Air Force on one side of the paper and the damage inflicted by the Germans on the city on the other side. That was so that people wouldn't get discouraged, John said.

* * * *

Before she knew it, a year had gone by and Pat was turning eight. The family had a quiet celebration for her birthday. There was no cake because her mother couldn't get enough sugar, so she made a bread pudding instead. Her father couldn't get home that day, and Pat was bitterly disappointed not to see him on her special day.

Then, rather suddenly in mid-September, the Germans appeared to change their battle plan and began to concentrate the worst bombing on London and its seven million people. The family listened every night to the news reports. Pat hoped that her grandmother and their other family members would be all right.

One night, Mrs. Q's street was bombed quite near her house, and she decided it was no longer safe to offer lessons there. So John and Pat no longer went to school, but worked on some lessons with their mother at home. Pat's dance school also closed, so she didn't even have that to look forward to.

More than ever now, Nora wanted John and Pat at home where she could be sure they were safe. She no longer allowed even John to go out with his friends unless she knew exactly where he was going and when he would return. This restriction on his freedom irritated him, Pat could tell, but he never disobeyed his mother and he did not argue with her. The only place they now went was Sunday school.

They spent a lot of time with the Marchant children. None of them were allowed too far from home these days, and the boys were told to watch over their little sisters. John and Alan talked endlessly about their friends, who seemed to be allowed to roam all over the city collecting military debris from bomb sites.

"You should see the collection Jeremy's got," Alan told John. "It makes this stuff seem like baby toys," he said as he and John arranged their lead soldiers in battle formations.

"Yeah, I don't know how they get it. The Home Guard and soldiers are all over the place trying to keep people out of the bombed-out places," John said.

"Jeremy says it's easy. He's got the best collection of shell casings and plane pieces. He trades with other guys for even better stuff."

"My mum says one of them is bound to get killed or blinded or something doing that one of these days. There's unexploded bombs and live ammunition all over those bomb sites and wrecked planes."

"My dad would box my ears if he caught me doing that," Alan said. "Say, your dad's not been around much lately, has he. Wonder what's going on."

"I guess he's just busy," said John.

One day at Sunday school, John was waiting outside to walk Pat home when the air-raid siren went off. "You kids run home as fast as you can," said the teacher. "There's no safe shelter here and your mother will be worried."

John took his sister's hand and they ran for home. "Come on, Pat!" John cried, pulling her along.

She could barely keep up with him. They were both out of breath and covered in sweat by the time they got to their house. Pat was so out of breath she couldn't even speak by the time they ran through the front door.

Their mother heard them and came out of the cupboard under the stairs. Baby Diane was crying, but Nora soothed her with a bottle.

"What were you doing running across the neighborhood with an air raid going on?" she asked. She was very upset.

"I had no choice," John said, panting. "The teacher told us all to run home because there was no shelter there, and our mothers would be worried. I didn't know where there was a shelter closer, so we just ran for home." He sounded afraid. Machine-gun fire and sirens could still be heard outside.

"That will be the last time Pat goes to Sunday school. You two are not to leave this road unless I'm with you, is that clear?"

"Yes, Mum, I'm sorry," John said.

"It's not your fault. You did what you were told to do. Sometimes even adults don't think when they're afraid for their lives."

Nora looked at Pat, who sat clutching a doll. Soon they heard the "all-clear," and Nora went to change Diane's nappy. Pat went up to her room and lay down on her bed, holding Topsy and her baby doll close before she fell asleep, exhausted by the day.

A few days later, she was across the street playing with a friend when the air-raid siren blared. The girl's mother tried to get her to run across the street to her house, but Pat stood frozen in the doorway. She couldn't get her body to move. Her arms and legs felt like lead. The siren and the sound of her heart pounding in her chest blocked out all other sounds. She could see her mother across the street with Diane in her arms. Her mother's lips were moving, but Pat couldn't hear anything. John ran across the street, picked her up, and carried her home. Once in the Anderson shelter, she relaxed and lay on the bunk, listening to the wireless until it was safe to come out.

That night her father came home. Her parents went into the front room to talk, but they didn't bother to close the door, so of course Patricia crouched on the steps and listened.

"I don't think it's safe for the kids to be here anymore, Arthur," her mother said.

"The Germans have occupied the Channel Islands now," her father said. "The threat of invasion is real, but I believe we can hold them off. They seem to have switched their attention toward London now. The RAF's done a heroic job."

"Whenever the sirens go off, Pat goes into panic. I'm worried that even if we don't get hit, she'll go off her head. That damp shelter's not a place for children to sleep during the winter, and there's no school."

"They're only taking school-aged children now, not mothers and infants like before," her father said. "That means splitting up the family. If it gets worse, you'll have to do what you need to. If I'm not here, I trust you to do the right thing."

"If we leave the house, we won't have the money to stay anywhere else, even if we can find a place," her mother said. "Certainly no one will want to buy it now."

"I know, but something will work out."

John came up behind Pat. He'd been listening, too, from the landing.

"Come on, you, get into bed or you'll be in some trouble for eavesdropping on things you don't need to hear," he whispered.

Once in her room, she asked him, "Why does Mum want to send us away?"

"Don't worry about that tonight. You heard Dad, everything will work out. Now go to sleep," John said, tucking her into bed.

A fortnight after her eighth birthday, on September 17th, her dad was home for lunch. They had just sat down to eat their meal, and baby Diane was asleep in her special tented crib in the front sitting room. It was a special infant bed that doubled as a gas tent to protect babies who were too tiny for gas masks.

Suddenly, both parents stopped eating and looked at each other. Simultaneously, they put their knives and forks down and listened. In the silence, the droning buzz of a plane could be heard.

"It's a German plane and it sounds close," her father said.

"Shelter!" her mother shouted, as she sprang from her chair and ran toward the sitting room.

John grabbed Pat's arm, but she wrenched it free, grabbing her dinner plate with both hands.

"No one's going to get my dinner!" she shouted as she ran out through the conservatory, John close on her heels, the door swinging behind her.

With her plate still in her hands, she jumped down the steps of the shelter. Her father and John were right behind her, but her mother and the baby had not come to the shelter with them. A massive explosion followed, shaking the ground beneath them. Pat sat on the shelter floor, still holding her dinner plate. She was proud that she had not lost one crumb of her lunch. She started to eat it with her fingers, having left her knife and fork on the table, but she looked up as her mother came down into the shelter, carrying the crying baby.

Nora just stood there, staring down at Pat. Her hands were shaking and her face looked pale.

"I've saved my dinner, Mum, see?" Pat said, but her mother didn't say a word.

Her father crouched down beside her and said, "Well done, Pat. Now let's sit here and you can finish your lunch, shall we?"

Pat ate her dinner, though it was now cold, and after she finished, her mother tended the scrapes on her knees. The all-clear sounded, and the family went back into the house to clear away the mess.

Nora said quietly, "Arthur, she'll kill herself. We've got to do something."

"Yes, we can't put it off any longer. Things are only going to get worse."

Pat had no idea what they were talking about, but it made her worry. So she just went up to her room and sang quietly to Topsy for a while.

Chapter Four

"Don't Let Them Separate You"

The next day, Mrs. Marchant and Nora sat at the Phillipses' kitchen table talking quietly over a cup of tea. Pat sensed something unusual, since the two usually had their chats over the garden wall. Even more unusual, her mother sent Pat and little Nora out to play in the garden by themselves. Nora got absorbed in settling the dolls in their prams, but Pat hung back in the conservatory, just out of sight. She listened as she crouched among the empty plant pots and baskets of root vegetables that were stored in this small glassed-in space off the kitchen.

"The paper says yesterday's attack was just one pilot offloading what bombs he had left before going back across the Channel. St. Alban's church is nothing but rubble," Mrs. Marchant said.

"Diane was just baptized there. John and Pat, too," her mother said.

There was silence as the two women paused to sip their tea.

"It's a good thing you taped your windows, Nora, or that baby would have been cut to ribbons. I didn't put much tape on mine, and there were glass shards everywhere. It took me hours to clear up the mess in my front room. Thank God no one was in there."

All that remained of the Phillipses' front-room windows were pieces of glass stuck to the frames with what was left of the tape.

"This one was too close," her mother said.

"Here's a pamphlet I picked up in town," Mrs. Marchant said. "It says what the kids should bring. Says here they will leave from the school."

Nora looked down through the list and read it aloud. "Gas mask, in box; ration card; identity card; toothbrush, flannel, towels, hairbrush, comb; fork, spoon; older pupils knife as well; a complete change of clothing including two pair of socks or stockings, handkerchiefs; jersey or jumper or pullover or blazer; one pair of sand-shoes or slippers; night attire (two sets); one vest; one pair of pants; one shirt and collar; one pair of trousers or shorts. For girls it lists one vest or combinations; one pair of knickers; tunic and blouse or dress. There's a whole paragraph of instructions."

Nora continued to read:

> *"Each child should carry food for one day: sandwiches, biscuits, oranges, apples are suggested. Bottles must not be taken. The child should wear an overcoat or Mackintosh and strong boots or shoes. No railway or bus fares will be charged...."*

"I guess they think they've covered everything!" Her mother stopped reading, put the pamphlet down, and sipped her tea.

"It's hard to believe one plane could do so much damage," Mrs. Marchant said. "The paper said it damaged buildings near the church, seriously injured four people, and twenty-three less seriously, but who knows what that means? The Ack-Acks shot it down and killed the pilot." After a pause, she continued, "I'm evacuating Nora and Alan. I'll only do it if they keep the two together, though. They aren't even telling us where they're taking them! I hate the very idea, but I just don't know what else to do."

Mrs. Marchant suddenly stopped talking and there was a long silence. Pat knew that her mother hated people getting "emotional," as she called it.

"Will you stay here with the baby?" Mrs. Marchant finally asked, her voice wavering.

"I have no choice. No one will buy this place under the circumstances, and I wouldn't have much in the way of rent for someplace else even if I found one."

"I see what you mean," Mrs. Marchant replied, getting up to leave. "I always thought you were so lucky to own this place. Now I see it's something of a burden, too. Anyway, Pat can come over and play with Nora after lunch, if that's okay. Might as well let them have as much time together as possible."

Pat slipped into the little toilet room off the conservatory so she wouldn't be caught eavesdropping. Her stomach felt queasy. When she finally came out, her mother was there.

"You were listening, weren't you?" her mother demanded. "What have I told you about that?…John, come in here," her mother called out the back door. "Come into the kitchen and sit down."

Pat did as she was told, and John came in and joined them.

"Yes, Mum?" he said.

"Sit down," their mother said. "This attack was too close. I'm sending you two out to the country to be safe. You'll be with a lot of other kids. The Marchant kids are going out, too."

"Why do we have to go? You need me here," John said.

"I need you to take care of your sister, John," mother said. "The time has come to get you two out of Portsmouth, somewhere there aren't bombs raining out of the sky and you don't sleep every night in a damp shelter. And you both need to go to school."

Pat started to cry. Her stomach felt sick, like it was all twisted up inside her.

"Don't cry, Pat," her mother said. "You have to be brave and do your part. Remember, that's what your dad told you, and John will be with you. It will be quiet in the country, no more air-raid sirens. It will be like a Sunday school outing every day."

Pat looked at her brother. He just sat and looked at his mother. She saw him swallow very hard, but he didn't speak. It was clear that their mother had made her decision and there was no arguing with her.

"What about you and the baby?" John asked, his voice breaking slightly, as it had started to do a lot lately.

"We'll cope here, for now. Unless something else opens up, we'll be here in Pompey. The evacuation is for school-aged youngsters now," she said. "Your job will be to look after your sister. I'll keep things going here so your father has a place to come home to when he gets time off."

"Will we be gone for long?" John asked.

"I don't really know."

"How will we say goodbye to Dad?"

"He's coming to the school to see you off," Nora said. "You can each bring one toy, so go to your rooms and we'll start getting your things together. We'll get Dad's old small case out of the loft for Pat, and you can use your rucksack. It will take us a day to get the things on this list together." She was very matter-of-fact, betraying no emotion, as she always was.

John got the suitcase down from the loft, and Nora told them to start gathering the things on the list, handing the pamphlet to John. He helped Pat pack her case and then went into his room to pack his rucksack. Nora began to assemble the documents and food items they would need to take with them.

Pat found it hard to choose just one toy. She knew she would never leave the house without Topsy, but worried that her other baby doll would feel sad about being left behind. She sat on her bed and talked to the dolls until it was time to go downstairs to eat.

That night, Nora made sure that their bags had each item from the list. If John carried the case, she said, and had his rucksack on his back, that would leave one hand free to hold onto his sister. Pat could carry her doll and the paper bag with their lunches. They would carry their boxed gas masks with the string handle around their necks as they always did.

Nora hated the idea of sending her children away to live with strangers. She'd heard already the horror stories of kids being abused or neglected. She'd heard that some of the evacuee kids were allowed to run wild and do as they pleased, living with people who didn't care what they did as long as they were not causing them trouble. At least if she put their things together and instructed John in no uncertain terms that he was not to be separated from his sister, it would be all right temporarily. Meanwhile, she was determined to do whatever she could to find a place for them *all* to be safely together. Arthur had told her he believed it would be a long, hard war, and the outcome was far from certain, despite Winston Churchill's confident speeches and the attempts to frame the news in a positive light. For now, she simply had to trust that somewhere out in the country there was a kind soul who would look after her children and keep them safe.

The next morning, Pat clutched Topsy tightly under her arm as she walked with her mother and John to the school. Nora pushed Diane in her carriage. There were other families gathered at the school when they arrived, but they quickly found Arthur in the crowd. He'd ridden his bike from the barracks to the school to see them off.

All the other children were also carrying toys or bags, and everyone wore their gas-mask boxes around their necks. Pat had the bag with sandwiches and biscuits their mother had made for their journey, and John had his rucksack on this back. As more people came, women carrying clipboards and wearing armbands organized the children and made lists. Parents had forms to fill out. Pat and John were given name tags to tie onto their coats, and Arthur helped Pat thread the string through her top buttonhole to tie it on securely. No one spoke of what was happening. Pat was confused, but she felt better with her father there.

"Excuse me, miss," her father said to one of the people organizing things.

"Yes?" she said. Though she looked quite busy, she stopped to speak to him.

"Can you tell me where the children are going?"

"I am sorry," she said. "You're a marine, so surely you'll understand that we must keep the evacuee reception areas secret. Unfortunately, there are spies. If the enemy knows where all the children are, those villages would become targets, too."

Hearing this exchange, Pat started to feel even more anxious. The crowd of people began to press in around them. She clutched her father's hand and tried to keep from crying.

Soon the woman in charge called out for the children to form a line to board the bus. There was very little time for goodbyes. Her mother gave Pat a quick hug; her mother did not believe in what she called "public displays of affection."

"You behave and mind your manners. Listen to John and stay with him," her mother instructed.

"You'll love it out in the country," her dad said, also giving her a hug. "There'll be farms and animals like cows and horses, and lots of gardens. You be my brave girl and do your part. We'll see you soon. Mind John."

"Yes, Dad," was all she could say. She had a lump in her throat and that now-familiar sick feeling in her stomach. She didn't understand why they were being sent away. She was trying hard not to cry because she didn't want to disappoint her father. She'd promised him she'd be brave. Other mothers and children were crying, and her own mother looked at them with disapproval.

Arthur turned to John and put his hand on his son's shoulder. "Mind yourself and look after your sister. We're counting on you."

"Yes, Dad," John said, and he swallowed hard.

"John," said his mother, "whatever happens, whatever anyone tells you, don't let them separate you."

"Yes, Mum."

Nora had repeated this several times between their home and the school, and each time, John had promised he wouldn't let anyone separate him from Pat. Looking after his little sister was second nature to him. He was now 13, and stood as tall as his mother. Leaving home was scarier to him than staying in the bombing—but he wouldn't let on that he was afraid.

Pat and John boarded the bus and stored the small suitcase and the rucksack beneath their seat. John held their lunch in his lap. Pat sat next to the window, holding Topsy. She tried to find her parents in the crowd, but she'd lost sight of them. Some mothers were waving white handkerchiefs, and the effect reminded her of whitecaps on a rough sea.

She had an awful feeling of heaviness in her stomach, and the lump in her throat wouldn't go down no matter how many times she swallowed. She was glad to have John beside her. She could hear some other children crying for their mothers.

"You won't be a crybaby like that, will you?" John said.

She didn't answer him, just shook her head no. She just wanted to get off the crowded and noisy bus and go home. Despite what her parents had said, she had a vague uneasy feeling that she'd done something wrong and was being sent away for punishment. Her mother had worn such a serious expression on her face, like she was angry about something. But why would she send John away, too?

The bus gears ground and the bus lurched forward. Pat caught one last glimpse of her parents before the bus pulled away from the school. Her mother was clutching her father's arm as though she might fall. Pat had never seen her parents touch each other in public. She'd occasionally seen them kiss, but never in public.

Pat and John had seldom been far from their home on Highgate Road, and had never been separated from their parents. Their closest experience of the country had been the annual Sunday school outing on Portsdown Hill. Pat vaguely remembered the last picnic before the war.

On the high plateau above Portsmouth, they'd had a picnic on the grass and played games. From the hill, they could look down on the city with the sea at its edge. It was like being on the rim of a huge green bowl with tiny buildings and roads at the bottom. Pat had no idea what was on the other side of the hill.

Bouncing along on the bus, she asked John if he knew where they were going.

"No, just that we'll be going to live with a host family somewhere away from the city in a country village."

"Will they be nice people? Will Mum and Dad be able to find us?"

"Mum gave me a stamped card to send her as soon as we're settled. They'll come out to see us, but with bus fares so high, it won't be too often."

"But who will we stay with?"

"I don't know any more than you do about that, but we'll be together and I'll look after you. Don't worry."

"Where are Nora and Alan?"

"I think they're on the other bus," John said. "I don't know. I lost them in the crowd."

The bus finally stopped at the train station, and all the children got off with their belongings and lined up at the ticket window. John got their tickets, which were stamped DESTINATION UNKNOWN. A uniformed porter told them which train to board. Though she'd seen and heard the train as it clanged by their back garden, Pat had only been on a train once before.

As the train pulled out of the city, she was surprised to see that on the other side of Portsdown Hill lay rolling fields of green and gold. In the distance, she could see a farmer plowing a field. A massive flock of birds circled and swooped up and down the neat rows he was making. Her curiosity about where they were going began to edge out the worry she'd felt leaving her mother.

Throughout the trip, the women in charge of the evacuation walked up and down the aisles of the train cars checking on the children. Some children were sick; others complained of being hungry. Very young children were crying for their mothers. Pat could tell by the smell that someone near her had wet pants.

When the train stopped, they all climbed down and crowded with the other children on the station platform. Pat held tightly to John's hand. She was glad to escape the stuffy, smelly train, but then they were herded onto another bus. The bus was also crowded and noisy, but she was so tired, she fell asleep on John's shoulder.

It was nearly dark when they climbed off the bus and were led up the steps of a gray stone house. It was the largest house Pat had ever been in. The front was lined with tall windows and someone was rolling down the blackout curtains. In the large entry hall, several people were gathered around a table shuffling papers. The lady from their bus spoke with these people, and then turned to the children to give instructions.

"Girls to the left," the lady said kindly as she pointed to one set of open double doors. "Boys to the right," and she pointed to the doors on the opposite side of the hall.

Pat could see that both rooms had rows of cots, each with a blanket and a pillow. John hesitated.

"Please, miss," he said to the lady in charge. "My mum gave me strict orders not to be separated from my sister."

"What's your name?" she said.

"John Phillips, miss. This is my sister, Patricia."

Pat hid slightly behind John and clutched the back of his shirt.

"Don't worry, John," she said reassuringly. "You're only staying here for one night. You'll all have a sandwich and a hot drink tonight, and a doctor or nurse will check you out to make sure you're all healthy. You'll be back with your sister first thing in the morning. We'll leave on another bus right after breakfast, to take you to the village that will be your new home."

John thanked the lady for her explanation, but he was still hesitant.

"I'll bring your sister to you in the hall in time for breakfast, I promise," the lady said. "Right now, there's a lot to be done, so I'll need your cooperation. As one of the older boys in the group, I'll need you to set a good example. Can you do that for me?"

"I'll do my best, miss," John said. "Come along, Pat, you heard the lady. I'll be right here in time for breakfast. Don't cry or be a baby about it. Remember what Mum and Dad said."

Pat certainly felt like crying, but she fought back the tears just as she'd done when she said goodbye to her parents. "Yes, John," she murmured.

"I'll see you at breakfast, then." And he went across the hall to the room where the boys were to sleep.

Pat hugged Topsy to her chest as a different friendly lady showed her to a small cot, one in a row of dozens of others in a large beautiful room. After a sandwich and a glass of milk, they all settled down on their cots to sleep. Pat could hear one girl near her crying into her pillow, but she didn't remember falling asleep.

The next morning, she was very glad when the lady came as she had promised and took her to meet John in the room where the breakfast was being served. After breakfast, the children were lined up and examined one by one by either the doctor or the nurse. Pat stood perfectly still when it was her turn. The doctor listened to her heart and asked her to stick out her tongue so he could peer down her throat with a torch. He was friendly and spoke with a gentle voice.

The doctor examined her head for lice. Her hair was still in the braids her mother had put in the day they left home, but the little ribbons were hanging loose. Pat prayed there were no bugs in her hair. It made her scalp itch just to think of them crawling on her head. Her mother always said only "dirty" children had bugs, so she was relieved when the doctor found none.

After they'd all gathered their belongings, they were lined up again and led out of the house to the buses parked in the circular drive out front. The kind woman who'd spoken to them the night before made sure, as she'd promised, that John and Pat were together.

"Good luck," she said to the children on the bus. "There will be someone where you're going who'll help you." She spoke to the lady who was riding their bus, and then waved to the children as she got off their bus to get on the one behind it.

They hadn't gone very far before they stopped in front of what looked like a large hall. The lady who'd ridden the bus with them stood at the front with her clipboard and addressed the children.

"We're in the village of Bramdean," she said. "We're going into the village hall. Your host families will meet you here to take you to your new homes. I'll need you to make an orderly queue. Once we're inside, find an empty chair along the far wall and sit down to wait for your host families. Be sure you have all your belongings as you get off the bus."

Then she went to the back of the bus and helped the younger children gather their things. John and Pat got off the bus and into the queue that was forming at the door to the village hall. Once the children were all off the bus, the woman with the clipboard led them into the hall. John and Pat sat down next to each other with their bags at their feet, and Pat held onto John's hand and clutched Topsy tightly.

Soon, a group of people came in and stopped at a table at the front of the hall. They gave their names, and the volunteers checked their lists. They were asked to confirm the number of rooms they had, and were told how many evacuees they were to billet. Some of the villagers complained that they really didn't have room, but most just came over to the row where Pat and John were and looked the children over.

Some of the people spoke kindly to the children, trying to make them feel welcome. A few of the people who had come clearly didn't want any evacuees at all, and there were one or two arguments between them and the evacuation officials.

"The rules were set by the government," one official replied to a protesting villager.

"There's a war on, you know. Everyone's making sacrifices—some more than others," said the woman who'd ridden on Pat and John's bus.

"You're required to take as many evacuees as you have space for. We have an inventory of all the houses and families in the village," another volunteer added.

"Who is going to pay to feed and clothe them?" one woman demanded. "I'm barely able to feed and clothe my own, with everything in short supply."

"The government will provide a stipend, and will assess parents who are able to pay for their own children's care directly. You'll be provided with a stipend either way. They each have their ration books, as well," one of the women at the table said.

Fortunately, though, most of the villagers seemed kind. Most said things like "happy to help," "poor little things," or similar words.

One woman said to another, "Must've broken their parents' hearts to send 'em away."

The people of Bramdean, mostly women, walked along the row of children and pointed, saying, "I'll take this one," or "We'll have this one." Then the child was told to follow them to the table, where the people in charge noted where each child was going. Pat noticed that the better-dressed or prettier children were chosen first. It made her wonder why no one picked her and John. It felt like being the last one chosen for a team on the school playground. She wondered what would happen if no one took them—where would they go? Would they be sent back home?

After a short while, there were only a few children left, including Pat and John. Then a new lady walked into the hall, stopped to see the woman at the table, and the lady with the clipboard pointed to them. The woman came over to where Pat and John sat.

"I'll take the little girl. What's your name?" she asked.

"Her name's Patricia, but my mum said we're not to be separated," John said, sitting up straighter in his chair and holding his sister's hand.

"I'm sorry I haven't room for you both. I have two little girls near her age and could just make room for one more little girl. Good luck," she said, and went to the next girl about Pat's age.

Some brothers and sisters were broken up, but the officials tried to keep the children in the same neighborhood, at least. Pat was very afraid they would be separated, too. John was firm, and whenever anyone came by them, he held tightly to her hand and said, "We have to stay together."

After about an hour, Pat and John were the only evacuees left in the village hall. The two people left running things looked at them as they spoke in low voices to each other. One was glancing at her watch. It must be near lunchtime, Pat thought. The rumbling from her stomach was so loud she was sure it could be heard across the room. John heard it, and seeing that they were the only children left and it wouldn't be impolite, fished in his rucksack for the two biscuits he'd saved from their lunch the day before. They ate their biscuits in silence, and waited.

"We'll have to find them a place before dark," Pat heard one of the women say, "even if we have to go door to door around the village."

"Maybe we could find somewhere just for the night, then contact some of these people on the reception list who haven't come in yet," the other said.

At last another woman came into the hall and approached the table. The volunteer lady greeted the woman with relief in her voice.

"You're just in time for these two lovely children," the volunteer said.

"Your name please, madam," said the other.

"Mrs. Barter, from the Common," the woman said.

The evacuation official checked for her name on the list in front of her. "Perfect," she said as she consulted the paper. "Says on the inventory you have two spare bedrooms and no children of your own. This is John and Patricia Phillips from Portsmouth. Their parents requested the two be kept together. We honor that request whenever we can," she said.

"I'll take the little girl, but I don't want any boys, especially not one that age," Mrs. Barter said curtly.

"I'm sorry, Mrs. Barter," said the woman, "but the rules are firm. You must take as many evacuees as you have spare rooms for."

"We only have one spare room," Mrs. Barter replied. "The other one's very small and my husband uses it to store vegetables and seeds."

"It says here that your cottage is tied to the Silks' farm, is that correct?" asked the woman, looking at her papers.

"Yes. My husband's a dairyman there. What's that got to do with anything?"

"A survey was done to inventory all the possible places in the village to billet evacuees. Mr. Silk indicated on the forms that you have a very comfortable cottage with three bedrooms and it's just you and your husband."

"You really have no choice, I'm afraid," said the other volunteer. "They seem like nice children, and the young man's keen to take care of his little sister. They come from a nice family, by the looks of it. I'm sure they'll give you no trouble. Their father's in the marines, after all, fighting for all of us."

It was clear by now that Mrs. Barter had to abide by the rules.

"Boys that size will eat you out of house and home, you know," Mrs. Barter huffed.

"Their parents will send clothes as they are needed, and will send money for their other needs. The government will give you an allowance for their food. The boy has their ration books," said the official.

"As I have no choice, let's get on with it," Mrs. Barter said.

The volunteers made notes on their papers, and Pat and John were called up to the table. The two picked up their things, and John took his sister by the hand.

"Children, this is Mrs. Barter, your new foster mother. I'm sure you'll get along fine," the lady said, handing John a card and an envelope with a stamp on it to let their parents know their whereabouts.

"Thanks, but my mum already gave me one," John said.

With that, Mrs. Barter turned and walked toward the door. John hesitated.

"Go on," said the evacuation lady. "It'll be okay."

John took their case and the two followed Mrs. Barter out of the hall.

So far, they'd traveled by bus, by train, and then by bus again. It had been a long two days, indeed. Now they were walking, following Mrs. Barter on the road threading out of the center of the tiny village, and Pat was growing tired. John carried their luggage while Pat held Topsy close as she walked beside him.

They trudged along behind the stocky figure of Mrs. Barter, their "foster mother," who just walked ahead of them without speaking. The late afternoon sun could barely penetrate the high hedges and towering trees lining both sides of the deeply rutted dirt road leading out of the village.

They walked without speaking for about two miles. It was about as far as Pat had ever walked all at once, but she dared not complain or ask when they would stop. She followed John's lead and was quiet. It was clear from every move she made and every word she didn't say that Mrs. Barter didn't want to be bothered with them.

Pat tried to look around as they walked, but it was hard to see anything through the thick, high hedges on either side of the road. It was like a big green alleyway. So she concentrated on the road in front of her feet. When they came to a wide, open fork in the road, Pat was astonished to see a large grassy field filled with grazing cows. Mrs. Barter led them to the left of this field, down an even smaller dirt lane with a tall strip of grass running right up the middle, creating what amounted to a path on each side of it. There was a field to the left, tiny cottages with gardens all around them to the right. Pat couldn't open her eyes wide enough to take it all in. The smells were like nothing she'd ever experienced.

Mrs. Barter finally spoke. "This is Bramdean Common, and up behind those trees is the farm where Mr. Barter works, for the Silk family. Local farmers graze their cows here in the Common, as you can see."

The cows munching grass appeared not the least interested in them as they passed by. Pat had seen pictures of cows in books and she knew cows gave milk, but she'd never seen a live cow. They were much bigger than she'd imagined; they were huge. Pat could tell that John was as amazed as she was, because he slowed down and stared at them, too. They smelled very peculiar, too, nothing at all like the smell of milk.

"That's the Battens'," Mrs. Barter said, pointing to the first cottage on their right. "Rosie Batten owns a couple of those cows."

Two cottages down the lane from the Battens' farm was the gate Mrs. Barter turned into.

"This is our house. The one on the other side is where the Norgates live," she said, pointing to the house to their left. These were semi-detached houses at the end of the lane.

As they walked up the narrow front path, they passed through the middle of the most amazing flower garden Pat had ever seen, and she recognized the strong scent of lavender. Her mother grew it in their garden back home, and each year picked and dried it in bundles to put between the sheets in the linen cupboard. Deep-pink roses climbed a trellis on each side of the bright-blue front door, their prickly thorns draped up over a little roof above the steps. The roses were still in bloom and their fragrance filled the doorway as they followed Mrs. Barter into the cottage.

Standing in the tiny entryway at the bottom of a set of narrow stairs, they saw a small room to either side.

"That's the sitting room," Mrs. Barter said, pointing to the right. "You don't go in there unless we're in there."

Pat looked into the room, which reminded her a little of their front room at home, as if no one ever sat there. There was a small fireplace with a grate for a coal fire, in front of which were two high-backed chairs. To the other side of the fire sat a small table with a lamp and a worn settee with a blanket draped over it. A wireless sat on a table in the far corner.

Pointing to the left Mrs. Barter said, "This is obviously the kitchen."

The kitchen table was draped with a square of shiny blue oilcloth, and four high-backed chairs were pulled up to it. In the middle of the table was an oil lamp with a smoke-blackened glass chimney, and the walls of the room were yellow that had been darkened by wood and coal fires. At the back of the kitchen stood a large black cook stove, and the sink was in a small scullery. Beside that was another door.

There were no electric lights, no boiler on the stove for hot water, and under the sink were two buckets filled with water and a third, larger bucket under a drain-hole in the sink. Pat wondered where the water came from. There were no pipes or taps at the sink.

Mrs. Barter said, "Bring your things and I'll show you where you'll sleep."

She led them upstairs to a tiny room at the right of a small landing. There was one double bed across from a fireplace, and a large dark wardrobe stood in the far corner.

"You'll have to share the bed. I only planned on one evacuee," Mrs. Barter said.

She walked to the wardrobe and opened it. There were three coat hangers on a rod across the top, but it was otherwise empty. "This is where you'll keep all of your things. I don't want to see them left about the house," she said.

Speaking for the first time, except for the occasional yes or thank-you he'd uttered at appropriate moments, John recovered his voice and his manners.

"Thank you for having us. We'll be no trouble and we won't be here long. My mum's going to find a place for us all to be together in the country very soon," he told Mrs. Barter.

Pat had never heard of such a plan, but she said nothing.

"I haven't any choice," Mrs. Barter replied, "But we've all got to 'do our part,' as they say. I'll expect a lad of your age to be of help around here. I also expect, since you refused to be separated from her, that you'll be in charge of looking after your sister. I'm a busy woman. I have my own war work, too, even here in the country. I haven't time for baby-minding."

"I'm not a baby," Pat retorted before she even realized the words were out of her mouth.

John shot her a look that clearly said "be quiet," so she said no more.

But Mrs. Barter smiled and said, "That's good to hear, I'll expect you to help around here, too. You'll be old enough to know not to answer back when you're spoken to. I'll show you the rest of the upstairs so you don't get curious and snoop around on your own. This room is the only one up here that you're to go into unless told otherwise," she warned.

John placed their bags on the bed, and they followed Mrs. Barter across the landing to the room she shared with her husband. A smaller room at the back of the house was full of gardening supplies. Seed trays, plant pots, and root vegetables were stored in baskets or hung from nails in the walls. Apart from having just one window, the room reminded Pat of their conservatory back home.

"This is Mr. Barter's garden storage room. Now put away your things and come to the kitchen. I'll see what I can scrape together for a bit of lunch," Mrs. Barter said.

With that, she left them in their room and went downstairs to the kitchen.

Pat and John did as they were told and put their few belongings in the wardrobe. They put their gas masks on the floor at the back. John took the paper labels off their coats and stuffed them in the outer pocket of his rucksack.

Actually it was a nice room, Pat thought. The small fireplace looked as if there had never been a fire in it. Pat went to the one large window, which looked out to the front garden and the field Mrs. Barter had called the Common. There were woods and fields as far as she could see, and she'd never seen anything like it.

She'd never shared a room with anyone, either, and she and John had never slept in the same bed. In this strange house, however, she was comforted knowing she and John would be together. She was afraid of the dark and she knew John was afraid of the dark, too, but he'd never admit it to anyone. Still, he didn't seem too pleased about the arrangements.

"It's the best we could hope for, I suppose," he said. "I'll fill out this card so Mum will know where we are, and that we're all right and together. Then we'll see if there's a postbox anywhere near this place. You've got to do as I say and not answer back to that woman. We don't need her getting cross at us. She doesn't want us here. But did you see this place? I can't wait to go look about. You'll have to stay right with me."

"Okay, John," Pat said.

She laid Topsy on her side of the bed. John put his lead army men at the bottom of the wardrobe next to their suitcase. He took the postcard from his rucksack and put the bag in the wardrobe beside the suitcase and the gas masks.

Pat was so glad she had John with her. She knew he was being brave and grown-up, and that made her want to be brave, too. She wasn't feeling so well, though. Her stomach was so empty she felt sick. The bus ride had made her queasy, and the tension of waiting in the village hall being looked over by strangers had her insides all in knots. She was tired and keyed up, all at the same time.

"Come on," John said. "We'll get something to eat and I'll see if she has a pen so we can post this card to Mum."

Downstairs in the kitchen, Mrs. Barter had made a cup of tea for John and there was a glass of milk on the table for Pat. There was a thick slice of bread, thinly buttered, and a small chunk of cheese on each of the two plates she set before them. They ate quietly, and Pat was glad to have something in her stomach. When they'd finished, Mrs. Barter told them to put their dishes beside the sink. John asked for a pen and what their address was, and he wrote it on the card.

Pat asked timidly where the toilet was. Mrs. Barter took her to the back door beside the stove and pointed to a small shed up a narrow path at the back of the garden.

"That's the privy," she said pointing to the shed. "You two stay outside now, out from under my feet, until Mr. Barter gets home from milking. We'll eat then," she said.

"Thank you," Pat said.

Reluctantly, she went up the path to the privy. She wasn't wild about exploring the outdoor toilet. She'd never even seen one before, but she was fairly desperate. It was a tiny shed, about the size of their toilet room at home, but definitely not a place she wanted to spend much time.

"Wow, I didn't know they didn't have flush toilets in the country," John said. "It stinks. Hope it isn't my job to empty that bucket."

"Me too," Pat said, wrinkling her nose at the thought.

Behind the house, there was a vegetable garden with neatly tended rows, very much like their allotment garden in Portsmouth. At the back of the garden, a tripod made of sticks held a huge bush of runner beans, just like those her father grew, the ones with the pretty red blossoms and the fat wide pods.

John said, "Let's go see the cows and explore a little."

It was a beautiful late summer afternoon, and they had until teatime to explore the area. There were no signs telling them to keep off the grass, so they walked all over the Common. John started to run, and Pat started after him. Soon they were laughing and stopping in turns to look at every flower or bush that caught their eye. It was all so strange and new.

They approached the cows, but not too closely. Each was tethered with a length of rope to a post in the ground. There were only six of them, spread out across the Common. As they walked near, John narrowly avoided stepping in a large brown pile. They didn't have to wonder long what that was, as the cow nearest them began to excrete a brown mass on the ground below its tail. It was like no smell they had ever experienced.

"I guess we don't want to step in that," John said, disgusted. "To think, we drink what comes out of them!"

Pat decided she would rather not think about that.

In the center of the Common was a little dell, a small hollow in the ground about five feet wide and sheltered by a grove of trees and bushes. Pat and John crept down into this shaded and private nook, and just sat in the middle of it.

"Just think of the games we can play here!" Pat said.

"There are no signs telling us to keep away," John said. He poked his head out of the bushes and looked toward the Barter cottage. "It doesn't look as if she's going to yell at us. She doesn't seem to care where we are," he said, looking a little relieved.

There was a small grove of trees a few feet from the dell.

"I'm going over there and climb that tree to see what I can see!" John said.

"Are you sure you should?" Pat said worriedly. "You've never climbed a tree in your whole life."

"I guess it's about time to try. How hard can it be?"

He crawled out of the dell and ran toward the trees with Pat running after him.

"What if you fall out?" she asked as she watched him start to climb.

"I'll land in all that soft grass, and some cow droppings, I suppose," he said, laughing as he slowly climbed from the lower limbs to the top of the first tree in the little grove.

Pat looked toward the cottage. She was sure that this time, Mrs. Barter would come out of the house yelling for John to get out of that tree. But not a soul or a sound came from the direction of the cottage, or from any of the surrounding cottages, for that matter. So Pat gingerly hoisted herself up to the lowest branches as she'd seen John do, and sat there dangling her feet and holding onto the branch above her. She looked up to see John near the top of the tree, which stood four times his height but was just a thin tree. The top was starting to sway a little under his weight.

"Whoa!" she said, laughing. "Be careful, John."

"It's an amazing view from up here! I can't believe this place. I've never seen anything like it!"

She'd never heard John sound so excited.

Pat felt a tingle of excitement herself as she climbed a few more branches toward where John was perched, looking out at the countryside around them. She pulled back some leaves and looked around. Even from that lower height, she could see how wide the Common was. There was a forest behind the Barter/Norgate cottage, and on the other side of the Common were other cottages of similar style and size. Pat wondered who lived there and if there were any kids their age in the neighborhood to play with.

She had never had such freedom to run or go where she pleased— Mrs. Barter had not told them anything they couldn't do or anywhere they couldn't go. Pat was more excited than she'd ever been in her life, more excited even than being on the stage at her dance recitals. Bramdean was the most fantastic place she'd ever seen, and she and John actually lived there now!

They climbed down from the tree and decided to explore some of the woods behind the cottages. A path behind the Barters' privy wound up a slight hill through a dense grove of trees. The ground beneath the trees was thickly carpeted with soft, green moss, and thick bands of ivy wound up into the trees. Pat had seen ivy before, growing up the sides of buildings in the city, but she didn't know it grew in the woods, too.

They followed the path until it came to a large iron gate with an "S" and a crest at the top. The iron and stone fence surrounded a two-story brick house. Lace curtains hung at the windows, and there were flowers growing along a border at the back. There were barns and other buildings beyond the house. No one was about, but John hesitated, afraid to trespass or open the gate, so he led Pat back down the path. The roof of the Barters' cottage was visible, so they knew they weren't lost.

All over the ground, under the trees, they found curious-looking things they'd never seen before, and they started to pick things up to take back with them. Pat quickly ran out of room in her hands, and her dress had no pockets. Under a massive gray tree with very smooth bark, she started assembling a little pile of these curiosities. One was a round green ball with little prickles on it; another was round and brown with a little cap on it, like some sort of nut. Still another was a little different, rounded but long and green with a smooth outside. There were sticks of unusual shapes and sizes. The roots of the tree were partially exposed through the hard-packed dark earth around it, and these thick roots formed a little nook to tuck their treasures into.

"I wonder if she'd give us something to put this stuff into," Pat said. "It might not be here tomorrow."

"I don't know, but why don't you go ask? She seems to like you better than me," John said. "All she can say is no."

"Okay," Patricia said, and she ran down the path to the back door of the cottage. Mrs. Barter was in the kitchen making the evening meal.

"Please, Mrs. Barter, may I have a small sack? We've found treasures outside," Pat said, slightly out of breath. "We'd like to save some before they're gone."

"Gone? Where would it all go?" Mrs. Barter asked, obviously surprised.

"I thought it might be like when it snows at home, it only lasts for a few hours," Pat said, starting to feel a little embarrassed.

"What an idea!" Mrs. Barter laughed, but she wasn't cross, as Patricia had feared she might be. Instead she went to a bin under the sink and pulled out a small paper sack.

"You can put as many bits of acorns or conkers in here as you want, but don't bring any of that rubbish into the house."

"Is that what they're called?"

"You're funny kids. Haven't you ever seen conkers before?"

"No," Pat said, shaking her head slightly.

"Well, I never," Mrs. Barter said. "After tea, Mr. Barter will tell you what they all are. Now get out and let me get the tea ready."

Mrs. Barter doesn't seem quite as unfriendly as she's been before, Pat thought. She hurried back with the bag to the place in the woods where John was still piling up things he'd found.

"Mrs. Barter says we're not to bring any of what we pick up into the house. She said Mr. Barter would tell us what it all is."

"Well, let's put one of each thing in the bag and carry the rest to the dell," John suggested.

"Mrs. Barter said they won't melt."

"Of course they won't melt," John said, "but I've never seen such things before."

They made several trips, and soon the piles grew in the little dell, which they now thought of as their very own secret hiding place. By the time Mrs. Barter called them from the cottage door, and they reluctantly left their treasures in the dell, the sun was low in the sky. The woman Pat supposed was Rosie Batten was leading one of her cows to the barn beside her cottage. She smiled and waved at them.

"Hello!" she called. "You must be the evacuees. You're welcome to come over any time and help milk my cows. I expect my mother could save a biscuit for you, too."

"Thanks," John said.

Pat just smiled and waved a little.

"What are your names?" Rosie Batten called to them, coming closer.

It felt strange to shout across the field, so Pat followed John as he walked toward the woman. He still kept a healthy distance from the cow she was leading with a rope as if it was a dog on a leash. Pat was awed by the sheer size of the beast. It seemed quite placid and took no notice of them at all.

"I'm John Phillips, and this is my younger sister, Pat. We're from Portsmouth," John said, extending his hand to shake hers.

"How do you do," she said, shaking John's hand. "I'm Rosie Batten. I live in that cottage and look after my mother and the farm. She thinks she looks after me, so it works out. You'll like my old mum. She'll be glad to have more kids nearby. So you're with the Barters? He's a nice man, very keen gardener and gives us lovely honey from his hives." She rambled on a bit.

"We haven't met Mr. Barter yet, we've only just arrived," John said.

"What have you got in your sack?" Rosie asked.

"Oh, bits and pieces we've collected," John said, coloring a little. He blushed easily.

"I don't suppose there's anything like this where you come from. I think you'll like Bramdean....Well, Mother will have tea ready and I've got to get these cows in for the night. I'll let you help me sometime if you like. Mr. Barter's a dairyman up at the Silk farm. I'm sure you'll learn your way around cows soon enough! Goodbye!" She turned and walked away, and the cow plodded along behind her.

Pat and John made their way back to the Barters' cottage and left the sack of treasures beside the door. They'd never gone into a stranger's house without knocking, so John opened the door a little hesitantly, not sure whether he should knock first. He didn't want to make Mrs. Barter cross.

As they stepped into the entryway, they saw a man sitting at the kitchen table drinking a cup of tea. The table was laid for a meal and Mrs. Barter was at the stove.

"There you are," said the man. "I'm Bert Barter. Nel's just told me about you. She tells me you're from Portsmouth, and your dad's in the marines." He smiled, stood up and reached out to shake John's hand. "You must be John."

"Pleased to meet you, sir," John said.

"You can call me Bert. This must be Pat," he said, turning to her. "How do you like our little neighborhood?"

"It's lovely," Pat said, feeling suddenly shy.

"You kids go out behind the kitchen and wash your hands in the bucket out there," Mrs. Barter said. "There's soap and a towel. That's where Bert washes up before he comes in. You can do likewise. Tea's ready."

Bert Barter looked a little older than his wife, but Pat liked him right away. His voice was gentle and he smiled at them when he spoke. He actually seemed glad to have them. Pat and John felt welcomed for the first time since they'd arrived. It seemed strange to Pat that the Barters had no children.

Pat and John had been raised to address adults as "Mister" or

"Miss," unless an adult was family. If the adults were very close friends, like George and Lillian Parker, they called them "Aunt" or "Uncle." Pat couldn't imagine calling the Barters "Bert" and "Nel."

After washing their hands, they came back to the kitchen and sat down at the table where they were told to. Nel served the tea—a large scoop of mashed potatoes on each plate, one half of a sausage each, and a large helping of green beans.

"I'll need your ration books before I go to the shops tomorrow," Nel said to John. "This will have to do for now. I didn't plan for two of you."

"I have them upstairs," John said.

"There's usually plenty of potatoes and other vegetables here in the country. It must be harder in the city," Bert said.

"My dad grows our vegetables on the allotment," John said.

"Oh, so you have some experience in the garden, then," Bert said. "That'll come in handy. You two can help me after tea, if you'd like, and I'll tell you what all the plants are, if you don't know them."

"They don't even know what a conker is," Nel said, chuckling.

"They'll learn fast, I'm sure," Bert replied.

They ate their meal in silence, just as their family did at home. After supper, John and Pat stood up to clear the table, as they were used to doing. Nel washed the dishes, using water from one of the buckets below the sink and hot water from the kettle on the stove. Pat and John dried the dishes, and Nel showed them where to put everything.

"There, now you know how, this is your job every meal that you're here," she said. When they finished, Nel instructed John to carry the dirty dishwater bucket out to Bert to water his plants with.

"After you do that, he'll show you how to fill the wash buckets from the cistern out back. The drinking water comes from the well. Your job will be to keep my buckets here in the kitchen full."

"Yes, Mrs. Barter," John said.

"Nel. Call me Nel. Calling me Mrs. Barter makes me feel old," she said.

Pat and John went out to the flower garden in the front of the house, where Bert was pulling a few weeds and plucking dead flowers from the plants. Pat had always helped her father with the deadheading. The little stone path through the garden, from the front step to the front gate, was neatly trimmed, and there was a wooden slat fence dividing the Barters' garden from the cottage next door.

As he pulled the very few weeds from his tidy garden and snapped the drooping buds from the flowers, Bert told them the name of each plant, flower, or herb he had growing in his border. Pat and John already knew many plants from helping their father in his garden. Bert showed them how to keep the path neat by twisting the grass tops off between their thumb and fingers. He was very friendly, and the time passed without their even noticing how late it was getting to be.

"I never use clippers," he said. "It doesn't look as nice that way…. This can be your job, if you like," Bert said to Pat. "You can keep this walk nice and tidy and that would be a big help to me."

"Yes, Mr. Barter," she said.

"You can call me Bert, seeing as you're going to live here," he said.

"Yes, Bert," said Pat.

"Nel tells me you've been collecting things and you want to know what they are. Let's take a look at what you found," Bert said.

John got their bag and tipped out the contents—nuts, berries, twigs, and now-wilting flowers—onto the front step, and Bert told them what each item was and what tree or bush it came from.

"Don't eat anything or even put it in your mouth until you check with me first," he warned them. "Some things look lovely but will make you sick if you eat them."

Being with Mr. Barter felt almost as comfortable as being with their dad at the allotment or in their own garden back in Portsmouth.

"It's getting late now; time to wash for bed," Bert said, as they came to the last item in the bag. "You'll be starting at the village school tomorrow. Oh, pardon me. John will go to the senior school, won't you? It'll be a big day, and I expect you're tired from all the traveling."

They used the privy, then followed Bert into the house after they'd washed their hands out by the back door, as he did. Once upstairs, Pat changed into her pajamas in their room while John waited outside the door. Then she waited outside the door while John put on his pajamas. When he was finished, he opened the door and they got into the bed, but were still sitting up, not really ready to go to sleep. Bert came up to say good night.

"Welcome to Bramdean. Sleep well," he said kindly, and went out, closing the door behind him.

It felt very strange to be sleeping in the same bed, and they could hear the Barters listening to the wireless in the sitting room below them. John extinguished the oil lamp on the bedside table, and the room was completely dark. There were blackout curtains at the windows, but no one had bothered to pull them down. No one was patrolling the neighborhood shouting, "Put that light out!" along Bramdean Common. Pat just couldn't settle down to sleep, and was still staring into the darkness of the room when she heard the Barters come upstairs to their room.

"John, are you awake?" Pat whispered.

"Yes. What do you want?" he whispered back.

"Did you hear that noise? It sounds like something scratching in the walls," she said.

"Mice, I expect," John said. "Go to sleep."

"Are you afraid, John?"

"There are no bombs and sirens, at least."

"I wonder if Mum misses us," Pat said. She could feel a lump in her throat again. She hadn't actually thought of her mother since she'd arrived in Bramdean. It felt like ages since they'd been home, even though it was just two days.

"I expect so. But she'll get out to see us as soon as she can," John said.

"Is she really going to find a place in the country? What will happen to our house?"

"Yes, she said she would, but hard telling when. You just go to sleep and don't worry," he said.

"Good night, John. I'm glad they didn't separate us."

"I would have walked us home first," he said. "Good night."

Pat lay awake long after John's regular breathing indicated he was asleep. The house was dark, and it was totally quiet, something she'd never experienced before. Back home there was always noise from trains, traffic, and factories running around the clock, the general hum of a busy city. As she listened to the quiet, she began to pick out strange noises. The noises got louder the more intently she listened and focused on them. She drifted off to sleep eventually, but woke with a startled scream.

Bert rushed in, dressed in his pajamas with a torch in his hand.

"What is it?" he asked.

John sat up, rubbing his eyes.

"I heard someone scream," Pat said, trembling.

"That's an owl," Bert said. "They have a hoot that sounds like they're saying, 'Whoo-o-o.' Just remember, there's nothing there in the night that isn't there in the day, so go back to sleep and don't worry."

He tucked the blankets around her and left the room, closing the door softly.

Pat finally dropped off to sleep.

Chapter Five

"Vackies"

When Pat awoke the next morning, the room was filled with sunshine and John was already up and dressed.

"Get up, sleepyhead, and get dressed," he said. "Mrs. Barter's got breakfast ready and we have to get to school."

Pat swung out of bed and jumped back when her bare feet hit the cold floor. She quickly found her slippers and helped John make the bed. She put Topsy on her pillow.

"I'll see you downstairs. Hurry up," John said, and went out of the room and shut the door.

Pat dressed in her school dress and hurried downstairs to join John and the Barters, who were sitting at the kitchen table. Nel put a bowl of warm porridge down in front of her.

"Thanks," she said. The warm porridge was just what she needed.

"It's Wednesday. I go to Winchester to do my shopping and see my sister. I'll need your ration books," she said to John. "The government's supposed to give me some money for your keep, but I don't know when I'll see that. In the meantime, I've made Pat a Marmite sandwich. They serve a hot dinner at the senior school, so that'll take care of you, John. There's a lady near the school who gives the kids a cup of hot broth and some milk to go with their sandwiches. All the kids who live too far from the school to walk home for lunch go there to eat. Just follow the other kids, Pat," Nel said.

"John, you'll catch the bus to Alresford at the village school. I'll walk you there today, but after this it'll be your job to get yourself and your sister there in the morning."

"Yes, Mrs. Barter—I mean Nel," John said, and he went upstairs to get their ration books.

Nel spoke more kindly to Pat. "Come here and I'll brush your hair. I can't have you going to school from my house looking a mess."

She brushed and braided Pat's hair. "I always thought it would be nice to have a little girl. My sister's got two girls about your age—Myrtle and Ivy. They sometimes come to visit me. Boys, on the other hand, are just a lot of trouble."

Pat thought, That won't be true with John.

When her hair was done, she went out to the privy and washed her hands with the water in the bucket by the back door. It was very cold, but she took a flannel from a peg near the bucket, wet it, and washed her face. She shivered and hurried back to the kitchen.

Bert was just leaving.

"Have a good first day," he said. "I'll be down this evening after the milking." He went out the door, wishing John well as they passed each other in the entryway.

John came back to the kitchen and put their ration books on the table. He also had their gas masks in their cardboard boxes.

"Oh, you won't need those here," Nel said.

"My dad said to keep them with us, just in case," John replied.

"Well, come along then, or you'll miss the bus." Nel's friendly tone of a few minutes before was now gone completely.

John and Pat followed her out of the house. She was carrying her shopping bags and handbag, and was dressed in a smarter dress, along with a coat and hat. She wasn't as neatly turned-out as her own mother, Pat thought, and she didn't have gloves on like her mother always wore to town. They walked the same route they'd walked the day before.

"It's two miles to the school, so let's get a move on," Nel said to John. "You can just go and see the headmaster at the senior school and he'll sort out what class you're supposed to be in. There's a lot of new evacuees at both schools, along with the ones who've been here since the start of the war."

When they arrived at Bramdean Village School, the bus for the senior school was already boarding. John said a hasty goodbye to Pat and told her he'd be there when she got out of school to walk her to the Barters'. Then he followed the others onto the bus.

It was the first time Pat had been separated from John since they'd left home, and she felt really alone. She stood with Nel as the bus pulled away from the school.

"Come along, and I'll help you find your class," said Nel.

Pat followed Mrs. Barter up the stairs of the small stone building. There was a vestibule as they entered, and beyond that was one large room with a curtain partition down the middle, dividing the space into two classrooms. There were two teachers, and a very large number of students of all ages sitting two to a seat.

Right away, Pat's attention focused on a grand rocking horse standing to one side of the large entryway. It had beautifully carved details and was painted just like a carousel horse, with a golden mane. She reached out and stroked its nose the way she always did to the carousel horse at the Fun Fair at the seafront. She longed to climb up into the little wooden saddle. It looked smooth and worn from use, and very inviting.

One of the teachers had seen them come in and came to greet Nel Barter.

"Good morning. I see we have another new student. I'm Miss Haversham," she said.

"Good morning, I'm Nel Barter. This is Patricia Phillips, an evacuee from Portsmouth. She and her older brother arrived with that group yesterday. He's gone up to the senior school in Alresford."

"How old is she?" asked Miss Haversham.

"She's just turned eight. According to a note from her mother, their school closed just before the war, and though they had lessons at some woman's house, her mother is a little concerned that she's behind her age group in spelling and arithmetic, but she reads well."

"We'll put her in with her age group and see how she gets on. We're a little overcrowded, but we'll do our best," Miss Haversham said.

"I'm sure you will. I'm off then, I have business in town," said Nel. She turned to Pat. "You do as teacher says and follow the other kids to Mrs. Brown's house for lunch. Your brother will walk you home after school."

With that, Nel left.

The teacher spoke kindly to Patricia. "I see you've already noticed our school mascot, our special rocking horse. Of course everyone wants to ride him, but only students who are especially well behaved or receive good marks are given that great honor. I'm sure you'll be a hardworking pupil and earn your chance," she said. "Now let's go in and you can join your class with Miss Smith!"

Reluctantly, Pat followed her to the other side of the partition, where the students were arranged in rows at small wooden desks. She would be among the oldest students in the group ages five to eight. The other students aged nine to eleven were on the other side. Miss Haversham introduced her to her new teacher, Miss Smith, and the two women spoke for a moment before Miss Haversham left to go to her side of the classroom.

"Class, please welcome Patricia Phillips, another of our new pupils from Portsmouth. You'll get a chance to introduce yourselves at recess. Meanwhile, prepare for our arithmetic lesson," Miss Smith said.

Pat struggled with the arithmetic lesson, but she kept thinking of the rocking horse in the vestibule. She was longing for a turn, so she worked very hard at her lessons. She was also anxious to go to the other class. She didn't want to stay in the "baby" class.

At recess, all the children crowded onto the small playground in front of the school. At the back of the school were the toilets—boys on one side, girls on the other. Like the Barter cottage, there was no indoor plumbing at the school. Instead there were pit toilets with sawdust lining the trenches below.

On the playground, the two teachers were organizing games.

"We must keep everyone busy and help the village children get to know our evacuees," said Miss Smith as she invited Pat to join the beanbag toss game.

Pat loved the beanbag toss game. The wide cloth bags filled with beans were supposed to be tossed back and forth between partners, but when the teacher wasn't looking, children tossed them into the big trees encircling the playground, seemingly with the purpose of getting them stuck up in the branches. The bags then had to be poked down with sticks, which everyone seemed to think was more fun than simply tossing them back and forth.

Pat had been paired with a girl named Joan Herbert, who lived near the Barters, and Margaret Moon, who lived at the other end of the Common. She liked both girls right away, and was so glad to learn she would have friends her own age nearby. As the students were poking their beanbags out of the trees, Pat listened to the children all around her. The country accent of the villagers was very different from the accent of the evacuees. It was easy to tell them apart straightaway.

She heard the older village boys call out, "Hey, Vackies!" The teachers stopped them, but the adults couldn't possibly see or hear everything with so many children on the playground. Despite Joan's and Margaret's kindness, Pat felt painfully out of place.

At noon, the children who lived in the village went home for lunch, and Pat followed Joan and Margaret to Mrs. Brown's house near the school, where several of the other children went for lunch. She met Margaret's brother, Ernie, there. He was 10.

"We'll all be able to walk home together," said Joan, "and play after school."

Pat liked her new friends. She did not, however, like the Marmite sandwich Nel had made for her. The dark, bitter-tasting vegetable spread had a strong, yeasty smell and an awful aftertaste. Nel had said it was "good for you," but Pat just couldn't make herself eat it. Mrs. Brown noticed that she hadn't touched the sandwich, but had drunk her cup of broth and eaten the apple she'd given her. She offered Pat some bread with a little jam on it, which she gratefully accepted.

Back at school, she again struggled with her lessons, this time with spelling. She felt ashamed to be so terribly behind the other students her age. When they came to reading and she was called on to read aloud, however, Miss Smith praised her for a job well done. Still, by the end of the first day at her new school, Pat was feeling discouraged.

"You'll be getting a ride on that rocking horse in no time, reading like that," said Miss Smith, and Pat felt a bit better. Miss Smith was very kind.

When Pat walked out of the school, John was at the gate waiting for her. She introduced her brother to Joan, Ernie, and Margaret, and the group set off on the journey home. John and Ernie hit it off right away, even though Ernie was a bit younger than John, and by the time they'd walked the two miles back to the Common, they were all friends.

"After chores, why don't you two come over to our house and we'll show you around," suggested Ernie, and Pat and John eagerly agreed.

Since Nel was in Winchester all day, there was no meal waiting for them at the cottage, only Oxo broth and a piece of bread. They ate, cleared their few dishes, and went out to fill the water buckets and gather sticks for kindling, as Nel had instructed.

The Barter cottage was heated with wood and coal fires, and Nel had told them it would be their job to keep the kindling-wood baskets in the kitchen and sitting room filled, and a pile was also kept in the small woodshed at the back of the cottage.

To carry the wood, Bert had given them a little wooden, four-wheeled pushcart made from an old baby's pram fitted out with handles and a wooden cover. The two pushed it all through the woods between the cottage and the farm, picking up sticks and fallen branches. As they gathered the kindling wood, they played "horse and cart" and other games. It didn't feel like a chore at all, and they decided to call it "wooding."

By the time they'd done their chores, Ernie and Margaret Moon had come to fetch them to go exploring. John and Pat followed and explored their new surroundings with the enthusiasm of pioneers setting forth in a new land. Every turn brought new discoveries, new wonders. What the others couldn't name for them, Pat and John put in a little sack to take home to show Bert.

In the woods behind the cottages were scattered piles of discarded household items people had dumped—old broken china, plant pots, and other assorted junk. The children poked through the piles and found bits and pieces to use in their games. Pat, Joan, and Margaret picked up old broken pots and teacups to bring to their little "house" in the dell. The girls built a little roof of sticks and branches over the top. Pat ran into the Barter cottage to get Topsy, to join the other girls for a doll's tea party. They mixed water with leaves and mud to make their "tea." It was great fun.

John and Ernie had gathered up their toy soldiers. There were wide, flat anthills dotting the Common, and they used these as battlegrounds, lining up the little toy soldiers into battle formations. They took turns being the Germans. Neither boy had any planes in their collection, so they made some out of sticks and twine, dropping stones on the ants scurrying for their holes.

"Did you see a lot of enemy planes in Portsmouth?" Ernie asked John.

"Yeah, the bombing was getting heavy."

"Must have been pretty exciting, being right where the action is.

Nothing ever happens out here."

"Lots of the fellows have collections of bomb fragments and pieces of planes that were shot down. They trade and swap for the best stuff. My friend Alan got a German pilot's glove in a swap. It's amazing," John said.

"Do you have a collection, too?"

"No. I had to stay close to home to help my mum with a new baby and a little sister, and my dad's in the marines," John said. He was embarrassed to say he didn't have such a collection.

"My dad's in the Home Guard, but he's a baker so he's exempt from the service—'vital jobs,' you know. Have to keep the country from starving, Dad says. Speaking of food, let's go see if my mum's got anything for us to eat," Ernie suggested.

The girls joined them, and they all went to the Moons' cottage, across the Common from the Barters'. Since Mr. Moon was the village baker, there was no shortage of food there. Mrs. Moon was very nice, and didn't seem to mind how many of them tracked through her house. The Phillips children would never have dreamed of bringing that many children home to their house in Portsmouth.

Mrs. Moon greeted them warmly when her son introduced them.

"Oh, you're from Portsmouth. I have a cousin down in Pompey. He's in the navy. You must be a little homesick, missing your mum. You come any time you like. The more the merrier, I always say." And she put glasses of milk on the table and heaped rock cakes she'd just taken from the oven onto a plate.

"Mr. Barter's a very kind man, you'll get on with him just a treat," Mrs. Moon went on. "I think he's always wanted children anyway."

She was silent about Mrs. Barter, Pat noticed.

Mrs. Moon chattered away with the children, wanting to know how school had been. When they finished their milk and the delicious rock cakes, Pat felt better than she had since leaving home. It was nearly time for Mrs. Moon to get the evening meal going, so she went back to her work and the children went back outside. John and Pat were grateful for her kindness, and for the extra food, as they'd still been hungry after the watery broth and thinly sliced bread Nel Barter had left for their tea.

When they finally did return to the Barter cottage, it was nearly dark. Bert was just coming down the hill from the Silk farm. He seemed genuinely glad to see them, and his weathered face brightened into a smile.

"How've you been getting on, then?" he asked.

"It's all amazing," Pat said.

"We've got things to ask you about, if that's all right," John said.

"Let's get something to eat first, and then we'll have a look," Bert said. "Nel won't be back until late, so we're on our own."

The children helped Bert put the cold leftovers from the previous night's meal onto the table. Soon the teakettle was whistling, and the stove threw out enough heat to take the early autumn chill off the kitchen. After they'd eaten and cleared away the dishes, John and Pat spread each twig, berry, nut, and flower out on the table. Bert knew the names of them all.

"Tomorrow you kids can come up to the farm at evening milking and meet Mr. and Mrs. Silk," Bert said. "I'll show you how to milk a cow."

Pat wasn't sure she really wanted to know, but John was quite enthused with the idea.

"There's so much here to see that I never knew about before," John said.

"I suppose everything's quite different to you kids, living your whole life in the town. I can't abide going to town. I can't stand the noise, the crowds—even the smell of town. My wife does all the shopping. She gets kind of bored here," Bert said.

This was the longest speech Pat had heard him make. When Nel was around, Bert was quiet and seemed content to let her do most of the talking. Pat liked being with Bert. He reminded her of her father, except that he was around all the time. She thought she might get along in this new place, after all. Just before they went to sleep, as they were lying in bed, she said to John, "I like Bert. He's nice."

"Well, don't get too attached. Mum told me she's going to get a place out here somewhere and we'll be together as a family again," he said, rolling on his side, away from her.

Pat was looking forward to more exploring the next day, and quite unconcerned about what her mother would do. During the day, her feelings of homesickness had been crowded out by the excitement of all the new wonders that remained to be seen in this new country, and her newfound friends. The freedom to come and go as she pleased was exhilarating. It was only when all was quiet and dark, alone with John in their room, that she missed her mother.

As she drifted toward sleep, she felt a vague sense that she ought to go out to the privy once more, but she didn't want to wake John. She ignored the urge and went to sleep.

Chapter Six

"Goodnight Children Everywhere"

The next morning, Pat was horrified to discover she had wet the bed. She could feel her pajamas and the sheets, and even the blanket, were wet through. She shivered from the wet and cold. She couldn't recall when such a thing had ever happened to her. She lay there, afraid to move, but heard John begin to stir. From downstairs she heard Nel and Bert talking and smelled something cooking. John awoke, and immediately Pat knew she wouldn't be able to hide what she'd done. She felt ashamed and started to cry. John sat up and looked at his sister crying in the urine-soaked sheets.

"You won't make things better by crying," he said.

Pat couldn't answer him.

Just then, they heard Nel's steps on the stairs. She knocked and opened the door without waiting for an answer.

"Time to get up for school," she said, and then stopped short. The smell of urine, John's expression, and Pat's tears summed up the situation. Nel looked angry, but she took a deep breath before speaking. Her voice was cool and calm.

"Hurry up and get this cleaned up or you'll be late for school. John, strip the bed and bring the bedclothes downstairs. Are you wet, too?" she asked him.

"No," John said. "She couldn't help it, she's only little. I'll take care of it."

"You get the sheets off the bed before it soaks into the mattress, then get yourself ready for school. She'll need a bath—she can't go to school smelling like that," Nel said.

They were talking about her as if she wasn't there. The tears streamed down her face.

"Stop crying and let's get you cleaned up," Nel said. "Come down to the kitchen and I'll get the tub ready. Bert's already gone."

Nel pulled the covers off the bed and waited. Reluctantly, Pat got out of the wet bed and followed Nel downstairs, her bare feet on the cold floor. She could hear John stripping the sheets and blankets off the bed as she left the room. She shivered because she was damp and the house was cold. Feelings of shame and homesickness swept over her, and her knees began to shake. She was afraid she'd fall down the stairs, but she made it to the kitchen.

Nel poured hot water from the teakettle into a stand-up bathtub and put a folding screen around it at the back of the kitchen.

"Hand me your wet things and stand in there. Here's a flannel and a cake of soap. Can you clean yourself?" Nel asked her.

"Yes," Pat said. Her cold feet hit the hot water and she shivered again.

"Hurry up, then. There's a towel on the peg behind you."

"John," Nel called upstairs, "bring your sister down some clean clothes."

John had dressed quickly and soon came downstairs with Pat's school clothes. Then he went back upstairs to get the soiled sheets and blankets. Nel was obviously very put out, but she didn't say much. As Pat washed in the tub, she could hear Nel getting breakfast. She dressed quickly, ate her breakfast with John, and was anxious to leave for school.

"You'll have to walk fast not to miss that bus," Nel said to John.

The other neighborhood children had already gone, and John and Pat had to run most of the way to get to the village school on time. John just made the bus to Alresford, and Pat had to run up the school steps to get into school before she was marked late.

After another difficult day at school, they came home to sheets flapping in the breeze on the clothesline. To Pat they seemed like flags announcing her shame, since everyone knew that *Monday* was washday, and this was not Monday. She felt her cheeks flush, but to her relief, the other kids didn't seem to take any notice.

"When you're through with your chores, meet us in the dell," Ernie said to John. "Bring your soldiers."

John went to fetch the drinking water so it would be ready when

Nel made their tea. The well was very deep, and it took a lot of cranking to get the bucket down to the water level and lots of harder cranking to get the full bucket back up again. For washing, rainwater from the roof was collected in a large cistern, at the back of the cottage. John had to pump the water from the cistern and carry it in buckets into the house. Even after it was used once, water was not wasted. Wastewater from the kitchen sink, the bathtub, and the washtub was re-used to water the vegetable and flower gardens. For baths and laundry, the rainwater had to be heated in large pots on the wood-burning stove.

As in Portsmouth, everyone had a bath on Saturday night. But at the Barters', everyone used the same water in turns. For the last person in the bath, the water was cold and gray. At home in Portsmouth, there was a gas water boiler attached to the kitchen stove, and running water from the faucets.

After they had done their chores, John and Pat went to play with Ernie, Joan, and Margaret until the evening meal. As they were organizing their games in the dell, a man came walking up the lane with a rifle in his hand. Pat was afraid and hid behind the bushes. She'd never seen a man carrying a gun unless he was a soldier.

"Don't be afraid. That's just Mr. Norgate. He lives in the cottage on the other side of you," Ernie said.

"Why is he carrying a gun?" Pat asked.

"Oh, that's typical out here. Farmers use them for hunting, or to shoot rats and magpies, you know—pests."

But Pat was still afraid as she watched Mr. Norgate walk past them.

"You'll be glad of that gun if he shares some fresh rabbit with you," Ernie said.

Pat couldn't recall eating rabbit, and she still didn't like the idea of anyone shooting a gun.

That evening, Nel gave Pat and John a clean pail to take up to the Silk farm for their milk, and Bert introduced them to Mr. and Mrs. Silk. Mrs. Silk had thick white hair. She looked up from the sewing she had spread out on the old farmhouse table and smiled at them as they came into the kitchen behind Bert.

"Hello, and welcome to Bramdean," Mrs. Silk said. Her voice was gentle and her face was friendly.

"Pleased to meet you," John said, rather formally.

"Mr. Silk's out in the barn with our son, Will. Bert will introduce you. Have you ever seen cows being milked before?" she asked.

"No, ma'am," John said.

"Well, by the looks of you, some fresh country air will do you a world of good. I can see you both could use some fattening up. You come in on your way back home, and I'll find you a fresh glass of milk and something good to go with it," Mrs. Silk said.

Pat liked Mrs. Silk immediately, but she was shy with strangers and was glad John could answer for them both.

"Thank you very much indeed," John said.

Bert led the children out to one of the larger barns beside the house. Cows were standing in stalls, and Pat practically recoiled when they entered the barn and the strong smell hit her nose. Bert put a tight-fitting white cap on his head before milking and explained that it was so he wouldn't get ringworm from the cows.

He squatted down on a short stool beside a huge cow. The cow didn't appear to notice as Bert leaned his head into her thick side and started pulling on her teats. White fluid squirted into the clean bucket he'd placed beneath the cow. The cow's tail switched at some flies buzzing around her, and there were gentle "moos" coming from cows in other stalls lining both sides of the large barn. When the cow's tail hit Bert in the head, he stood up and tied her tail to the gate of the stall.

"Don't want her to knock the bucket over," he said, as he resumed milking.

Suddenly, warm milk was trickling down Pat's face, and Bert started laughing. He aimed and squeezed the cow's udder and squirted milk at John, too, hitting him on the lips. The children were startled and then laughed with him.

"I'm known to be a pretty good shot with an udder," he said.

An older man with thinning gray hair and another man Pat supposed was Mr. Silk's son came toward them. They were both carrying full pails of milk. Bert stood up and introduced the men to John and Pat.

"Welcome," said Will, who had a friendly smile like his mother.

"What do you think of my cows?" the older Mr. Silk asked.

"I've never seen anything like it," John said.

"They're awfully big," ventured Pat.

"Oh, they won't hurt you," laughed Mr. Silk. His voice was gruff and booming. He made Pat a little nervous. "Just don't stand behind them or get under their hooves," he said.

He needn't have worried: Pat had no intention of going near the huge smelly animals.

The men got back to work as the children watched Bert milk cow after cow, completely fascinated. Bert filled the bucket Nel had sent with them, and John carefully carried the bucket of still-warm milk down the path through the woods to the Barter cottage.

Each day, the ritual was the same: school, chores, and playing with their new friends, and then going up to the farm to watch or help with the milking. Pat and John took Mrs. Silk at her word and stopped by to see her regularly. Pat was no longer shy of Mrs. Silk and Will, but she was a little afraid of Mr. Silk and kept out of his way. Every time they visited, Mrs. Silk gave them a biscuit or a rock cake, along with a glass of fresh milk.

Yet of all the differences between their old life in the city and their new life in the country, it was the darkness that Pat and John minded the most. Bert tried to reassure them.

"There's nothing there in the night that isn't there in the day," he repeated patiently. Still, the country darkness, unbroken by streetlamps or traffic or the lights of nearby buildings, unnerved them.

The privy was always dark, even in the daytime, for it was shaded by a dense clump of brush and tall trees at the edge of the woods. At night, when Pat walked up the garden path, she had to keep her torch pointed carefully on the ground just in front of her, because even in the countryside the blackout was strictly observed. She imagined all sorts of terrible creatures lurking in the darkness all around her, wild animals that would tear her to bits. She hated going up there at night.

She couldn't understand how it happened, but she wet the bed again on several occasions. It was so humiliating. Nel scolded her and made her help wash the bedding as a punishment. She was not allowed to drink before bedtime, and Nel make her go to the privy just before she got into bed.

As autumn turned to winter, the privy was not only dark, but also freezing cold. The awful smell seemed frozen in the air when she shut the door behind her. Her hands were rough and raw from washing them in cold water in the bucket outside, and from hanging wet sheets and blankets on the clothesline every other day.

Through it all, John was patient with his little sister. He never complained about having to help with the laundry, and he protected her as best he could from Nel's anger. He was terribly homesick and missed his mother, home, and friends, and wrote to his mother faithfully every Sunday afternoon. Nora wrote often to say how important it was that he and his sister stay where they were in Bramdean, where they were safe and could go to a real school. Though the war did not touch them directly in the country, they heard the news on the wireless and heard adults talking about it. John was hungry for news and worried about his father and mother and baby sister back in the city that was still being bombed regularly.

In mid-November, everyone in Britain was horrified at the news that the city of Coventry, in the north of England, had been severely bombed. The wireless reported that more than five hundred people had been killed in a raid that lasted more than ten hours. The great cathedral there was bombed to ruins.

In the meantime, John and Pat focused on adapting to country life. So much was new and different, they had little time for homesickness. In the autumn, everyone who was able was expected to help with the harvest and other farm work, even children. Pat and John joined the other village children in collecting acorns to feed the pigs.

The older children John's age helped on the farms with the potato and corn harvests. They walked behind the tractors and harvesters and picked up what the machines left behind so that it could be used for animal feed. There were also fun things to do, such as collecting beechnuts. Once the beechnut pods opened, they looked like little flowers with four petals. Pat and her friends painted the beechnuts bright colors and glued pins to the backs to make brooches. These were very important status symbols to wear to school, to trade, and to give to friends.

To her great relief, within a few months of being with the Barters, Pat's bedwetting stopped. The weather was turning cold, but Pat and John still spent most of their free time outdoors. Their mother had sent several parcels of warm clothes and money for Mrs. Barter to buy them winter boots.

Even though Nel Barter was not motherly and spent very little time with them, Pat had begun to feel quite comfortable in the Barter home. Nel wasn't warm and kind like Mrs. Moon, and apart from combing out her hair each day, she didn't take care of Pat the way her own mother did. But she allowed Pat to go wherever she wanted, and this was heaven for Pat. And, as Nel grew accustomed to her, she actually began to favor Pat and treat her like her own child. She did not extend this caring to John, and she continued to make it quite clear that she didn't care for him being there at all. John didn't seem to care either way. Both children grew very fond of Bert, who spent a lot of time with them in the garden or milking cows at the Silks' farm.

One morning in late fall, Pat woke up feeling sick to her stomach. She started down the stairs to go to the privy, but before she was halfway down, she threw up all over the stairs. Nel appeared at the bottom of the steps and looked with disgust at the mess dripping down the walls and steps. Pat was horrified and didn't know what to do. Without a word, Nel walked back to the kitchen and returned with a bucket of water and two rags.

"You made the mess, you can jolly well clean it up," she said, and returned to the kitchen, leaving Pat standing there in her nightdress on the stairs.

Pat had never cleaned up vomit before. Her mother had always taken care of her when she was sick. She took a rag and started to wipe the mess from the wall beside her. The smell and warmth of it made the nausea rise in her stomach and she was nearly sick again.

John came to help her. When they'd finished cleaning up, he sent her back to bed and took the bucket out to the edge of the back garden to dump it. Pat was embarrassed, but her stomach felt better. John brought her some weak tea, and put the bucket beside the bed in case she felt sick again. At that moment, she missed her mother more than at any time since they'd been evacuated. She was so glad to have John with her. He missed school that day to take care of her. It was Nel's day to go to Winchester, and she had made it clear that she wasn't changing her plans. Pat slept the rest of the day and woke the next morning feeling better.

At night in Bramdean, when it was so dark in their room, Pat thought of her home and her parents. She hugged Topsy tighter, and with John's familiar breathing next to her, was comforted. Sometimes she felt that her mother had sent her away because she had done something terribly wrong, though she had no idea what that bad thing could have been or why John had to come away, too. Some nights, from the sitting room below them, the wireless brought Vera Lynn's soothing lullaby into the darkness of their room:

> *Goodnight children everywhere;*
> *Your mommy thinks of you tonight.*
> *Though you are far away,*
> *She's with you night and day.*
> *Goodnight children everywhere.*

At school, Pat continued to struggle with her arithmetic and spelling. Missing so much school had put her more than a year behind her classmates in these subjects, but her reading was good because she loved to read. The teacher was kind, but she had so many pupils to work with, Pat was left to struggle on her own most of the time.

John helped her at night by drilling her on her spelling words, but he had his own catching up to do. Never a scholar, he nonetheless worked hard. He was anxious to finish school and help with the war effort somehow. He was quite certain he would finish school at 14 and go directly to work, as most working-class boys did.

Both John and Pat made friends easily, and quickly settled into village life. There were several evacuees in the village from Portsmouth, London, and other cities. The local children continued to call all the newcomers "vackies," and often made fun of their city accents. Local names for things were different, and Pat couldn't always understand people when they spoke to her. The Bramdean kids played tricks on the evacuees who were unfamiliar with village customs and ways. Most of the teasing was good-natured and didn't bother Pat and John too much.

The two also spent many happy hours helping Rosie Batten tend her cows. Rosie's elderly mother was kind to them, too. Like Mrs. Silk, she thought it was her duty to feed these "poor little evacuees" whenever she saw them. Naturally, they visited her as often as she'd have them. She always had a glass of milk for them, and often offered them something she had just baked. It was their ritual after school to stop and say hello to Mrs. Batten.

"Sit down, young man," Mrs. Batten would say to John. "I'll bet you've grown an inch since yesterday. You look hungry." And John would happily accept second helpings of rock cakes or ginger biscuits and another glass of milk.

Pat loved sitting in the old lady's kitchen and being fussed over. It was like having a grandmother nearby, something she hadn't experienced before. Rosie welcomed the children's interest in her cows and gave them small jobs to do. The Battens had chickens, too, and they shared fresh eggs with the Barters.

In December, Pat and John saw their first real snow. It rarely snowed in Portsmouth, and it melted quickly when it did. In the country, there was more snow, and it drifted and piled up. On the first snowy morning, Ernie and Margaret had left early and John and Pat were lagging a bit behind because they'd had some extra chores to do. As they hurried up the road toward the village, they were assaulted from both sides with missiles of snow. Several other village children had been waiting behind the hedges with large stockpiles of snowballs to ambush the unsuspecting newcomers, laughing and shrieking at their startled victims.

"Hey, vackies, don't you know how to make snowballs?" came a voice from behind the hedge.

Pat and John had never made snowballs before, but they quickly learned. Soon all the kids were tossing snow, running and laughing—and they were all thoroughly wet and cold by the time they reached the schoolyard.

Two weeks before Christmas, a package arrived from their mother. In it were warm gloves, hats, socks, and scarves she had knitted for them. There was also a wrapped Christmas present for each of them, with a note saying they were not to be opened until Christmas morning.

At school, the teachers let the children decorate with paper chains, paper snowflakes, and other decorations made with materials found outdoors or around their homes. Beechnuts that had been collected earlier and made into pins were now painted as angels or stars, and these were hung from the windows and shelves. The children sang Christmas songs and read Christmas stories and made Christmas cards out of scrap paper, glue, and whatever embellishments could be found during wartime.

The evacuee children were to be given a Christmas party at one of the big houses in the village. Miss Smith said that Father Christmas was to make a special appearance to cheer up children who were separated from their families and unable to go home or have their parents visit. Pat did feel homesick when she thought about Christmas.

The Barters, with no children of their own, knew very little about putting on any sort of Christmas, and Bert said they had never had a Christmas tree. At home with their parents, no matter how lean the year might be, the Phillips family always had a Christmas tree. Even if Arthur carried a leftover one home from the market along with the turkey on Christmas Eve, they had always had a tree. Nora had a box of special glass ornaments that were brought out to decorate it, and they would string whatever was at hand for garlands.

One morning about a week before Christmas, Pat overheard Bert asking Nel if they "shouldn't do something for the kids at Christmas."

"The local Women's Institute is going to throw the kids a party so they can feel all good about themselves for helping the 'poor evacuees' on Christmas," Nel said. "I'm not changing my ways for kids I didn't want in the first place. Their mother's sent a parcel; that's all they need. I'm going to my sister's. You do as you please."

Bert said nothing and Pat thought that would be the last of it.

On the Sunday before Christmas, John and Pat walked to the village to attend the Christmas party. They met a group of other evacuees at the school and walked together to the biggest house in the village. The children were all dressed up in their Sunday clothes.

Pat and John knew most of the other evacuees from school. When they knocked on the door of the big house, a maid in a uniform opened the door, and a footman took their coats and hats before they were led to the large drawing room where the party was being held. There were about twenty children and a few adults, mostly host parents, at the party. The lady of the house greeted them, and they were invited to help themselves at a large table in the dining room spread with goodies of all sorts. Pat had never seen such a beautiful room.

In a huge fireplace, a blazing fire warmed the elegantly furnished room, and a lady was playing beautiful music on a grand piano at the far end of the room. In the center of a large bay window was the biggest Christmas tree Pat had ever seen. It was twice as tall as John, and beautifully decorated with velvet ribbons and sparkling glass ornaments. A shining star rested on its top, and under the tree were brightly wrapped presents.

After refreshments and carol singing, someone exclaimed, "Father Christmas is here!" All the children turned to stare at the jolly figure dressed in red coming through the door.

"Happy Christmas!" Father Christmas called, as all the youngest children ran to greet him.

The older children like John stood back and watched, and Pat stayed next to John, unsure of what to do. Eventually, the white-bearded gentleman came up to where the older children were standing, and he greeted each one warmly, in turn, and then addressed the whole group.

"I know you children are away from your families and loved ones this Christmas, and many of your parents are serving our country bravely in this hour of need. Their Majesties, the King and Queen, have asked me to visit you and send their warmest wishes. We all wish you a happy Christmas, and we applaud you for the brave way you are facing this separation from your families, especially at this time of year."

When Father Christmas finished his speech, the adults in the room applauded. The woman at the piano started playing "We Wish You a Merry Christmas," and everyone sang along. At the end of the song, Father Christmas handed each child a little bag of goodies and waved goodbye. Everyone cheered and waved and wished him "Happy Christmas!" as he left.

Patricia looked inside her bag and found an orange, some nuts, and several bright red-and-white peppermints. It was a lovely present. She hadn't seen a fresh orange since the war had started.

"Let's save ours for Christmas morning," suggested John.

Pat reluctantly agreed. She longed to eat the orange right then and there, but she was full from the treats at the party anyway. Then they walked over to the lady of the house, politely thanked her for the lovely party, and left to walk back to the Barters' cottage with full stomachs and a lovely sack of goodies to look forward to having later.

"John," Pat asked as they walked along, "do you believe in Father Christmas?"

"Of course I do. You saw him with your own eyes today, didn't you?"

"Well, yes, but was he the *real* Father Christmas or just someone dressed to look like him? I mean, the older kids at school say only babies still believe in Father Christmas."

"Well, I guess you can believe them or believe me and your own eyes. I choose to believe he's real, and you can decide for yourself. Even if that man was only dressed up to look like Father Christmas, there are worse things to believe in, in this world," John said.

Pat decided that, as usual, John was right. So much of their world had changed beyond recognition. Their new life among strangers in a strange place made her think about the Christmas story she'd so often heard in Sunday school back in Portsmouth. Maybe Mary and Joseph had felt the way she and John had felt the day the villagers came to the hall to choose evacuees. Some complained they had "no room," and some were happy to invite the evacuee children into their homes. Perhaps she and John were better off than the baby Jesus, who had to be born in the cow barn. But it sure wasn't at all like home. She wondered whether her mother and father would still have a Christmas tree, and whether Father Christmas—the real Father Christmas—would know where to find them to fill their stockings.

When they went to bed on Christmas Eve, John pulled from the wardrobe a branch of a fir tree he had put in a pot of dirt. He had placed a paper star on the tree, and he put the branch by the window of their room. Then he carefully placed the wrapped parcels from their mother under the tree before he climbed into bed.

"There," he said. "We'll have our own Christmas."

"Maybe now Father Christmas will know where to find us," Pat said.

"No matter what happens, we're together, and someday soon we'll be back with Mum and Dad again. Sleep well," he said, and pulled the covers up around them.

"Good night," Pat said, and she fell asleep thinking of her mother and father, wondering if they missed her and John as much as they missed them.

When dawn came on Christmas morning, Pat woke to the smell of frying sausages, and she and John got up to get the parcels their mother had sent. Pat opened hers first. There was a coloring book, a small package of colored pencils, a new blue cardigan for her with a matching one for Topsy, and a little bag of individually wrapped sweets and nuts. John opened his parcel, which also contained a sweater, along with three comic books, some new lead army men, and a bag of sweets like Pat's. Pat was very happy with her present—she'd colored every page of the book her mother had sent in the last parcel. She pulled Topsy out of the bed and began to dress the doll in the new cardigan.

The smells from downstairs were making her mouth water, and she realized she was very hungry. A gentle knock came on the door, and Bert stood at the doorway, a big smile on his face.

"You should come downstairs," he said. "Something's been left for you in the front room."

With great curiosity, the two got their slippers and robes and followed Bert down the stairs. Nel had gone to Winchester to spend Christmas day with her sister and her sister's family while Bert had stayed home with John and Pat. Nel wouldn't be back until the next day.

As they came into the sitting room, Pat spied two wool stockings lying on a table near the fireplace.

"Go ahead," Bert said. "I assume Father Christmas left them here for you."

Pat and John each took a stocking. Both stockings were bulging with something round inside the toe. Inside, they found a handful of gobstopper candies, which were Pat's favorite, a round rubber ball—hers was red and John's was blue—and in the toe of each sock, a perfect, shiny red apple.

"Where did Father Christmas get such a lovely apple this time of year?" Pat wondered aloud.

"I guess he must have a special place he keeps them," Bert suggested. "Now," he announced, "I have a special Christmas breakfast ready; come on."

Bert seemed as excited as the children, but in his own quiet way. At the kitchen table, three places were set, and keeping warm under three upturned plates were an egg, a sausage, fried tomatoes, and grilled bread for each of them. It certainly wasn't the Christmas feast they were used to at home, but it was clear that Bert had gone to some trouble to prepare this Christmas breakfast. They ate their breakfast feast while the wireless in the parlor played Christmas music.

A wave of homesickness swept over Pat as she thought about what they would be doing if they were still at home with their parents. She looked at John and could see he felt the same way. Neither of them wanted to disappoint Bert after the trouble he'd gone to, so they ate and thanked him for the lovely meal. Then the three of them quite companionably washed and put away the dishes.

John and Pat spent the remainder of the day at home with Bert. He still had to go milk the cows at the Silks', but otherwise they spent the day together. Pat carefully chose a page in the new coloring book, and John arranged his soldiers on the floor of their room. They listened to the King's Christmas speech, as they always did at home. Princess Elizabeth came on the wireless with a special message to the evacuees, telling them they were brave and doing their part for the war effort.

The Germans, it seemed, had now turned their attention toward London, and that city was undergoing terribly heavy bombing. There was a bit of quiet for Christmas, but everyone said it would not last. That night before bed, they sat down and wrote letters to their mother, thanking her for their Christmas gifts and telling her how they'd spent this most unusual holiday in the country.

Chapter Seven

A Growing Distance

By the turn of the New Year 1941, Pat and John had settled into a routine at the Barters'. They went to school, did their chores, and helped Rosie with her cows. John helped Bert up at the farm and stayed out of Nel's way. Pat couldn't understand why Nel disliked John so, since he made every effort to be helpful and was always polite. Still, she secretly liked being her favorite. Nel started taking Pat with her sometimes on her trips to Winchester when she went to the market and to visit her sister. Nel's nieces, Myrtle and Ivy, were great playmates. Pat felt a little guilty that John was left behind, but he told her not to worry. He didn't care any more for Nel than she did for him, and as long as Pat was taken care of, he was happy to help Bert with the cows and learn to work on the farm. Most of all, Pat loved the freedom to come and go as she pleased. With John up at the farm with Bert, she could roam the neighborhood and visit her friends and Rosie as often as she wanted to.

Every Sunday afternoon, they sat down to write to their mother. Pat only wrote a few lines and drew pictures, mostly of cows and trees, to put with John's letters. Their mother's letters were full of family news, and John usually read them aloud to Pat in their room before bedtime. Nora wrote often, and her letters reassured them that the family, especially their dad, was fine and they were not to worry. There were parts that John didn't read out loud about how hard the city was being bombed. Nora wrote these things so that John would know why it was important for them to stay in Bramdean until she could find a place for them all to be together. She told them she would be out to visit them as soon as she could.

With one letter in early January came the news that they were expecting a new baby brother or sister in March. This news seemed strange to Pat. It felt like hearing about someone else's family. It seemed ages since she had seen her mother and father, and she had begun to think of the Barters as her parents. One day, she actually called Bert "Dad" before she caught herself.

That night in their room, John scolded her.

"These people aren't your mum or dad, remember. They're strangers who took us in because they had to," he told her.

"They're nice," Pat retorted, "and no one's telling me what to do all the time—except for you."

"Our mum would not be happy to see how you're behaving," he said hotly.

"Our mum sent us away and I like it here. Nel and Bert don't boss us all the time," said Pat. She felt quite bold now, to tell her big brother what she thought, as she'd never done before.

"Mum sent us away because she had to, to keep you from going off your head from the bombs and to keep us alive," he said. "Do you think this is easy for her?"

Pat rolled away from her brother and pulled the covers over her head. She didn't want to listen anymore. John rolled over to his side and did the same. The next morning, neither John nor Pat mentioned their argument of the night before. For her part, Pat wanted to forget all about it. She was just settling into a new life, and she didn't want everything all changed again. She was happier going about her own way.

She had loved her dance classes at Miss Cannoway's before the war changed everything, and her mother had sent the Barters enough money to pay for dancing lessons in the village. Sometimes the dance classes were held at the Bramdean Village Hall, but occasionally they went to the dance teacher's house, in a small studio that had once been a barn. It was not like Miss Cannoway's, but dancing was great fun, and Pat looked forward to it each week. Her favorite dance was the "Sailor's Hornpipe."

She loved dancing and music of any kind. When the war was over, she would take piano lessons, her father had said. Everything good would happen "after the war." No one seemed to have any idea when that would be, but Pat heard people talking about it a great deal.

News of the war barely touched her life now, and it was a huge relief to her not to hear air-raid sirens day and night. Life back home began to feel like it had been another world, someone else's life altogether. She felt sorry for John and tried very hard not to give him any trouble. One aspect of the war that touched everyone in the country was rationing. Food had become very scarce as the war dragged on, and rationing was strictly observed, even in the country, where food was generally more plentiful. Nel was rigid about food rations. In fact, this was the one area in which Pat felt that Nel was really out-and-out mean to John. She doled out each person's butter, jam, cheese, and margarine allowance at the beginning of every week, and there was no flexibility, even if there was food to spare.

"It's your responsibility to make sure your rations last the week. Don't come crying to me if you eat it all in one day. If you eat all your butter on Monday, you'll go without the rest of the week," Nel warned them. On this point, she would never budge, but they could eat as much bread, potatoes, and homegrown vegetables as they wanted. There was a paper posted in the kitchen, cut from a government pamphlet, listing exactly what was allowed under the rationing system:

> Meat, 1/2 pound
> Bacon or ham, 4 ounces
> Cheese, 2 ounces
> Butter, 2 ounces
> Margarine, 4 ounces
> Milk, 3 pints
> Tea, 2 ounces
> Sugar, 8 ounces
> Jam, 4 ounces
> Dried eggs, dried milk, and canned fish, as available.

When the allotted portion of jam or butter or margarine ran out, it was too bad, Nel said; they'd eat their bread plain. Most days, it was one slice with butter, one with margarine, and one plain. If Nel made a cake, she would take a portion from each person's rations to make it—such as the eggs, milk, and butter. She wasn't a great cook, either, like their mother, so neither John nor Pat minded if she didn't bother with cakes at all and left them their rations.

Where Nora had a talent for making a little food seem like so much more, Nel lacked this talent completely. Pat found herself dreaming about bananas or peaches. Soft fruits had become so rare since the war began, even a canned peach was an exotic treat. Pat had no idea where they came from, but every now and then, Nel would produce a tin of peaches when she returned from her weekly trip to Winchester.

John was a growing teenager, and he was hungry most of the time. Pat could hear his stomach growling when they were in bed at night. She shared with him what she could of her own rations because she felt sorry for him. The first time Nel saw Pat give her brother some of her jam and butter, she reached across the table and took it from him and put it back on Pat's plate.

"Nope. You had your allocation, John. You should have made it last," she said crossly. "You needn't be eating your sister's portions. As for you, miss," she said to Pat, "if you don't want it, I'll keep it until you do."

After that, Pat had to sneak food to John when Nel wasn't looking. John and Pat were all the more grateful for the baked goods and milk they got from the kind neighbors—Mrs. Batten, Mrs. Silk, Mrs. Moon, and Joan's mother, Mrs. Herbert.

At their evening meals, there were only small portions of meat, if there was any meat at all. Instead, Nel filled their plates with bread, potatoes, and whatever vegetables Bert had grown in the garden. These were kept in the storage room upstairs. Pat did learn to like the taste of rabbit. It was a bit like the dark meat on a chicken, she thought. Mr. Norgate from next door frequently traded the rabbits he'd shot for a few of Bert's vegetables, since the Norgates' garden never produced as much as Bert's did.

When Nel returned from town, she would tell Bert stories of the long queues for things in the shops. She complained bitterly that "some people" seemed to get whatever they wanted, rationing or not.

"It's who you know that counts these days," she said over their very meager supper one night. "There's stuff hidden under those counters most of us never see."

"This war's made a lot of people step out of character, or maybe show their *true* character," Bert observed.

"If you've got enough money, or the right connections, you can buy anything you want on the black market," Nel said.

"That's if you don't get caught," Bert said. The subject seemed to drop there.

One day, Mr. Norgate came by with a brace of pigeons and rooks he had shot, and traded them for some turnips and carrots. Pat was horrified at the idea of eating the gentle pigeons. She dearly loved all birds. Bert told her these birds were considered pests on farms. "But they're very good eating if you have enough of them," he added. "Meat is meat." So Pat overcame her hesitation and became pretty good at eating whatever was put in front of her.

However, she never acquired a taste for the Marmite sandwiches Nel insisted on giving her for lunch every day. As she grew bolder in her behavior, she began to argue with Nel about them.

"I hate that stuff," she said one day. "It's bitter and horrible. It leaves an awful taste even hot broth or milk can't wash down."

"It's good for you—full of vitamins," Nel said.

"Can't I have just plain bread? I won't eat that stuff," Pat said stubbornly.

"You'll eat it, or you'll go hungry. There's people dying to bring food to this country, and it's against the law to waste food."

"Yes, I know, so why waste bread putting that awful stuff on it?"

She was afraid she'd crossed the line this time and that Nel might actually hit her. John interrupted the escalating battle by reminding his sister that they had to leave or be late for school. Pat took the lunch Nel handed her without another word, but on the way to Mrs. Brown's house, she pitched the Marmite sandwich over the hedge and the kind lunch lady gave her another sandwich with jam. Every day thereafter, she did the same, and Mrs. Brown gave her whatever she happened to have on hand. Pat was grateful that Mrs. Brown never told Nel, or worse, reported her to the police for wasting food.

More and more regularly, Nel was not around when John and Pat came home from school. There was nothing in the house for them to eat, so they usually ended up at the Moons' house or with Mrs. Batten. These snacks held them until Bert got home from the evening milking. Their mother had taught them to cook, but they weren't used to getting their own meals, and the country kitchen was vastly different from their kitchen at home.

One Wednesday when Nel returned from Winchester, she carried a large bag and announced she had a "special treat" for supper that night. Pat wondered what it could be, but Nel guarded the parcel like a Christmas present. When they all sat down to the table, Pat expected something amazing as Nel placed the platter in the middle of the table with great ceremony and evident pride.

"The butcher in town saved it for me, and he may be able to get them for me regularly. It comes all boiled and ready to eat," she said.

"Oh, well done," Bert said, obviously very pleased.

Pat and John just stared at the platter. There on the table was a cold, boiled animal's head! Pat stared into its empty eye sockets and was truly horrified. They'd never seen, let alone eaten, anything like it before. Nel and Bert started picking bits of meat from the skull and eating it, licking their fingers as though it was the most delicious treat in the world. Pat and John both hesitated, not knowing what to do. Their mother had never let them eat with their fingers—at least not since they were babies.

"Eat," Nel commanded. "This is what we're eating and you should count yourselves lucky to have it. It's sheep, and just as tender as you please!"

"It's really good," Bert said. "Try it."

So first John, then Pat, gingerly tore off a piece of the sheep's head and tasted it, and Pat had to admit it was delicious. After that, they looked forward to this unusual treat. Sometimes Nel was able to procure pigs' feet, or "trotters." The first time they tried these, Pat and John were equally dubious. Pat finally decided that as long as you put out of your mind what a thing was, these strange foods weren't too bad, especially if you were hungry!

That February, they learned that their mother would make her first visit to them in Bramdean. Grandfather Thompson had a moving job from Portsmouth to nearby Cheriton, and he'd offered to bring Nora out to see the children for a few hours. John was so excited he could barely wait for the day to arrive. They had not seen their mother for five months.

The Phillips family didn't own a car, nor did any of their neighbors or friends, and even if they'd had access to a car, petrol was tightly rationed and very expensive. Bus fares were also very expensive, and it was a long journey full of stops, too much for a pregnant woman with a small child. Nora had also wanted to let her children settle in before she came out to Bramdean. John's letters telling her how "wild" Pat was getting had her very worried, however, and she decided that before her new baby came, she'd have to get out to Bramdean and see the situation for herself.

Mrs. Marchant agreed to look after Diane, who was now nearly a year old. Nora didn't want to take her along this time, especially in the removal van.

It was a Saturday, so the children would be home from school, and Nora arrived at the Barter cottage about midday. Nora's father dropped her at the gate, and told her he'd be back to see the kids himself when he'd delivered his load.

When Nora arrived, Nel was at the cottage to greet her, and invited her in for a cup of tea. Nel had no idea where the children were, she told Nora nonchalantly, but they'd turn up presently, she was sure. Nora was not pleased that Nel didn't know the exact whereabouts of her children. The two women sat and talked awkwardly, their conversation dotted with uncomfortable silences, until Pat and John came in at lunch-time. Bert had also come down from the farm to meet Mrs. Phillips.

Pat didn't realize her mother was already there when she came bursting into the house calling for "Mum" and "Dad"—of course meaning the Barters. She turned toward the kitchen and saw her own mother, and was momentarily confused and embarrassed. The angry look on Nora's face made words unnecessary. John went and hugged his mother and Nora hugged him back. Pat had rarely seen her mother so emotional. She went to hug her mother, too, because she felt she would be expected to.

Bert cleared his throat and introduced himself, offering his hand. Nora shook it formally. They all sat in the front parlor, the adults making stiff, polite conversation. It was awkward, and Pat could tell straight away by her mother's strained politeness that she disliked Nel.

"I suppose you'd like some time with your children," Bert said. "Nel and I are going next door for a bit."

"I've left some sandwiches and tea on the table. Please help yourselves," Nel said.

The Barters rose to leave, but Pat didn't want Bert and Nel to go and leave her alone with her mother and John. She was afraid she was in trouble, and as soon as the Barters left, she realized she was right.

"What are you doing calling them Mum and Dad? They're not your parents," Nora said hotly.

"I don't know," Pat said, looking down at her dusty shoes. One of the laces was untied.

"Look at you! You look like some sort of wild thing," Nora said. "Come here and let me fix your hair."

Pat stood before her mother, as if being inspected. In the old days, their father would line them up for inspection, marine style, but it was just a game. This did not feel like a game.

Nora reached into her handbag and pulled out a comb. She undid Pat's untidy braids, which she had done herself that morning. They were loose and coming undone. Her mother combed and tidied her hair. It hurt Pat's scalp a little, as her hair had not been thoroughly combed since it had been last washed at her bath the week before. She was certainly in need of a bath again, a fact her mother duly noted.

"You've got twigs in your hair, Pat. How did your hair get into such a state? It's clear to me this woman has no idea where you are most of the time and that neither of them has any idea how to raise children," Nora said.

Pat deeply resented her mother's criticism of Nel, and especially of Bert, but she could think of no way to respond. She only hoped her mother would not notice her scraped and filthy knees.

"Bert's really good to us," John said, "and I always keep my eye on Pat."

"It's a good thing you do," Nora said. "My conversation with this woman gives me all I need to know of her character. I'm going to see about having you moved until I find a way to get out of Pompey and bring us together again. I knew this would happen. You can't trust strangers to care for your kids—especially people who have never raised children. I had no choice," she said, and her voice cracked a little.

Pat thought her mother might cry, and the very idea unnerved her. John had noticed it to.

"We're all right now, Mum, really. It would be worse to be moved again. I'm very nearly through school. I'll be fourteen in May, remember. After I finish school, I'll be looking for work," John said.

"Yes, John, I know," Nora said.

Their mother had dark circles under her eyes, which made her look tired. Her skin was pale. Her stomach was barely covered by her dark woolen dress. Pat remembered her mother looking that way just before Diane was born—which seemed like another lifetime.

"Things have been hard in Portsmouth?" John asked quietly.

"Yes, but we're okay, don't worry, and so is your Dad," Nora said. "He sends his love."

After a pause, Nora turned to Pat, who had moved a few feet back from her after her hair had been combed. It was all very awkward. Pat had really missed her mother, and part of her longed to throw herself into her arms and be held like a little baby. The huge bulk of her mother's belly, however, frightened her a bit, and she didn't dare, in case it should hurt the baby inside. She still had no idea how that baby was going to get out, any more than she'd known how Baby Diane had been born.

Her mother's expression softened a little.

"Let's eat our sandwiches. It would be rude to leave them, and you may be permitted to run wild here, but I hope and pray you haven't shamed us by forgetting your manners," Nora said.

"I'll put the tea on," John said. "You must be ready for a cup of tea after that journey in Granddad's lorry."

"Yes. First though, Pat can show me where the toilet is," Nora said.

"The privy's out back," Pat said. "I'll show you."

Nora followed her up the path through the back garden to the cold, damp privy.

"Well, this is certainly primitive," she commented dryly. "I'll meet you back in the kitchen. Don't forget to wash your hands before you eat. Where do we wash our hands?" she asked looking about her.

"There's a basin by the back door." Pat pointed back toward the house, then left her mother and went back to the kitchen.

After lunch, John and Pat showed their mother around Bramdean Common. They met Rosie Batten, and took Nora in to meet Mrs. Batten. The old lady was delighted to meet her.

"You poor dear, come sit by the fire and let me make you a cup of tea. You should be so proud of your kids. They're both lovely children. John has grown two inches since he's been here, and Pat is such a sweet little girl. And now you're expecting another—how wonderful, but so hard in wartime. Is it so awful in Portsmouth?"

Mrs. Batten didn't get much company, and fired her questions rather rapidly. Nora, who was normally a very private person, was initially a little overwhelmed. She was glad of the warm kitchen and the hot tea, as her feet had begun to swell a little, making her shoes feel tight and her feet pinched. It was such a relief to sit down, and she did not want to go back to the Barters' just yet.

"I'm so glad the children have such nice neighbors," Nora said, gratefully sipping the hot tea.

"Yes," Mrs. Batten said. "We love children out here. I know country life is so different from the town, but I think the fresh air and country food has done them both a lot of good. They looked a little pale, begging your pardon, when they first came. I just can't imagine how awful that constant bombing must be. You have another child, too, John told me."

"Yes. Diane's nearly a year old. This one's due late in March. My husband is posted at the barracks out on Whale Island, but he gets home regularly. I never know when it will be, but I like to be there for him," Nora said.

"Of course you do, dear, of course. Such brave men we have. What awful times. I remember well the Great War…."

Mrs. Batten launched into one of her many stories, and Nora only had to nod and say "Really" now and again.

Pat was glad to have a place outside the Barters' to sit for a while. Mrs. Batten, as usual, had set out fresh glasses of milk for her and John, and had laid a plate of biscuits on the table, which they were happily munching through. After what seemed a short time, they heard a big lorry turn down into the Common and pass the Batten cottage.

"Oh, that must be my father, back from his removal job. I'm afraid we must leave. I'm so glad to have met you," Nora said, standing and shaking Mrs. Batten's hand.

The old woman slowly got out of her chair and led them to the door.

"I hope to see you again. You can be sure we're all looking after your kids," Mrs. Batten said.

"My father says more and more people are getting out of Portsmouth, away from the coast. He'll likely have many more jobs this way. After my baby is born, I'll be back out," Nora said.

She thanked Mrs. Batten again before they left the Batten cottage and turned up the lane. Grandfather Thompson's big removal lorry was parked in front of the Barter cottage. The big man himself stood beside the vehicle, watching them approach. Pat ran to hug him, and her grandfather picked her up and swung her around just like he always had.

"Hello, Pat! How are you?" He hugged her and then set her down again. He turned to John and shook his hand. "You've become quite the man in a few months. Look at you!" Grandfather Thompson said.

John flushed slightly at the attention and said, "It's good to see you, Granddad. Thanks for bringing Mum out."

"No trouble, my boy. We'll get out again this way. Lots of folks are trying to get out of Pompey now. You can buy a house there pretty cheap if you've got the money.... 'Course it might not be there in a month, thanks to the Germans!"

Nora gave her father a look that made it obvious she did not want him to continue discussing that topic. She quickly changed the subject.

"Do we have to get going straightaway, Dad?" she asked him.

"Afraid I do. I have another small job to do when I get back to Pompey. But as I said, now we know where you are, we can get out again."

Pat suddenly felt all pulled apart inside. She didn't want to say goodbye to her mother again, but at the same time she couldn't wait until her mother left. Nora seemed all out of place here. Her grandfather gave them each a few of their favorite sweets and a handful of coins for "pocket money."

The Barters came out of the cottage when they saw that Nora and Mr. Thompson were about to leave. Their grandfather told Pat and John that the next time he was out that way he'd bring their bicycles so that the trip to the village would be easier. John was excited about this because he was sick of walking everywhere he wanted to go, and besides, all the other boys his age had bikes.

Before Nora left, she said to John, "I've asked the Barters to see that you two go to church. Bert says they don't go regularly themselves, but there's a church in the village you can get to with a neighbor. Please see that you do that. Keep writing me letters, and I'll see you again as soon as I can."

She kissed John on the cheek, and did the same with Pat. It was not something Nora did often, so it felt a little alien to Pat. Then Nora said a polite but cool goodbye and thank you to the Barters.

"Behave, Pat, and try to act like a little girl, not a tomboy," she said.

"Yes, Mum," said Pat.

Grandfather Thompson helped their mother up into the lorry, shut the door, and hugged Pat, patted John on the shoulder, and waved goodbye to the Barters.

"I'll be by again soon with those bicycles," he shouted as he put the truck in gear.

Pat and John stood and watched as the old lorry rattled up the rutted lane and out of sight.

Having her mother visit was very confusing for Pat. She had just begun to settle into life with the Barters and had put out of her mind all the bombs and destruction of her past life. Now she and John would have to go to church every other Sunday, weather permitting, because their mother said so—and John always did whatever their mother said.

Bert was anxious to please their mother, too. He'd grown very fond of the children, and liked having them around. So that first Sunday, he arranged for them to walk with Mrs. Herbert to the village church in Bramdean. Pat didn't care to walk the two miles each way to church, but she went along to please John, and because Bert said she should.

John and Pat got occasional letters from their father, too, though they were usually short because he had little time to write. He couldn't tell them much about what he was doing or even where he was. John explained to Pat that letters from servicemen like their dad were carefully censored to be sure they contained no information about the whereabouts of ships or troops or other vital news that would be of interest to German spies. "Loose lips sink ships" said the posters hanging in the village.

In March, their mother wrote to say that their new brother, Michael, had been born. It seemed strange to Pat that she now had a brother she'd never seen. It was a great comfort, however, to know that the family back home was safe, after the news of heavy German bombing raids reached the village.

According to the wireless, over a three-day period in mid-March, the Germans had concentrated heavy bombing over Portsmouth. Military posts were hit, as were hospitals, shops, and homes. Many people were killed and even more were wounded. Hospitals were full of both military and civilian casualties.

Their baby brother had been born at home during one of these air raids. A letter from their mother to John told how it happened. There was no time to get to the shelter when the sirens blared and the bombs started. Right after the birth, Nora and their newborn brother were rolled under the bed for safety, and Mrs. Marchant and the midwife waited for the all-clear in the cupboard shelter under the stairs. The electricity was down again.

Shortly after Michael was born, Nora and Arthur decided it was time to try to get the rest of the family out of Portsmouth and to bring Pat and John back to be with them. Nora wrote to John to reassure him they were all safe and to tell him she would be actively looking for a place out in the country near them. Grandfather Thompson, she said, was also actively looking for a place for them when he was out in that area doing moving jobs. John couldn't wait to be back with his own family and away from Nel Barter.

* * * *

After her visit, Nora tried to find her children a more "suitable" foster home. However hard she tried, though, evacuation officials told her that homes for evacuees were scarce. The fact that her children were climbing trees and were not kept clean enough was not their problem, the officials told her. Unless she could provide evidence of real abuse or neglect, she should be grateful that her children had a safe place to live. (Pat now felt the Barters were her family, and the cottage and its neighborhood were her home. She could never admit this to John, but she was happy to be right where she was.)

Also shortly after that first visit, their grandfather brought their bikes out to Bramdean as he had promised. He delivered them while they were at school, so Pat and John were totally surprised to come home one day to find the bikes parked out behind the Barter cottage. Bicycles made getting places, to school, to church, or to visit friends, so much easier. Unlike the old days at home, there was no one in Bramdean to set limits or boundaries on their freedom, and Pat rode when and where she pleased. So long as their chores were done, Nel Barter didn't interfere with anything John and Pat did.

* * * *

Spring was fully upon them and Bert's seed trays began to fill the tiny spare bedroom. One of John and Pat's new chores was to collect the dirt from the tops of the molehills that peppered the common.

"Molehills?" John had said to Bert the first time he asked them to go out with their pails and hand trowels.

"Those clever moles dig their holes and tunnels and burrows under the Common, and as they do, the dirt they pile up outside is just right to start seeds in," Bert said, crumbling a handful into the pail over the first molehill they came to.

"Look how finely crumbled and sifted it is. I don't have to sieve it through a screen to make it loose for my seedlings. The moles have done it for me," Bert said.

All across the fields and the Common, there were these tiny heaps of soil, evidence of the industrious moles. It was actually fun, walking along with their pails and trowels, scooping up the precious loosely crumbled soil.

Bert also kept bees in several hives at the back of his garden. This at first terrified, but then fascinated Pat. She wasn't overly fond of insects, but the first time she watched Bert put on his special hat and prepare the little pot of smoke he carried up to the hive, he invited her to come and watch.

"Don't make sudden moves; just follow my lead," he said.

He gave her a veiled hat and some gloves to put on, and she timidly followed him to the hives.

"The bees pollinate the garden. They make all of our plants and vegetables flower and bear fruit. Then the bees turn the pollen to honey. Here, taste it." He handed her a piece of honeycomb. It was sweet and delicious. Her mother had cooked with honey back home, but it wasn't as delicious as this honey, fresh from the hive.

"What does the smoke do?" Pat asked.

"It sort of lulls them into a dopey state," Bert said, "but they don't bother me either way."

Pat didn't like the feeling of the bees swarming around her head, and was glad of the little veiled hat she had on.

"If you don't harm them, they won't harm you," Bert reassured her.

There didn't seem to be anything about country life that Bert didn't know. Pat helped him tend his seedlings, and helped plant them out in the garden when frost was safely past. John helped Bert dig over the flower and vegetable beds. Once the plants were in the ground, the two helped keep them weeded and watered with the rainwater from the cistern and the wastewater from the kitchen.

The weather got warmer as spring came into full bloom. Pat loved to ride her bike as fast as she could pedal, the wind whipping through her hair and in her face. One day, she sped down the hill from the Silk farm, through the woods, beside the Norgates' cottage. She didn't see the old piece of fence wire under the leaves. The wire caught her front wheel and she was thrown from the bike into a patch of plants appropriately called "stinging nettle." Miraculously, she had no broken bones, but her skin soon began to itch and burn all over.

When she arrived home crying, Nel was not very sympathetic.

"That's foolish to be riding through the woods at such a speed. Go out back and find a dock leaf," she told Pat. "Spit on the leaf and then rub it on the stings. It'll take the burn and itch out."

"Where do I find dock leaves?"

"Conveniently enough, right near the stinging nettle, and you obviously had no trouble finding those, so you'll find the cure easily enough."

Though it seemed quite odd, Pat did as she was told because she was desperate—and she was surprised to find that this strange procedure worked, just as Nel had said it would. But the next day, her skin stung again, so she had to repeat the process regularly for a few days, until the fall and the stings were just a memory. However, the day after her fall, she was right back on her bike, riding as fast as she could, but she was careful to avoid the stinging nettles.

After Easter, the new school term began and Pat studiously applied herself to her schoolwork. She desperately wanted to be moved up to the next class, where her friends were, but she continued to struggle with arithmetic and spelling. John helped her at night, though he had struggles of his own to try to finish school in the summer term.

April saw another month of heavy German raids on Portsmouth. John and Pat listened to the news on the wireless, and John was very worried about their family until Nora wrote to reassure them that they were unharmed. She also told John she would try to get out and see them the next month, around the time of his birthday.

When John turned 14 in May, their mother did manage a visit, as she'd promised, coming out with Grandfather Thompson on another of his rounds. She brought a gift for John and a little treat for Pat as well. As before, the visit was a thrill for John and confusing for Pat. Nel wasn't even there this time, so that made things a bit less awkward. Bert served Nora a cup of tea and then left so the children could visit with their mother.

John had asked his mother if he could finish school at the end of the term and go get a job so he could help the family move. Pat just sat quietly and listened. She didn't want to attract any unwanted attention from her mother.

"I'm fourteen now," he said, "so I should be going to work. I don't like school anyway."

"No, John, I think you should stay at school through this next year. You missed so much when you were still in Portsmouth. You'll need that education later. Besides, you need to stay where you are and look after Pat. Lord knows, no one else is," Nora said.

Pat squirmed uncomfortably in her chair.

"How is the house search coming?" John asked.

"There's not much housing available," Nora said. "Everyone's trying to get out of Portsmouth, London, and all the places that are getting hit so hard by the bombing."

"How are Grandma Phillips and Aunt Winnie?" John asked.

"They've been bombed twice. London is taking it hard now. If I can find a place out here, they'll take the house, and it'll be a relief to them to get out of London. As bad as it is for us, it's been worse for them. Your father would still have family to go to when he gets time off, and if we head out this way, it might still be possible for him to get out this far to see us," Nora said. "He says he's going to try to get out here to Bramdean to see you two, if he can. Things are pretty intense right now, but he's safe, thank God. Unlike those poor men on the *Hood*," she said. There was a long silence.

"What did Dad say about that?" John asked. His voice was unusually quiet. "We heard the news on the wireless."

"I've never seen your dad so upset, even as much as has happened in this awful war. He trained some of those men, and served with some of the others. They're all feeling this deeply. The whole navy has vowed to destroy the German *Bismarck*," she said. "More than thirteen hundred men went down. Only three survivors were found as they searched the waters off Greenland."

After a short silence, John said, "If I can't finish school with the summer term, maybe I can finish by Christmas. I don't want to be fifteen and still at school. I need to get to work."

"We'll just see how things go, John. If you go to work here, and I don't find a place that's within easy distance, you'll have to give the job up. I want you here to keep an eye on your sister," Nora said.

It was settled, then, that John would stay at the senior school in Arlesford for the next term at least, and Pat had endured another awkward visit with their mother. She put the idea of moving again completely out of her mind. She didn't believe she'd ever live with her mother again, which didn't upset her. She was only eight and a half years old, yet so much had happened to her since the war began. As long as she had John, and Nel and Bert continued to treat her as if she were their own child, she was quite happy for things to carry on exactly as they were. Her mother's visits only upset her, and she argued with John more afterward, when he tried to impose their mother's rules on her again.

After much hard work, Pat was able to pass her schoolwork for the term and would be promoted to the next class. She was delighted. As a reward, her teacher let her have a "ride" on the beautiful wooden carousel horse in the school vestibule. She'd longed to climb onto it since her first day at the Bramdean Village School. Her best friends were there to see her, as it was the end of the school day, and they all cheered for her.

As she sat upon the beautiful wooden horse, Pat felt so proud of the work she had done. She suddenly wished her dad could be there to see her; he always had a way of making her feel special. She tried to imagine his face, but the details seemed fuzzy. She imagined for a moment that she was on the carousel at the Fun Fair, back along the seafront. She could hear the organ music in her mind, but she couldn't really remember what life had been like before the war. It felt like a dream life or someone else's life that she'd read about in a book. She climbed down off the wooden horse, patted its painted wooden mane, and said goodbye and thank you to her teacher. She was looking forward to the summer holiday.

When that summer of 1941 arrived, Pat and John found to their delight that in addition to the school holiday, they no longer had to walk the two miles to the village to go to church. There was a very special church, only open in the summers, right near the Common, and Bert walked Pat and John there on that first Sunday. The Church in the Wood, the tiniest church Pat had ever seen, sat in a clearing of dappled light in the woods beside the Bramdean Common. No bigger than a cottage, the church was so small that the surrounding trees dwarfed its slender steeple. The outside was painted a brilliant shade of green, accented with lacy white wood trim along its steep eaves. Inside, there were a dozen rows of wooden pews on either side of the center aisle, and on the steep eave wall above the single altar table was a brilliantly colored stained-glass window in the shape of a rose.

The Church in the Wood was not even as big as the chapels inside the great Winchester Cathedral. Nel had taken Pat to see that awe-inspiring architectural wonder when they were on one of their shopping trips just before Christmas. The cathedral's vast vaulted ceilings had made her feel small, and her neck ached from looking up at them. The Church in the Wood felt like a fairy church, and Pat was immediately charmed by it.

"I've never seen a church so tiny," John whispered to Bert as they sat halfway back on the left side of the row of pews.

There were only a handful of other people in the church, and Pat didn't recognize any of them.

"I'll tell you all about it after the service," Bert whispered back.

Pat knew that Bert and Nel didn't attend church regularly, as they had not gone once since she and John had been there. Bert had suggested the Church in the Wood as the way to "oblige Mrs. Phillips," since the two children could walk there by themselves for the twice-a-month services. Pat was happy not to walk the two miles to town with Mrs. Herbert every other Sunday.

After the brief service, Bert led them out of the church with the other villagers, and they all shook the vicar's hand as they left. A sign beside the door said the church had been built in 1895. As they walked back across the Common, Bert told them about the Church in the Wood.

"The church was built for the Romany gypsies so they'd have their own church when they're in residence on the Common," Bert said.

"Who are the gypsies? Where are they now?" Pat asked.

"They come to this area in early spring or summer, the same family groups each year. We usually see their brightly painted horse-drawn caravans just after the snowdrops come to the woods. They set up camp here in the far end of the Common," Bert said. "They're a little late this year."

"Are they friendly?" Pat asked.

"Oh, yes. Some of the villagers will say 'lock up your chickens and watch your eggs' when the gypsies come, but that's not the ones who come every year that steal or make trouble. Those are the Diddakois. They come in motorized vans and will steal anything that isn't nailed down. Those are the unknown bands of 'travelers,' as they're called, and you have to watch out for them," Bert said. "But the gypsies are quite harmless. The regulars keep to themselves, except when they sell their wares."

"What do they sell?" John asked.

"The menfolk cut witch-hazel branches in the thick woods, and they carve wooden clothes pegs. Nel says they're the best pegs you could ever find, and she always buys them when they come 'round," Bert said. "They also carve trinkets and jewelry from wood. Nel has a brooch of a carnation flower carved from cedar wood she's very fond of. The women," Bert went on, "make paper flowers they sell by the bunch. They pick wild white heather and make little bouquets to sell, too. They come door to door, dressed in their bright-colored clothes, and in their sing-song voices say, 'Buy my heather and be lucky all your life,' and Nel always buys a bunch."

Pat loved the Church in the Wood and couldn't wait to see the gypsies for herself.

John appreciated Bert's friendship. Bert had already taught him a lot about farming and country life. He hoped to get a job on a farm, preferably driving a tractor, as soon as he could finish school. Everything about motors and engines interested him, and he wanted to drive a lorry like his grandfather. When he was old enough, he'd join the services, but not the marines like his father. He wanted to join the army and learn to drive tanks.

John and his friends kept track of every detail of the war, from the deserts of Africa to the sea battles in the North Atlantic, where the family supposed Arthur was serving. In the year since France had surrendered to the Germans, virtually every European country had been overrun by the Nazis. With air bases just across the English Channel, the Germans could easily bomb any British target.

"There's just the Channel between them and us now, and it looks like we're on our own," Bert said to John one night as they sat and talked after supper.

"It says in the paper that Hitler has turned on his so-called Russian friends, and his armies have marched into Russia. I have a hard time telling who our allies are and who the enemies are," John said.

"The Germans, Italians, and Japanese are the enemy at this point. It's hard to see where Russia stands, but as Germany's now turned on them, they'll probably be helping us beat the Germans back," Bert said.

"Things have gone a little quiet in London and in Portsmouth, according to my mum's last letter," John said.

Pat didn't understand much of the war, partly because so little of it touched them directly in the country. In June, everyone was issued "Clothing Books," as clothes had to be rationed, too. For any new clothing item, shoes, or boots, a coupon had to be presented with the money to purchase the item. The Women's Voluntary Service organized clothing swaps in the village so that families with growing children could keep them in clothes and shoes.

One day when Pat and John went up to the Silk farm, there were six olive-skinned men at the farm whose language Pat did not understand. She was frightened and hid behind John.

"You don't have to be afraid of them," Bert said. "Those are Italian POWs—prisoners of war. They're here to help earn their keep."

"Won't they try to escape?" asked John, as Mr. Silk was leading the men to the back rooms above the farmhouse kitchen, where they apparently now lived.

"No; they're friendly enough. Most of them don't want to be fighting us anyway, but their crazy dictator Mussolini thinks he's going to get an empire if he stays on Hitler's side," Bert explained.

"Why are they here in someone's house?" John asked.

"Well, there were a lot of Italian soldiers captured in Egypt in December, and few places to house them. Can't have them going back to fighting us, so we may as well put them to work where we can," Bert said.

At first, Pat was quite shy of the "I-ties," as everyone called the Italian prisoners. But they were such warm and friendly men that she soon got used to them and even learned a few words of Italian. The prisoners were anxious to learn to speak English, and practiced with Pat whenever they saw her.

"The Italians love children," Mrs. Silk said as Pat and John sat at her kitchen table one day. "They all have large families at home and they miss them terribly, but they don't seem to miss being soldiers."

Just then, one of the prisoners brought in a large pail of milk from the barns, tipped his cap to Mrs. Silk, and smiled at the children.

"Good afternoon," he said in his thick, rich Italian accent. He put down the pail and went back out to work.

The Italian prisoners definitely seemed to like farming. Pat couldn't picture any of these friendly young men carrying guns, much less actually shooting anybody. She hadn't realized how many countries were at war. She was confused about who Britain's allies were and who their enemies were, apart from the Germans and that bad man named Hitler.

Chapter Eight

Their Darkest Hour

There had been no air raids in the countryside since Pat and John had come to the Barters'. Actual bombs were quite rare in their area, but planes could be heard overhead. To be on the safe side, people always stopped to listen to be sure they were friendly. John could tell by the sounds of the engines which were British planes and which were German. He could even tell what types of planes they were.

"That's a Spitfire," he'd say with authority, or "That's a Hurricane."

One day in the middle of summer, a little war excitement did come to Bramdean village when two German planes were shot down nearby. One plane crashed in a field with a bomb still on board, and its impact left a huge crater with pieces of metal everywhere. The pilot was killed. Pat and John got out of bed to go see the crash site.

The second German pilot managed to bail out of the plane and parachute to the ground. He was captured with great ceremony by the local Home Guard brigade.

"A bunch of local women were fighting over his parachute, or so I heard," said Nel that night at supper.

"What would they want that for?" Pat asked.

"That parachute's pure silk fabric, that's what they want, to make undergarments with—can't get anything that even *looks* like silk these days," said Nel. "Wish I could have come by a chunk of that myself," she added wistfully.

"Oh, by the way, Jean's boy, Tom, is coming to stay for a week, starting Friday," Nel announced. "You remember Tom, don't you, Bert?" she asked. "He's been up north for a while."

"Yeah, I remember. What's he coming here for?" said Bert, who did not seem pleased by this news.

"Oh, don't be like that," Nel said crossly. "He's all right, got into a little trouble a while back, but he's sorted that out now," she said. "He won't be here long, and I couldn't say no. We've taken in strangers, for goodness sake; we can't say no to family."

"He is not family," Bert protested.

Pat had never seen Bert argue with Nel.

"Still, he's coming Friday. He's a bit older than you, John, coming up to sixteen, I think. I'm sure you'll all get on—or you'd better," she said, a bit of warning in her voice.

"Where are you going to put him?" Bert asked.

"Well, that potting room upstairs is mostly empty now. I'll put a cot in there. He'll be fine for a few days," Nel said. "He's going to work down at the dockyards in Southampton, but he's staying here on his way down."

"Why isn't he working in one of the factories up north? They want people badly up there, too," Bert said.

"There was a little trouble, and his mother wants him to have a fresh start," Nel said.

"I can just imagine. I don't want him here long, Nel, I don't even want him here at all," Bert said.

Bert seemed to like everyone, and Pat couldn't imagine him speaking in such an unfriendly way about anyone, much less standing up to Nel about this person.

"It's not his fault people don't like him," Nel said, getting very angry now. "I haven't got much in the way of family now, Bert, and even though Anne's only a distant cousin, she was also a close friend of mine growing up. I feel I owe it to her to help her son out. Tom is my godson. Things haven't been easy on him," Nel said, "even before the war. That father of his was cruel. I don't know how Annie ever put up with it."

Bert sighed deeply, got up from the table, and went out to his garden without saying another word. So the subject was dropped and Pat and John began clearing the plates.

That Friday, when they got back from their last day of school before the summer holidays, "Tommie," as Nel called him, was already moved into the spare room across the hall and was sitting at the kitchen table, talking with Nel.

"These are John and Patricia Phillips, the evacuees I was telling you about."

"Hi," John said, the old shyness of strangers making him flush slightly, and Pat said "Hello" very quietly.

"Hi," Tom said, without getting up from his chair.

"I'm sure you'll all get on well for the weekend. John, you can show Tommie around the neighborhood," Nel said.

"That won't be necessary, I remember my way around," Tom said.

To Pat, Tom looked much older than Nel had described him to be. He was fair-skinned, with dark, deep-set eyes and a thin, finely chiseled nose. His hair was dark, and he was dressed in traveling clothes. He regarded them coolly, as though they had just entered his house, not him theirs.

"I've got some old friends down in the village. I'll see you at supper, if that's all right, Aunt Nel," Tom said.

"Oh, take John's bike. It's out back of the shed. It'll be quicker," Nel said, not even looking at John.

"Thanks," said Tom, looking at John but clearly expecting no reply.

Tom put his dark wool cap on and went out the back door. Without saying a word, John went upstairs. Pat could tell he was furious, and she didn't really want to go upstairs after him, but she had to change out of her school clothes.

Up in their room, John was already changed and sitting on the edge of the bed, staring out the window.

"I don't like him any more than Bert seems to. Acts like he owns the place. How dare she lend him my bike, without even asking me," John said. His face was flushed scarlet, as it always was when he was really angry.

"You can use mine, even if it's a little small," Pat said, trying to be helpful.

"Thanks, but that's not the point. We'll just have to stay out of the way for a few days," John said.

It was now July, and Pat had been so looking forward to their summer holiday. Now the start had been ruined by this stranger in their midst. John said he'd wait for her in the dell. He wanted to be away from

Nel before she gave him even more chores to do. Pat changed into her play clothes, hanging her school clothes carefully in the wardrobe. She grabbed Topsy off the bed and went out to the dell. She and the other girls were having a tea party at the Moons' house to celebrate the start of the summer holidays.

That night, it was very late when Tom came home. Everyone was in bed asleep, but Pat heard him creep quietly up the stairs to the little room across the hall. She'd awoken with a start and thought at first there was a burglar in the house, until she remembered Tom was staying with them. When he hadn't come home for tea, Bert had said something to Nel. Then they'd gone outside and had a heated argument. Pat couldn't make out what they said, but she'd never heard Bert get really angry before.

Pat heard Tom stop outside their door, and she thought for one terrible minute he was going to come into their room. In a few seconds, she heard the door to the spare room open, then close. Soon the house was quiet again, and she fell back asleep.

The next morning was Saturday and she woke to see a cloudless blue sky and sunshine outside. She and John had planned a bicycle ride and picnic with Ernie and Margaret Moon after their usual Saturday chores were done.

When they came down for breakfast, Tom was sitting at the kitchen table drinking tea with Nel. Pat had forgotten about him, as if he had been a bad dream from the night before. Nel was in her going-to-town clothes, and the two were laughing when John and Pat came into the kitchen.

"Oh, there you are," said Nel. "I was just about to wake you. There's porridge on the stove."

She went on talking to Tom while Pat and John dished up their breakfast and sat down at the table to eat.

"I've got a list of chores for you after you've done your breakfast," Nel said to John. "Bert and I are going to Winchester. We'll be gone the night. Tom's agreed to be in charge and keep an eye on things while we're gone. Don't you give him any trouble, either," she warned, looking right at John.

Why she would say such a thing to John was beyond Pat's imagination. John had never given her a minute's trouble since they'd been there.

"You'll also need to go up and help with the milking at Silk's while Bert's away," Nel said, with the usual tone of voice she used with John, as if he was a hired hand.

Pat noted that to her "godson," Tom, Nel showed every kindness, getting up to refill his teacup, and they began to talk again as if no one else was in the room.

"Tom, I'm sure you can find something to do while we're gone," Nel said.

Pat had known for a week that they were going to Winchester because she had heard Bert protest that he didn't want to go to the wedding they were attending in the first place. She had assumed that Tom would be going with them, but now her stomach began churning and she found it hard to swallow the porridge that was congealing in her bowl. However, she knew better than to waste it.

"I'm sure I can," Tom said.

"Did you meet some of your old mates down at the pub last night?" Nel asked him.

Pat didn't think Tom was old enough to go into the pub, but this apparently did not disturb Nel. She had clearly expected it.

"Yeah, we played some darts. I hadn't seen a couple of them since they came out to work on the farm over near Cheriton," Tom said. "It was a good time, but I've a bit of a head this morning."

"I'll bet you do," Nel said, laughing.

Pat thought for an instant of what her own mother would say about such a situation. Nora never took a drink of alcohol, except for a little brandy in her tea when she had a cold. Arthur never drank, either, and always traded his sailor's rum ration for extra chocolate to bring home. Whenever her mother mentioned anyone who "drank," it was mentioned quietly and with obvious disapproval. None of that seemed to occur to Nel.

"Well, you nurse your bad head with another cup of tea. We'll be going up after lunch, so you're on your own for a while." She turned to Pat and John. "And you two can get to your chores."

So John and Pat went about their usual chores. Just before lunch, Ernie and Margaret came by for their picnic, but John had to tell them they couldn't go. The additional chores Nel had given them would take well into the afternoon. Then John had to go up to help with the milking. Mrs. Moon had made a cake and had sent a piece for John and Pat for their picnic. Margaret handed the cake, all wrapped up picnic-style, to Pat.

"Here, you can at least have the cake as a treat later. I'll see you tomorrow at the Church in the Wood, then," Margaret said.

Margaret and Ernie went off sadly, and Pat and John went into the house for lunch. Pat put the cake up in their room and came back downstairs. The Barters were just heading for town.

"We'll be back tomorrow afternoon. Tom's in charge," Nel announced.

Bert seldom accompanied Nel on her town trips, and he didn't look as though he wanted to go. He looked extremely uncomfortable in a starched shirt with a collar. He said goodbye and thanked John for helping with the milking. Then they were gone, and John and Pat were alone with Tom.

Pat cleared the lunch dishes off the table and she and John started washing them without saying a word. It was not a comfortable silence. Tom continued to sit at the kitchen table, watching them, not saying anything. He did not offer to help. At the sink, her back to him, Pat could feel him looking and it made her very uneasy, though she could not figure out exactly why. She was relieved to finish the dishes and go outside to weed the garden. Tom had still not said anything to them.

The usual tradesmen who made their rounds on Saturdays had come and gone. The butcher had delivered their few bits of meat, and the coal man had left his load early in the morning. John had the drinking water to draw. Pat weeded the garden and picked the vegetables that were ripe. She didn't want to go into the house because Tom was there, and she didn't want to be alone with him.

When John had filled the drinking and cooking water jugs from the well, he took them into the kitchen, and came back out to help Pat with the weeding. Then it was time to do the watering, so Pat helped John tip out the wash water onto the plants, and when those buckets were empty, they filled the watering jugs from the cistern at the back of the house. Still they saw nothing of Tom. Pat missed having Bert there, as they usually did the gardening with him.

After the gardening, John had to go up for the afternoon milking at the Silks', and Pat went with him to fetch the Barters' milk. She didn't want to go back into the house alone, so she quietly put the milk in the kitchen larder on the old cold stone where it was kept until John could help her lower it into the well. That's where the milk was kept cool during the hot weather. Then she practically ran to the Battens' to get their eggs from Rosie.

She was happy to dawdle at Rosie's, helping her with the cows. Mrs. Batten had her glass of milk all poured when she came back from the barn. There was also a plate of biscuits, and Mrs. Batten told Pat to help herself and take some home for John. Mrs. Batten chatted amiably, and soon it was time to go home. Pat supposed they'd have to cook their tea themselves, and she also supposed John would be back from the Silks' by then. She said her goodbyes to Rosie and her mother, and went home with her basket of eggs.

Pat came through the back door and called John's name. There was no reply. She felt uneasy. She put the basket of eggs on the back step and went up to the privy. Then she went back through the woods to the Silk farm to find John. When she got to the farm and asked for John, the only person in the cow barn was Mr. Silk.

"John went home a half hour ago," the old man said, in his usual gruff manner.

Pat didn't stay around to ask more questions. She hurried back through the darkening woods to the Barter cottage. The summer days were longer, but the woods always got dark earlier, and though she was now used to the woods, and in fact had grown fond of the peaceful quiet there, she felt the need to hurry.

When she came by the back door, she noticed that John's bike was gone. She froze for an instant. She was sure John would not have gone off and left her alone with this stranger. Still, she entered the house quietly, through the front door this time, and ran on tiptoe to their room. The house appeared empty. In their bedroom, she noticed that the carefully wrapped parcels of cake were not on the stand where she'd left them. Instead, the empty paper was crumpled where they had been left.

"John?" She called quietly. The door to the spare room was shut. She went downstairs. As her feet hit the kitchen floor, she heard a noise from behind the kitchen. It seemed to be coming from the direction of the coal cellar, the dark cupboard at the back of the house where the coal was stored.

"John?" she called again. This time, she heard his voice, and it was definitely coming from the coal cellar. She went out the back door to the outside door that led to the coal storage area.

"Pat?" It was John's voice. The door had been shut and bolted. How could he be in there with the door shut and bolted? Alarmed, Pat struggled with the bolt and opened the door. John was there alone, with a frightened look on his now very pale face.

"I wondered where you'd gone," he said, looking much relieved.

"What're you doing in there?" Pat asked. She knew he hated the dark and hated going into the coal cellar, even though it was his job to keep the coal scuttle next to the kitchen range full for Nel.

"I came in to fill the scuttle. I couldn't find the torch, so I propped the door open with a stone so I could see in there. Before I knew it, the door was shut behind me and bolted. I shouted. I thought it was you playing a prank. I kept calling and no one answered. I knew it wasn't you then."

"Who do you suppose...?"

"It was that Tom. I didn't like him the minute I saw him. Bert was right about him," John said.

"Well, he's gone now, and so is your bike," Pat said.

Neither she nor John knew what to do next. They had no place to go, and they couldn't prove that Tom had shut John in the coal cellar. They weren't entirely sure he had. But who else would have done such a thing?

"We'd best not say anything to anyone about this. Nel will only say I was lying—she hates me and she dotes on that Tom. The Barters will be back tomorrow. Let's just go get our tea. We'll be in bed by the time he gets back from wherever he's gone—the pub, probably—on my bike." John looked really upset.

"Let's go get our supper," Pat said. They were both anxious to get away from the coal cellar.

It was getting late, and they were hungry. In the kitchen, they made a meal out of whatever they could find, and Pat told John about the cake.

"I've got biscuits from Mrs. Batten, though," she said.

They'd never found themselves in such a situation before. They ate their meal in silence, then washed and put away the dishes.

"Probably ought to do our baths, just the same. Tomorrow's

church," John said.

"Do we have to, John? Can't we just have a quick wash and pretend we did?"

Pat didn't know why, but she felt she didn't want to be taking her bath in the kitchen not knowing if Tom would come in while she was behind the screen in the stand-up bathtub.

"I think we can get away with that," he agreed. "Nel doesn't care if you're clean anyway. We'll just heat the teakettle and have a wash."

Pat was relieved, and the two did their quick wash-up. It wasn't even quite dark when they were up the stairs, in their room, in their pajamas, and shutting the door behind them. Pat wished they had a bolt on the door to lock themselves in. There wasn't even a chair in the room to put against the door. She was afraid, and clearly, so was John.

Pat climbed into bed. The light of the twilight was fading, so John drew the blackout curtains and turned on the oil lamp next to their bed. They sat side by side in bed, propped up on pillows reading—and listening for sounds of Tom's return. When he didn't come, they relaxed a little bit. The lamp oil was getting low.

"I need to go to the privy," John said. "I'll have to take the torch. Do you want to come down with me, or do you want to wait here?"

Patricia didn't want to be alone in the dark bedroom, but neither did she want to stand in the dark outside the privy to wait for John.

"I'll be quick. You wait here," John said. "That would be the easiest thing."

"OK. But hurry, John," Pat pleaded.

It wasn't at all cold, but after John left the room Pat shivered and hugged Topsy down under the blankets. She heard him go outside and then it was quiet except for the usual night sounds. John seemed to take forever. She strained to hear him come back, unsure how much time had actually passed. In a while, she did hear footsteps on the stairs, but didn't see a light come under the door. She lay as if frozen in the bed and heard the door open.

"John?" she said quietly. There was no response. Someone slid into the bed beside her, and even though the room was inky black, she knew it wasn't John.

"Nice and cozy in here," said a voice. It was Tom. What was he doing in their bed, and where was John?

Tom slid across the bed until he was pressed into her back. She had curled herself into as tight a ball as she could, still clutching her doll. She could smell his sweat and the beer on his breath.

"Scared, are you?" he asked. His voice was mocking her. "Where's your big brother? Supposed to look after you, isn't he? He must like that coal cellar. He's shut in there again. Wonder how that happened."

Patricia thought about leaping out of the bed to run, but Tom seemed to read her mind and reached over to hold onto her, pressing into her even harder. His hands were rough and roamed over her nightdress. She started to cry and felt sick to her stomach.

"Don't you ever tell anyone or I'll come and find you and your big baby of a brother. Then I'll really hurt you. No one will believe you anyway. Certainly not my sweet Auntie Nel," Tom hissed in her ear.

Pat couldn't speak or move. She couldn't even resist the hands that groped her private places. She felt sick and ashamed, and was very worried about John. The things that came next were like a nightmare she never wanted to think about again, but she knew that no matter how hard she tried, she would never in her whole life forget what Tom had made her do.

In a little while, Tom got up and went downstairs. She didn't know whether to run or where she would go. She still had not moved since Tom had come into the room. She had no idea where John was, or what Tom would do to them if they told anyone.

A few minutes later, the door opened again and she jumped. But it was John. She relaxed for the first time. He sounded as terrified as she was.

"Pat, are you all right? Has he done anything to hurt you?" John came over to the bed and found the matches to re-light the oil lamp.

"I'm okay, John," Pat lied. "Where is he?"

"I don't know. I worked on the bolt on the coal cellar until I could open the door. The torch fell on the ground when he shoved me in, and there's no moon so it's pitch black."

"He pushed you in there?" asked Pat, horrified.

"He came running up to the privy and said he'd shut you in the coal cellar. He was laughing, and pretty drunk, I think. I ran into the coal cellar to find you and he pushed me in and locked the door," John said. His hands were shaking as he tried to light the lamp.

"He said if we told anyone, he'd really hurt us, John," Pat said, choking back tears.

"No one's going to believe us anyway. Did he hurt you?" John asked again.

"No," Pat lied again. John was already scared enough. She couldn't find the words to say what had happened there in the dark, she just felt so sick and ashamed. "What do we do now?"

"Let's take our blanket and go out and hide in the dell. He won't find us there. Bert will be back tomorrow, and Tom won't try anything while he's around."

So they took the blanket off their bed and put their play clothes back on. Pat grabbed Topsy and followed John out into the darkness. He had found Bert's other torch in the Barters' bedroom, and led her to the dell under the trees. Without speaking a word, they huddled down under the blanket and fell asleep, unmolested, for the rest of the night.

At dawn, Rosie's rooster crowed and woke them. The night had been a warm one. They carefully folded their blanket, making sure no twigs or leaves had stuck to it, and tucked it behind a bush. Without stopping at the cottage for breakfast, they ran across the common to the Moons' house. No one was up yet, so they used the privy at the back of the Moons' garden. John fixed Pat's hair into some semblance of order, and they sat on the Moons' front steps until they heard Mr. and Mrs. Moon get up and start moving about the kitchen.

John knocked quietly on the back door. Mrs. Moon opened the door, clearly surprised to have a visitor this early on a Sunday morning.

"My goodness, what are you two doing up so early on a Sunday?" she asked.

"Nel and Bert are up in town at a wedding. Can we come in for a bit, until we go to the Church in the Wood?" John spoke quickly, afraid he'd lose his nerve.

He'd never barged in on anyone uninvited before, not even the Moons, as many times as he'd been in this very kitchen with Ernie and Margaret.

"Of course you can. Imagine them leaving you there on your own. You could have stayed here," Mrs. Moon said.

John was afraid Mrs. Moon would say something to Nel and they'd get into trouble. He regretted coming now, but wanted his little sister to get some breakfast before church.

"It's all right. We wanted to stay on our own. Please don't mention it to Nel," he added hastily, then lied yet again. "I just had trouble getting the stove lit, is all."

"Sit yourselves down. Ernie and Margaret will be up soon. Your secret's safe with me," Mrs. Moon reassured him. "I suppose now that you're fourteen, Nel thought it would be all right to leave you. Still, I wouldn't go off and leave my kids. There's a war on, even in the country."

Pat was glad to sit at the Moons' kitchen table and put the awful night behind her. Sitting there with Mrs. Moon bustling about, a wave of relief came over her. At that moment, she missed her parents more than she ever had since the first night she and John were evacuated. She swallowed a lump in her throat and helped Mrs. Moon lay the table for breakfast. They ate breakfast with the Moons, and then Ernie, Margaret, John, and Pat walked to the Church in the Wood. Neither Pat nor John mentioned Tom or the events of the previous night, and they were most happy to accept Mrs. Moon's invitation to Sunday lunch when they got back to the house after church. They spent the afternoon playing games with Margaret and Ernie.

Just before tea, John and Pat reluctantly went back to the Barter cottage. Nel and Bert were back, and when John and Pat came through the door, they saw Tom sitting at the kitchen table drinking tea and chatting animatedly with Nel.

"Didn't give you any trouble, did they, Tom?" Nel asked.

"No trouble at all," Tom said coolly.

Nel didn't take any notice of Pat and her brother, just continued with whatever story she was telling Tom about their visit to town. In a few minutes, Bert came down dressed in his work clothes. He was happy to see Pat and John.

"Thanks for doing the milking for me while I was gone," he said to John. "Would you like to go up with me now?"

The two were happy to get out of the cottage and gladly followed Bert up the path. He seemed as happy as they were to get away from the house and his "guest." It was such a relief to have Bert back, but neither said a word to him about what had happened while he was gone. They were too afraid.

Mr. Silk told Bert that John had been a big help while Bert was away.

"We'll make a countryman of him yet," the old man said, laughing his husky laugh.

Mrs. Silk was in her kitchen, putting the bones from the Sunday roast on to boil for soup the next day. Her kitchen always smelled wonderful and felt warm and comfortable. Mrs. Silk let Pat help peel potatoes. It was such a comforting ritual, Pat thought. Mrs. Silk chattered away, telling stories about when her son was a little boy, learning about the cows and how to milk them, and Pat pretended to listen. She just enjoyed the security of the farmhouse kitchen. She really didn't want to go back to the Barters', but at least Bert was home.

Too soon, John came to the kitchen to get his snack and said it was time to go. They walked with Bert back through the woods to the cottage. When they came into the kitchen, Pat was relieved to see that Tom had gone.

"Tom's decided to leave a little early and stay with some friends over near Cheriton. He'll go on to his new job from there. I expect he'll pop in again to visit one of these days," Nel said sadly. "I'm sorry I didn't get more time with him, but we had to go to that wedding."

"I'm glad to see the back end of him, I'll say that much," Bert commented.

Nel slammed a pot on the stove, but she didn't say anything more about Tom.

Pat and John set the dishes on the table without speaking. Bert went into the sitting room, sat down in his chair, and switched on the wireless. The newsman was reporting that Britain and Russia were signing some sort of agreement in Moscow.

"Looks like the Soviets are in the war on our side, now that Hitler double-crossed them," Bert said to John when they joined him in the front room.

John and Bert talked about the war and listened to the rest of the news before they sat down to their supper.

Chapter Nine

Mixed-up and Confused

Whenever Nel mentioned Tom's name, or the possibility that he might visit again, Pat felt a wave of nausea come over her. The thought of him terrorized her more than any bomb or air-raid siren she'd ever heard in the city, and she knew she would never tell a soul about that horrible night. John had warned her not to mention Tom's visit to anyone, and she was more than happy to obey. The vague, uneasy feeling that somehow it was all her fault—the same feeling that had come over her when they were evacuated—came over her whenever she thought of Tom. She was determined to put all memory of it out of her mind, and John seemed to feel the same, for they never spoke of that night again.

It was easy to put fearful thoughts out of her mind during the beautiful summer days of the school holidays. Pat could go wherever she pleased, whenever she pleased, so long as her chores were done, and she spent her days playing with her friends, helping Rosie with her cows, or riding the country roads on her bicycle.

But her favorite activity was helping Bert in the garden. Bert was knowledgeable and a patient teacher, and under his tutelage Pat grew to love digging in the dirt and watching things grow. She had always enjoyed gardening with her father back in Portsmouth, but her dad had not been around as much as Bert was. Now Pat was learning the names of every flower and tree in the surrounding country. Bert no longer had to show her how to weed or water or mulch the plants. She helped to pick vegetables and fruits, and was happy to help Nel preserve the produce and make jams and jellies.

Life in Portsmouth now seemed a million miles away. Pat hardly thought about her life there anymore. When she did think about home, it was usually only after hearing John read their mother's letters aloud each week. It was frightening to think about her mother and all the people they knew still running to the shelters whenever the air-raid siren sounded. When her mother's letters described what Diane was doing or learning, or what baby Michael was like, Pat felt as though she was hearing news of someone else's family.

John continued to learn country life from Bert, and he became a useful farm laborer at the Silk farm, for Rosie Batten, and for other neighboring farms. He worked as much as he could, and was anxious to please. He was also anxious to stay out of Nel's way, since she continued to treat him as an unwelcome guest.

Near the end of the summer, it was time to pick gooseberries. These plump green berries grew in profusion in Bert's garden. After working all morning at the farm, Bert came home for his lunch and to tend to his own gardens before going back for the afternoon. These summer afternoons picking gooseberries together were great fun for Pat and John.

"The first rule of gooseberry picking," Bert told them as he handed them each a pail, "is to keep whistling all the time you're picking. This is very important." He was quite serious as he said this.

As odd as this sounded, neither of the children questioned it, so as they picked berries, Bert led them whistling a chorus of "Hang out the Washing on the Siegfried Line," and the two joined in with gusto.

The first time Pat stopped whistling, Bert said, "Are you picking those berries or eating them?"

Pat swallowed a guilty mouthful, laughed, and resumed whistling while she picked. Between choruses, she and John still managed to sneak a few mouthfuls of berries, but found it was hard to whistle when you wanted to laugh.

Each evening, Pat went up to the Silk farm to fetch their milk in a pail, carrying it down through the peaceful woods at the back of the cottages. John helped her crank up the special bucket it was kept in deep down in the well, and lower the full milk pail down so it would stay fresh and cool. John would pull it up again in the morning for their breakfast. It took ages to crank the bucket up out of the well, and he had to be very careful not to spill the milk. It was certainly a lot more work than putting a bottle of milk in their electric refrigerator back in Portsmouth.

John never called Nel and Bert "Mum" and "Dad" the way Pat did, and he stopped reminding her that these people were not her real family; she wouldn't listen to him when he did. Otherwise, Pat did whatever John asked her to do, and when he occasionally reminded her of something that was "bad manners," the way their mother might have done had she been there, she rarely answered him back, but said, "Yes, John."

Pat still didn't like taking baths in the kitchen and complained and dragged her feet about doing so. She became very modest about taking her clothes off, and wouldn't let Nel help her at all. Everyone had to be out of the house before she would take off her clothes and step into the tub. Nel thought she was being ridiculous about the whole thing, but humored her because it was the only way to get her to bathe. Nel did still help Pat wash her hair over the sink. Her hair was getting long and thick, and it took some time to rinse, comb, and braid every Saturday evening. Nel didn't seem to mind helping Pat with this, and it was the only motherly thing she seemed interested in doing.

Nel was gone a great deal, but Pat didn't know where she went most of the time. When she was at home, she was very kind to Pat, and chatted with her while they worked together in the kitchen. Occasionally, Nel took her to Winchester with her. Winchester was a large market town about an hour's bus ride from Bramdean. According to the plaque on the statue of the Saxon King Alfred at the bottom of the High Street, the city was the ancient capital of England. Winchester had so far received little air-raid damage. Though no one was sure why the city was spared the German bombs, the local story was that Hitler, in his arrogance, was sure he would defeat the British, and he wanted to be crowned the new "Saxon" King beneath the ancient vaulted ceilings of Winchester Cathedral. Pat never heard the story without wondering what kind of man could be evil enough to start such an awful war—and then want to be a king.

During that summer of 1941, John worked every day on neighboring farms, wherever extra hands were needed, and he was able to save a little money to give to his mother. Farms all around the area needed help with harvesting corn and potatoes. John wanted to learn to drive a tractor, but local boys with farm experience weren't interested in giving up such prime jobs to "vackies" like him. Instead he had to work behind the tractors with the girls and younger boys, picking up the potatoes or ears of corn the big machine harvesters left behind. This was called "gleaning," and it was backbreaking work, but John never complained. He liked knowing he was doing something to help. Pat helped with harvesting, too, and though children her age didn't work as many hours, all hands were required for the harvest. Though they were officially exempt from the draft, many of the laborers from the farms had voluntarily gone into the fighting forces, and the farms were shorthanded. Women from the cities came out to replace them on the farms, and they were called the Women's Land Army, or "Land Girls," for short.

All that summer, the war raged on with no end in sight, but things were quiet in Bramdean. Pat and John received occasional letters from their father along with the letters from their mother, who wrote to them faithfully every week. Their dad's letters were very short and mostly said how much he missed them and how they needed to be brave and help with the war effort by staying put. Every Sunday evening, Pat and John dutifully wrote to both of their parents.

A few days before her ninth birthday, Pat received a parcel with a new skirt her mother had made along with a green wool jumper she'd knitted. Included with her gifts was a doll's dress for Topsy in material to match Pat's skirt. But Pat didn't play much with Topsy anymore. She preferred riding her bike or playing games outdoors. She still loved to read, and her mother had also sent an illustrated book of fairy tales for her birthday—a used one in very good condition. Pat sat by the hour reading it in the cozy dell on late summer days.

In September, when school started again, she returned to Bramdean School. She was happy to have moved to the upper class with her friends, but she still struggled with spelling and math. John was 14, and he really wanted to go to work, but he had to go back to the school in Alresford because he still had catching up to do from all the school he had missed in Portsmouth. There were other evacuees his age who were in the same situation, so at least he was not alone in this.

More evacuees continued to pour out of the cities, and the Bramdean School became overcrowded. Though Pat had lived in the village for nearly a year, and had made good friends, she still felt like an outsider. On the first day of school, she heard one of the older village boys ask a new evacuee boy from Portsmouth the riddle, "Adam and Eve and Pinch-me went down to the river to bathe. Adam and Eve were drowned. Who do you think was saved?" Before Patricia could warn him, the Portsmouth boy answered, "Pinch-me," and got pinched hard in the arm quick as a flash, much to the merriment of the other village children on the playground.

In fall, every able-bodied person in the countryside helped with the harvest, including school children. With the Germans sinking supply ships in the Atlantic, the nation's food supply was uncertain, even in the country. Growing and putting by food would be the difference between going hungry or eating during the winter months. Even Nel Barter, who wasn't nearly as organized a housekeeper as Nora Phillips, spent the fall putting up vegetables and jams, chutneys and pickles. Pat watched in fascination as Bert harvested honey from the beehives. Some of the sweet amber syrup was stored in jars in the spare room, along with the root vegetables and jars of vegetables and preserves. Bert sold some of his honey to neighbors or traded it for other items of food the family needed. Several jars were traded with Mr. Norgate next door for small game such as rabbits and birds. This meat supplement was very important to the Barters with everything in the shops so tightly rationed.

John continued to work hard at school, and sat long hours every evening doing his lessons at the kitchen table. He was determined to finish school and find a job so he could help his mother afford a place for their family away from the bombing in Portsmouth. Pat read books from the school's tiny library and listened to her favorite programs on the wireless, and tried not to think about the war too much.

In early December, the wireless broadcast carried the startling news that Japan had attacked the American naval fleet anchored at Pearl Harbor in Hawaii, all the way across the world in the Pacific Ocean. The Japanese had declared war on both the United States and Britain, and had joined the war on the side of the Italians and Germans. That week at school, there was a buzz of excitement among the teachers. Pat wondered why such a terrible event was being treated like good news. She knew America was Britain's friend, had heard all about it from Bert and from school, but the United States hadn't yet become part of the war.

"America is a vast country with many people and great wealth. With them on our side, we can win this war sooner," Pat's teacher explained. There was hope in the teacher's voice. There was hope everywhere, for the first time since the war began.

For Pat, this major event was overshadowed by the news that after long months of searching, Nora had finally found a place to live in the country and was moving out of Portsmouth. She would be renting two rooms at the back of a small farmhouse in the nearby village of New Cheriton. The farmhouse itself was a converted army supply hut made of corrugated metal, left over from the Great War. There was barely enough room for Nora and the two younger children, and it wouldn't be available until just before Christmas.

"Mum says we won't be able to leave the Barters' until she finds a bigger place, but at least they'll be out of Portsmouth, and we can visit every weekend," John told Pat when they were alone in their room that night. He was happier than she had seen him in a long time.

Pat could not even pretend to be excited about the prospect of living with her mother again. She didn't want to leave the Barters.

"What about our house in Portsmouth? What about Dad? Where will he go when he gets time off?" she demanded.

"Grandma Phillips, Aunt Winnie, and her Stella were bombed out of London for a second time, and they're fed up. They're moving out to our place because they have no place else to go. Obviously, Dad can still go there, and stay with his mother. Aunt Katie's husband, Uncle Steve, has been sent to the Pacific," John said. "She might move down there, too."

"But there's bombs falling on Pompey, too," Pat said.

"Not nearly as bad as in London," John said. "You don't seem too excited about being with your own family again."

He was confused by Pat's reaction, but no more so than Pat herself. She didn't want to make John angry, and she couldn't understand, let alone explain, how she felt.

"I can't wait to get out of this place," John said.

Pat had never seen John dislike anyone the way he disliked Nel Barter. He never referred to Nel by name, only as "she" and "her." And he still gave Pat a very cold look when she called the Barters Mum and Dad, so she was careful not to let that slip out when he was around.

"These people are not your family," John said. "I can't wait to have us all back together again, where we belong. Now the Yanks are in the war with us, we'll whip the Germans and the Japs." Softening a little, he added, "You'll be all right once we're settled with Mum again. Everything's going to be all right now."

When John was being all bossy, Pat could talk back, but when he was looking out for her, being his usual kind self, she couldn't do anything but go along with him. So she said nothing more about it. The fact that they weren't going to leave the Barters right away allowed her to put it out of her mind. It was easy to do because she was busy all the time, between school, doing her chores, and playing with her friends.

* * * *

A week before Christmas, Nel took Pat to Winchester, where they stayed the weekend with Nel's sister and her family. Nel showed Pat off to everyone as though she was her own child, always calling her "my Pat." They shopped together in the market and Nel indulged her with special treats, and Pat felt guilty that John was left behind. John was only too happy to stay home with Bert, but Pat tucked aside some of her treats to take back and share with her brother.

Just before Christmas, Nora settled into the two tiny rooms in New Cheriton. Despite the cramped quarters and primitive conditions, she was relieved to get out of the city. Arthur was to be posted to a ship patrolling the North Atlantic. He'd not been home much for the last few months and would be gone most of the time now. It might be some months before she could find another place large enough so that she could bring John and Pat to live with her, but at least she could be nearer to them and see them more regularly, as well as get her other two children out of harm's way. She was glad to be away from the bombing.

Her older children hardly knew their younger sister and brother, and Nora was tired of feeling that her family was scattered. At least she could see Pat and John on weekends, and Arthur could take the bus to see them all when he had a shore leave. On his last home visit, he'd told her there was renewed hope throughout the British ranks now that America was in the war.

On Christmas Eve, Pat and John took the bus to see their mother's new home for the first time. John was thrilled to be leaving the Barters even for a couple of days, but Pat was not excited at all. She felt confused and guilty for not feeling the way John did. She could tell that Bert was sorry they were going away for Christmas, and she couldn't meet his eyes when they left the cottage to walk to the bus station. He'd be alone at Christmas because Nel had gone to Winchester as she had the Christmas before.

Bert wished them "Happy Christmas" as they left.

Pat hugged him. "I'll miss you," she said.

When they arrived at their mother's new place, Pat was amazed at how tiny it was. There was one bedroom, with a small bed for her mother, a cot on one side for two-year-old Diane, and a crib on the other side for nine-month-old Michael. An old folding army cot was set up for Pat, and there was just enough room left to walk sideways between the beds. It was impossible to make the beds with any semblance of the neatness Nora still insisted upon. Another army cot was set up just at night in the other room for John.

This other room served as kitchen, dining, and sitting room, and contained a small table and chairs, a stove, and a small sink. There were two open shelves above the sink for a few dishes and utensils. Everything else Nora had managed to bring out from Portsmouth was stored in boxes stacked against the far wall. With all five of them in the two rooms, it was very crowded. Since it was cold and damp outside, Pat wasn't able to go outside to escape the confining atmosphere.

"We won't be able to have a proper Christmas tree," Nora told Pat and John as they sat for supper on Christmas Eve. "But Mr. Giles said we can cut some branches from some of the trees out back. I've brought a few of our decorations from home."

John was happy to be with his own family. "That's okay, Mum. We can make the place look good for the holiday, can't we, Pat?"

Pat wasn't feeling very jolly, but she tried to pretend a little, for John's sake.

"Yes," she said, mustering a smile.

She knew she should be pleased to be with her mother, and she had not seen her baby sister since they'd been evacuated. Diane hadn't been much older than Michael was now when Pat and John had come out to Bramdean. Now Pat was expected to help look after this toddler who didn't know her at all, and who seemed determined to get into everything and put everything in her mouth. Pat had never seen Michael, and he cried when she tried to talk to him the first time.

"He'll get used to you," Nora said, picking him up and shushing him while he howled. "There, there," Nora cooed to the baby, "this is your big sister."

Pat looked at his chubby, tear-stained face and felt like crying, too, but she held back her tears. She longed to have her mother pick her up and hug her and reassure her that everything would be all right. But her mother was preoccupied now with the younger children.

Nearly as soon as they'd walked into the house, their mother had chores for John and Pat to do. They actually knew more about country living than Nora, who was accustomed to the modern conveniences of the city, like electricity, a gas hot water boiler, and indoor plumbing. John was eager to help and did his chores with great energy. Pat was much less enthused. She was expected to amuse the little ones while her mother made meals and did other chores, and everything took longer because Nora was used to the conveniences of the city. Pat wasn't used to little children, and she grew bored with them very quickly.

Her mother made no secret of her intentions for Pat now that they would be coming to her place every weekend.

"You've been allowed to run wild. That woman doesn't know a thing about raising kids, and you've become quite a tomboy," her mother said. "We'll soon change that."

Mr. Giles, the farmer who owned the house, was a kindly landlord. He kept pigs on his small farm. He came by to say Happy Christmas and to tell Nora that any time she needed a ride, he'd be only too happy to offer his farm lorry. He offered to fetch John and Pat from Bramdean, too, since he was frequently over that way. Otherwise, they would have to take the bus to Cheriton and walk the three miles from town to get to the farm. Nora was grateful for his offer.

Christmas morning, John and Pat opened a parcel with a letter from their dad. Included with the letter was a bar of chocolate, some nuts, and a scarf he had knitted for each of them. There were treats in their stockings from Father Christmas. The family listened to the King's Christmas speech and their favorite programs on the wireless. For a Christmas tree, Nora had placed a few fir branches in an old jug decorated with paper decorations and the few ornaments she'd brought from Portsmouth. It was too far to walk to church, and Mr. Giles was not a churchgoing man, so the day passed quietly. Pat missed Bert and wondered if he was lonely at the cottage all by himself. Her brother and mother were talking about Christmases past.

"Do you remember the parties at the barracks before the war?" John asked as they ate their small Christmas dinner. "And the trips to the pantomime?"

"Yes," Pat said.

"I have a surprise for you," Nora said. "Mr. Giles has kindly offered to bring you into Cheriton tomorrow so you can attend the Christmas show at the village hall. It's a special Boxing Day performance for evacuee children. Won't that be fun?"

John and Pat were glad to have something to look forward to. For Pat, it was a chance to get out of the cramped bungalow and away from her mother. She felt guilty for feeling this way, but she couldn't help it. She missed the Barters.

Her own mother only seemed to see her as someone to watch the little ones, a job Pat grew tired of the very first day. She couldn't seem to do anything right. She resented being criticized for not doing chores the way her mother "had taught her," and was very defensive of Nel and Bert when her mother spoke critically of them. She had been with them for more than a year, and they felt like her family now. She and John would be returning to the Barters' after the pantomime, taking the bus from Cheriton to Bramdean, and Pat couldn't wait.

She was sent to bed at almost the same time as the little ones Christmas night, but John was allowed to stay up. Pat would have resented this more had she not been anxious to get to her cot, where she could escape into her new book, which she read by torchlight under the blanket. She could hear Nora talking to John as if he were an adult.

"Don't worry, I'll find another place soon, and we'll all be together again. Pat will settle down once we're all under one roof. I'll certainly have to take her in hand, I can see that."

The next day, Pat and John said goodbye to their mother, and Mr. Giles took them in his rickety old lorry to Cheriton. The village hall was full of children, and had been transformed into a makeshift theatre. There were fir boughs and handmade decorations. At one end was a table with refreshments for the party after the pantomime, and there was a curtain hung lengthwise at the other end of the hall to make it look like a stage.

Pat sat next to her brother and was totally absorbed in the panto-mime. Her laugh was so loud people turned to look at her. John shot her an embarrassed look, so she tried to control herself. Everyone got excited when the "Prince" told the audience to warn him when the "wolf" was there—and all the children shouted at the appropriate time, "He's be-hind you!" The hour seemed to fly by.

On the refreshments table there were fruits and candies they hadn't seen since the war started. There were other evacuees from neighboring villages. Pat didn't know any of them, but it was nice to hear kids speak-ing with the Pompey accent again. She'd had a wonderful day and didn't mind too much the bus ride back to Bramdean, or the walk back to the Barters'.

"Did you have a good time with your mum and your little brother and sister?" Bert asked them that night when they went up to the Silks' to help with the milking.

"Yes, thanks," said John.

Pat said "Yes, thanks," too, but without nearly as much enthusi-asm.

She was glad to spend the rest of the Christmas holiday at Bram-dean. Once they were back with their friends at the Common, things felt normal again for her.

As the New Year 1942 began, the long gray winter settled in. Pat and John were expected to spend most weekends with their mother, and Pat dreaded these visits. She missed the Barters and her friends at the Common, and she was bored to death minding her baby brother and sister. She couldn't help being secretly amused by her mother's struggles adjusting to country life. It took Nora several months to get used to oil lamps, pumping drinking water from the well, and lugging wash water from the rain barrel. Nora especially hated the bucket toilets, and ap-preciated very much that John would empty and bury the waste for her when they were there. Nora complained about how "unfriendly" the people in the village were to strangers, especially from the towns.

"They seem so suspicious when you go into the shop. Do they think I'm a German spy or something?" she often wondered out loud.

But she tried very hard to fit in and become part of the commu-nity. She wasn't naturally a person who joined clubs or socialized, but she decided to join the local Women's Institute, and was now helping with knitting and other work for the war effort. No matter how hard she tried to fit in with the women in the village, she was still an outsider, just as John and Pat were always "vackies."

Her mother hadn't lost her sense of humor, though, much to Pat's relief. When they were together, she tried to spend time with John and Pat playing their old favorite games in the evenings. It suddenly seemed to Pat that her mother was actually making an effort to talk with her when she wasn't ordering her about or scolding her for something.

One Saturday night, after their baths and after the babies were put to bed, Nora had Pat and John in fits of laughter as she told them about an incident during the previous week with one of Mr. Giles's pigs.

"The other day, I had to bring in the washing quickly—it was about to rain. Diane was playing on the floor, and Michael was asleep in his cot. So I left the door propped open so I could see her when I went out to fetch in the washing. I turned my back for just a moment—but I guess I must have been distracted for a few minutes.

"When I turned around and came back through the kitchen door with the washing, one of Mr. Giles's pigs, that old fat sow, was standing in the middle of my freshly washed kitchen floor! There was Diane, sitting over there, not four feet away, pointing at it and saying, 'Piggy! Piggy!'

"I was horrified—you know how afraid I am of that thing. Then I got angry when I saw the track of muddy prints on my floor. I grabbed the broom by the door and got myself quick between that old sow and Diane. I was terrified she'd step on her. I yelled at the pig, 'Get! Shoo!' and I waved the broom at her. She just stood there staring at me with this dumb expression in those bulgy red-rimmed eyes. I was afraid to move for fear of upsetting it and having it charge at me, with Diane, whom I'd now picked up and had on one hip with the broom in my other hand. I didn't want to yell so loudly I'd wake the baby in the other room. Mr. Giles was in town, so there was no use yelling for him to help."

By this point in her story, John was almost rolling on the floor laughing. Pat was laughing so hard tears were in her eyes. It was like their old storytelling days, when they were home, before the war.

"I didn't know what to do, really, so I poked that fat sow with the broom on her backside and shouted for her to 'shoo' again. This time, she'd obviously decided there was nothing worth eating in here. She just turned and ambled her way back through the kitchen door, taking no other notice of me whatsoever. She'd tracked mud all over the floor and my washing was all over the floor in it, where I dropped it when I ran in. My hands were shaking and there was sweat rolling down my forehead.

"I guess we need to be sure to close the kitchen door behind us from now on," she said. "I suggested to Mr. Giles in as polite a manner as I could muster that he needed to keep his pigs in their pens!"

That weekend was one of their better visits. Nora had adjusted pretty well to country life and had finally relaxed enough to laugh the way she had done back in Portsmouth. It was still confusing for Pat to go back and forth each week between the Barters' and her mother's in New Cheriton. Usually, she was relieved to be back with the Barters because she missed Bert. He never even went as far away as Alresford unless he had to, or to Winchester unless Nel wore him down. He was pretty much within walking distance all the time—either at the cottage or working up at the Silk farm.

With the Barters, she was spoiled like an only child. Bert treated John as an adult, while Nel ignored him. With her own mother, Pat felt like one of a group, and someone to help with the little ones and do chores. She wanted to stay with the Barters in Bramdean, not be up-rooted again.

Her mother frequently complained to John about how hard it was to find a place in the area big enough for all of them, and if she did, it was too expensive. John was anxious to make the move, but Pat hoped she could put the idea of moving out of her mind for a long time.

Chapter Ten

Taming the Wild Child

The news broadcasts and newspapers tried to shed a positive light on the war to keep morale up, but everyone knew things were going badly. Even with America and Russia fighting on the British side—the "Allies" or the "Grand Alliance," as Mr. Churchill called it—the Germans, Italians, and Japanese seemed to be gaining. The War in the Pacific was going especially badly. In February, the Allied forces surrendered in Singapore. The Japanese captured thousands of civilian and military personnel, among them Arthur's brother-in-law, Steve.

That month the government also required women—married, single, or even pregnant—ages 18 to 60, to register with the Ministry of Labor to be assigned whatever war work they could do. Only women who had children at home under the age of 14 were exempt. Pat's mother, even with young children at home to care for, made time to knit and roll bandages along with other local members of the Women's Institute. Of course, every weekend they visited their mother, Pat had to look after her little sister and brother so her mother could get all of her work done. Diane was two and Michael was now one year old.

For some weeks, the family did not hear from Arthur, and the news on the wireless from the Atlantic was grim. German U-boats had stepped up their efforts to destroy the critical shipping supply lines between the United States and Britain, but Nora kept saying, "No news is good news."

By the time school closed for the summer holidays in July, sweets were among the many items on ration, but this did not affect Pat and John much because they had so little pocket money. Bus runs between towns became much less frequent, and people were no longer allowed to take pleasure drives in their cars—fuel was too precious to waste. Mr. Giles's old lorry was a farm vehicle, so he could get extra petrol coupons, but it was expensive, so he drove only when necessary. To visit their mother on weekends, John and Pat now had to ride their bikes. For her part, Pat was always happy to get back to the Barters' on Sunday night.

Nel still went to Winchester every week, but Pat stopped going with her. Nel was frequently gone overnight at least one night a week, and for reasons unknown to Pat, she was no longer inclined to take her along. Pat was happier at the cottage with Bert, playing with her friends, and riding her bicycle. She continued her chores, and helped Bert in the garden and Rosie with her cows.

John turned 15 in May and finished school that term. He went to work as a day laborer at various farms in the area, but had not found a permanent job. He had become a skilled farm worker, and with shortages of labor, boys his age and the Women's Land Army were critical to the production of the nation's food supply.

Pat was nearly 10 years old. She would have one more year at Bramdean School before going to the senior school in Alresford. She was now the oldest girl in her class at the village school—no longer one of the younger kids. She was settled and had several good friends, and very much looked forward to her summer holidays. John wouldn't be around much, so apart from the weekends she had to spend with her mother, she would be free to play in the dell or ride her bike as far as she wanted.

When she was visiting her mother, she had to stay close to the bungalow, help her mother, and mind Diane and Michael—especially Diane. Pat couldn't go anywhere without Diane. If she started out the door, her mother would say, "Take your sister outside to play, but mind her." Patricia counted the hours until she could get back to the Barters'. John and their mother would talk about his jobs, or the news, as if Pat wasn't even there. She missed having John to herself. He was grown up now, and she felt the loss of him keenly. The only place she felt she fit in now was with the Barters, at the Common.

One weekend in August, they arrived to find their mother happier than they'd seen her since the war began. She couldn't wait to tell them her news.

"I've found a bungalow to rent at the top of Harnham Hill," she said. "That's the road going into Cheriton. It's only four rooms, but we'll have it to ourselves and there's a large piece of ground with it—almost three-quarters of an acre!"

"Well done, Mum!" John said. "How soon can we move?"

"In a fortnight, soon enough so that Pat can start the new school year in her new school, the Cheriton Village School."

Pat was not excited about this news; quite the contrary. She simply stood there, staring at her shoes. Taking no notice of her, Nora continued to talk with John about all the plans she had for their new home.

"I'm going to get some chickens so we can have fresh eggs, and we'll have a vegetable garden."

Nora had also secured a regular job for John on a nearby farm. Once he was in Cheriton full time, he'd have regular wages at just one job. He was thrilled.

"Maybe I'll get to drive the tractor, like the older lads," he said. Things were finally turning out as he had hoped.

After lunch that day, Pat cleared the table and helped dry the dishes without saying anything. No one took any notice of her anyway. Soon it was bath time, and seeing to the younger ones took every bit of Nora's attention until bedtime.

The next day, when John and Pat went back to the Barters', their mother and the two little ones came along in Mr. Giles's lorry, as he had business over that way.

When Nora told the Barters that her children would be coming with her in a fortnight's time, Bert and Nel were clearly devastated. John and Pat had been with them nearly two years.

Nel, visibly shaken by Nora's announcement, pleaded with her to let Pat stay. "You have your hands full with the two little ones. We'd be glad to keep Pat. She's become like our own. She's only got another year at the village school, and she's doing so well it seems a shame to uproot her again."

"She's not 'your own,'" said Nora stiffly. "I know what's best for my daughter. Her place is with her own family."

"We'd adopt her and take good care of her. You've got three others." Nel was crying now.

Nora's face registered the shock of this suggestion, but with great effort she controlled her rising emotions.

"Pat and John will move with us to Cheriton in a fortnight. Thank you for having them during this difficult time. We've all had to make many sacrifices in this awful war." Nora stopped. She was starting to get angry.

Pat could feel the intensity of the emotions all around her and wanted to run for the dell. But she stood there as if glued to her spot on the kitchen floor of the Barter cottage. There followed a very uncomfortable silence. Nel started to sob.

Bert spoke quietly to Nora. "We'd be glad to have them visit any time, if that's all right by you," he said.

"I'll let you know," Nora said, getting up to leave as she heard Mr. Giles's lorry rumble down the lane to stop in front of the cottage.

John helped their mother hand Diane and Michael up into the cab of the lorry.

When her mother had gone, Pat ran out to the dell to be alone. She was upset at the prospect of leaving the Barters and her friends at the Common. It made her sick to her stomach to even think about starting over at a new school.

Over the next two weeks, Pat spent as much time as she could with her friends.

"Cheriton's not that far on my bike," Margaret Moon said. "Mum will just have to let us ride over to see you."

In the meantime, their room at the Barters' would not remain empty—Nel's nieces, Stella and Brenda, were coming out from London. Nel was happy about this arrangement because it meant she wouldn't have to take in any more evacuees and it would fill the void Pat's departure would leave.

"When you visit, you'll have them to play with," Nel told Pat.

Pat was jealous that someone would be coming to take her place in Nel and Bert's affections, sleep in her room, and play in her dell. Nel and Bert would soon forget her, she thought gloomily, and then there would be no place she would fit in.

Before she knew it, moving day dawned, a lovely summer Saturday. The sky was clear and the air perfumed by the roses climbing the front of the Barter cottage. The flowers and shrubs were abuzz with busy bees. Mr. Giles drove up to the cottage with his lorry. Their mother had come herself to collect them. John and Mr. Giles loaded their few belongings and their bicycles, and soon the goodbyes Pat had been dreading were upon her. She had a lump in her throat and couldn't speak.

John shook Bert's hand and said, "Thanks for everything."

Nora shook Bert's hand. Mr. Giles helped Nora put Diane and Michael back into the cab of the lorry. He got in and started the engine.

Pat struggled not to cry.

Bert said to John, "Good luck in your new gardening job," he said. "Where did you say it was?"

"Beauworth Manor," John said. "It's been taken over by a London orphanage, a Dr. Barnardo's Home."

"Oh, yes, of course. That's a good start for you. You know your way around a farm now," Bert said.

"Yes, thanks to you," John said. He too found it hard to leave Bert. But to Nel he only said politely, "Thanks." Turning to Pat then, he said "Come on. Let's not make it any harder than it is already."

"They're welcome to visit any time," Bert reminded Nora.

"Thank you. Come along now, Pat," Nora said.

Nel stood wiping tears from her eyes, and Pat gave her a quick hug.

Pat said to Bert, "I'll visit and help with the garden and the bees," but her voice broke and she threw her arms around his neck and hugged him.

Looking up at Nora, he gently pulled Pat away and helped her up into the back of the lorry. John swung up behind her, the old truck clunked into gear, and they pulled away, up the deeply rutted lane along the Common. From the back of the lorry, Pat watched Bert's slightly stooped figure get smaller, until he disappeared from sight as they turned a bend in the road.

The small brick bungalow that Nora had rented was three miles from Bramdean on the top of a hill at the convergence of two roads. Going inside the first time, Pat saw familiar things she'd not seen since she and John had left Portsmouth. Everything looked smaller to her, though, and oddly out of place in this unfamiliar house. Their old corner cupboard was in the front sitting room with her mother's Chinese tea set. Beside it was her mother's piano. Her parents' bed was along the other wall.

"Grandfather brought our things up on his lorry," Nora said.

Pat walked to the piano and gingerly touched one of the keys. The presence of these familiar objects made her feel slightly more at home, but in all other respects, she felt as unsettled as the day they'd been evacuated to the Barters'.

"I'm glad to have you both home," Nora said.

"The place looks great, Mum," John said.

Pat was quiet.

"I'll put the kettle on," Nora said. She was clearly hurt that Pat was unhappy, but she said nothing.

Pat felt guilty, so she tried to act more interested in what her mother was saying to John. Nora had many plans for the bungalow.

"As soon as I can, I'll have one of those fold-out beds for your dad and me, the ones that are a sofa during the day. Then we can have a proper sitting room," she said.

"With my wages, we should be able to save some money," John offered.

Nora showed them the rest of the cottage. There were two smaller bedrooms off the kitchen.

"This one's for the boys," Nora said, showing them the first tiny room. John's bed and his bureau from Portsmouth were along one wall. Michael's baby's cot was on the opposite wall, and there was just room enough to walk between the beds. John dropped his rucksack on his bed.

He smiled broadly. "It's great," he said.

"This other room is for you and Diane," she said to Pat, opening the door to the other small room. There was Pat's bed with her old coverlet. Her mother had cut down the matching curtains to fit the small window above the chest of drawers from her old bedroom back home. There was a very small child's bed on the other side of the bureau for Diane.

"You can put your things away while I make lunch," Nora said.

Pat didn't feel like unpacking. She felt like getting on her bike and riding as fast as she could back to Bramdean, but she knew better. She put her clothes neatly in the two empty drawers and stacked her books on the chest beside the bed. Topsy was at the bottom of the bag. Pat took the doll out and looked at its well-worn face. One eye didn't open anymore. Pat had long ago outgrown the skirt that matched the one the doll was dressed in.

She tossed the doll onto Diane's bed, and the little doll's one good eye closed as it lay where it landed. Pat turned away and went to the kitchen.

She sat down to lunch with the rest of the family and ate without speaking. Her mother spoke to John, and cut up Diane's food. Michael was in a little seat, eating his food with his fingers. Behind him was a window that looked out to the back garden. Pat stared out the window, and her mind wandered as Nora and John talked about the possibilities for the garden. She wondered how soon she could get outside to explore on her own. She didn't have long to wait.

"As for you, Pat," her mother said, "you're old enough to be of help. You certainly won't run wild, as you've done with those people. I've worried myself sick about you. You've become quite a tomboy. From now on, I will know where you are, and with whom, at all times. Is that clear?"

"Yes, Mum," was all Pat could say.

She tensed up even more as her mother added, "Otherwise, any visits to Bramdean will be out of the question."

After the lunch dishes were done, Nora sent Pat outside with Diane, giving her explicit directions to mind her little sister and keep her amused while she put Michael down for his nap and did her work. Pat spent the entire afternoon keeping the toddler from putting everything she picked up on the ground into her mouth. She looked longingly at her bike propped against the back of the cottage, and had to resist the urge to jump on it and ride away. She knew there would be no point. If she tried to run away, she'd lose any chance of visiting the Barters and her friends at the Common.

Pat knew her mother well, and she had not changed. She was also right: Pat *had* been free, and liked it that way. When Diane was down for her afternoon nap, Pat did her chores as quickly as she could and sneaked off to a secret hiding place she'd found in the hedge. There was just enough room under a clump of flowering bushes for her to curl up with a book, and just knowing that she had at least one place to hide made it all a little easier to bear.

"Where have you been?" her mother demanded when she came inside. "I've been calling to you for ages."

"Just outside, finishing my chores," Pat said. She wasn't really lying, even if she *had* finished the chores an hour before. She felt great satisfaction about her secret hiding place, and thereafter sought its sanctuary as often as she could.

That first Sunday in Cheriton, Nora announced at breakfast, "We're going to church. Put on your Sunday clothes. I don't wish to be late and it's a mile walk into the village."

When they were ready, Nora pushed Michael in the pram and John pushed Diane in the pushchair. Pat dawdled along behind.

The River Itchen wound through the center of Cheriton Village, and willow trees bent over its flower-covered banks. The village center was a cluster of houses and thatch-roofed cottages on both sides of the one road, which followed the shallow river past the tiny village green. There were small arched footbridges over the river, which in some places was no wider than a stream.

The Phillips family walked up the gravel path to the little brick and flint-stone church, St. Michael and All Angels, which sat at the top of a small green hill encircled by an ivy-covered stone wall, and skirted by the churchyard, beneath which lay the bones of past generations of Cheriton's inhabitants. Ancient, thickly mossed tombstones leaned amidst the newer stones in the churchyard. As they passed from the bright summer sunshine into the dimly lit vestibule, Pat's eyes took a few seconds to adjust. Once inside, she could see that the church was not dark at all, but full of softly filtered light. Nora led them to a pew near the back, on the right-hand side of the church, and they all took their seats.

As the vicar's sermon droned on, Pat's attention wandered to the worn stone floor where the sun streaming through the stained-glass windows made lovely rainbow patterns. She stole surreptitious glances at the people sitting in the pews around them. With her mother sitting beside her, she had to be careful not to get caught. Nora had Michael on her lap on one side of her, and John was on her other side with Diane on his lap.

St. Michael's seemed a friendly church, Pat thought, not quite like the lovely little Church in the Wood back at the Common, but small enough to feel cozy. St. Michael's wasn't grand and awesome, like Winchester Cathedral, and there were no tombs of kings and bishops here. There were no familiar faces, either.

Music was the only part of church Pat liked. Sitting in the choir stalls in front of the altar was a choir of boys and girls, some older, some younger than herself. The children were arranged by height in two sets of carved wooden pews on opposite sides of the altar facing each other.

They were dressed in red robes topped with starched white surplices, and their voices filled the church as the organist pounded out the notes of the closing hymn on the old pipe organ. The congregation stood and joined in a rousing rendition of "I Vow to Thee, My Country," one of Pat's favorites.

As the congregation filed out of the church, the vicar stood at the door outside to shake everyone's hand. As she stood and waited beside her mother, Pat could hear him making polite inquiries into people's health, and asking for news of their families.

As Nora stepped up to him, the vicar greeted her warmly.

"Good morning, Mrs. Phillips. I'm so glad to see that you and your children are reunited. It must be a great consolation to you."

He smiled kindly from a deeply lined face, his bright blue eyes in stark contrast to his pure white hair.

"Thank you, Vicar. I'm glad to have my children back with their family where they belong," Nora said.

"We have many families who have come out from Portsmouth. Most evacuees haven't yet been reunited with their families. God has blessed you, indeed," he said.

"Yes," Nora said. "This is my son, John, who starts work tomorrow at Beauworth Manor."

"How do you do, sir," John said politely, shaking the vicar's hand.

"This is my daughter, Patricia, who will be ten in September. She's very musical, like her father, who has been in the Marine Band since he was in the Boy's Brigade. Could you use another voice in the choir?"

The vicar smiled at Pat as she looked up to shake his hand.

"Yes, of course. We'd love to have her. It would be a good way for her to make friends in the village. Just see our choir director, Mrs. Katie Cross. She's still inside, I think. Rehearsals are Thursday evenings."

So it was that Pat joined the choir at St. Michael's. It was just like the old days at Portsmouth—Nora made the decisions and Pat was expected to do as she was told.

When Thursday came, her mother told her to get ready for choir practice. There was no point in refusing. Before she left, her mother warned her, "Come straight home and don't dawdle on the way, or next time John will have to walk you to the village and wait for you."

Pat said, "Yes, Mum," then set off for the one-mile bike ride to the village.

As she rode her bike to town, it was a relief to be away from her mother's watchful eye. When she came to the church door, however, she hesitated before going in. The big oak door was propped open, and she could hear the sound of voices and rustling papers. When she shyly stepped in, everyone turned and looked at her. Pat wanted to turn and run, but she glanced across the crowd and saw two girls with friendly faces smiling at her.

"Ewh, hellew, Priscilla, is it? The vicaahr said we were to have a new voice in the choir. Are you a soprano or an alto?"

"It's Pat," she said quietly, "and I don't know."

"Let's try you with the altos, then, and see how we get on," said Mrs. Katie Cross.

Mrs. Cross spoke with the strangest accent Pat had ever heard, drawing out her words in an affected, nasal voice. She had heard comedians on the wireless speak something like Mrs. Cross, but she'd never heard anyone speak that way naturally. And Mrs. Cross continued to call her "Priscilla."

Pat stepped up to an empty spot made for her by the two friendly girls in the front row. From the other half of the choir, across the altar, while Mrs. Cross wasn't looking in his direction, a tall, fair-haired boy in the back row made a face at her and laughed, nudging his friend next to him and pointing at her. Pat shot back her haughtiest stare.

After choir practice, the friendly girl beside her said, "Oh, don't pay him any mind. That's Charlie North. He's a practical joker, but he's all right. I'm Jean Ray. I was evacuated out of Portsmouth, too. Mrs. Cross said before you came in that you and your family were from Pompey, and your dad is in the marines. My dad works at the dockyard."

"Hi," said Pat. "How long has it been since you were home?"

"I came out just before the war started, with the entire school and our teachers. My mother was sure the Germans would land in Portsmouth Harbor as soon as war broke out," she said. "When did you come out?"

"I was just eight," Pat said. "My brother and I have been in Bramdean. I'll be ten in September."

"Well, I turned ten in January, so I'll show you the ropes around here, but I've got to go now. I'll see you at school, though," Jean said with a smile.

"Yes, thanks," Pat said shyly.

She was grateful for a friend. She'd been missing her friends at the Common almost as much as she missed her freedom. She knew her mother would be expecting her home, so she pedaled back up to the cottage on Harnham Hill as fast as she could.

"How was choir practice?" her mother asked when she came through the door.

"Fine," Pat said.

"That's a good start, then," her mother said.

Pat didn't mention Jean Ray. She decided to keep her new friend a secret, in case her mother disapproved. But Pat felt sure that she and Jean would be friends. She didn't know how she knew it, she just did, but she didn't want her mother to know it because that might spoil everything. She remembered that in Portsmouth there had been girls her mother allowed her to play with, and those whom her mother found "unsuitable." Pat wanted to decide for herself. She had so few choices now.

"I will make a good girl of you, one way or the other, before it's too late," Nora said.

Pat spent the rest of the summer trying to be helpful and to stay on her mother's good side. Every time she displeased her mother—which felt like most of the time—her mother said that if she didn't "straighten up" she would not be allowed to visit "the Common," as she always called the Barters'.

Pat missed Bert terribly. She missed Rosie and her cows, and eating biscuits in Mrs. Silk's kitchen. She even missed Nel, who never told her what to do or with whom she could play. It seemed to Pat that, with her mother, she could do nothing right. She tried, but nothing she did seemed to turn out as her mother wanted, from changing Michael's nappies, which she hated, to keeping the water buckets filled. As often as she could, Pat disappeared into her little hiding place in the hedge, losing herself in the pages of a book. She pretended not to hear when her mother called her, and this infuriated her mother all the more.

Pat spent a great deal of her time looking after her little sister. Diane was a sweet, chubby-faced toddler who was happy most of the time, but she tried to put everything she found on the ground into her mouth. And if Pat didn't keep a sharp eye on her, she wandered off.

Though she was nervous about starting at a new school full of strangers, Pat was looking forward to at least getting away from her mother by going to school. Until school began, all she had to look forward to was seeing her new friend Jean at choir practice on Thursdays. Sometimes, when she was especially lonely, Pat would look at her mother rocking Michael to sleep in the old chair that used to sit in their kitchen sitting room at Portsmouth, and wish that her mother would just hold her and rock her like that. But she was too old for that now. There was always work to do and Pat felt she had to earn whatever praise her mother could spare for her.

"There's a war going on and we all have to do our part," her mother constantly reminded her.

Still, it seemed unfair to Pat that she was treated so differently from the little ones or John, who was working and was treated like a grownup. At least Nora had received a letter from their father recently, and that improved her mood for a week or so, Pat noticed. Their dad couldn't tell them where he was, but they knew he was still in the North Atlantic somewhere, trying to keep supplies and troop convoys safe from the German U-boats, which were sinking ships all over the seas.

Morale seemed low everywhere, despite the rousing speeches and upbeat programs on the wireless. Everyone knew from the bare shelves in the shops when the supply ships had gone down, John observed. Letters to Nora from Mrs. Marchant or Grandma Phillips were full of the awful news that some friend or neighbor had had someone killed in action, or in the bombing.

Pat thought that the date on the top of her father's letters was the most important news in those letters. As of that date, at least, they knew he was alive and all right. Pat tried not to think of him in any other way. She hadn't seen her dad since she'd been evacuated—nearly two years. Without the picture of him in his uniform on her mother's dresser, she wouldn't remember the details of his face. She could still remember how his voice sounded telling his old stories of the places he'd been before the war. The war had changed everything and everyone. Pat wondered when, or if, it would ever end.

On the first day of school, she rode her bicycle into Cheriton to the village school, crossing over the river on a small bridge in the center of the village. The school was next to a lumberyard. The school building had steeply pitched gables and was slightly larger than the Bramdean School. Pat parked her bike in the rack outside and found Jean Ray on the school grounds.

The bell had not yet rung, so the schoolyard was full of boys and girls—and Pat and Jean were among the oldest. The rude boy from choir, Charlie North, was with a gang of other boys.

Charlie spotted her and yelled, "Hey, Townie!"

Pat ignored him.

Jean chattered away, explaining who everyone was and telling her all about the school. "Over there are the toilets. Those are the boys' toilets on that side, and those are ours on the other. They don't have flush toilets, of course. That's one thing I really missed from home," Jean said quietly. "These are pit toilets with sawdust from the lumberyard at the bottom. They scoop it out and put new sawdust in there," Jean said, wrinkling her nose. "I'll never get used to those."

"Me neither," agreed Pat.

The bell rang and the students lined up by classroom, boys on one side, girls on the other, and filed inside. Pat followed Jean. The teacher was at the door of the room to greet them as her pupils came in to take their assigned places. She looked at Pat and smiled. Pat recognized her at once.

"Hello. Patricia Phillips, isn't it? Do you remember me?" the teacher asked.

"Of course. I couldn't forget you, Miss Carpenter! You were at our school in Portsmouth," Pat said. She was thrilled to see a familiar face.

"Yes," Miss Carpenter said. "I came out with my students in the first evacuation. You must have just come out?"

"No, I've been at Bramdean for almost two years," Pat told her.

"Well, it's lovely to see you again. Your place is over there. Settle in and we'll catch up at the lunch recess."

Miss Carpenter pointed across the room to an empty seat. Pat's momentary delight at the familiar face of Miss Carpenter vanished as soon as she saw that she would be sitting in front of none other than that horrible Charlie North, who grinned from ear to ear as she took her seat and turned her back to him. The desks were all attached to one another in long rows, two students to a desk. Each had its own inkwell and pencil tray, and the slanted top opened to a space for books and papers.

The morning was spent on arithmetic, still Pat's most difficult subject. She spent the morning huddled in concentration over a set of problems she found especially hard. When the bell rang for lunch, she moved her head to look up, and when she did, she felt something odd and heard Charlie and his friends laughing. She knew they were laughing at her. Miss Carpenter had stepped out of the room for a moment.

"Oh, Charlie, you nasty little brute!" the girl beside her said.

Pat realized with horror that the end of her long braid had been dipped in Charlie's inkwell directly behind her, and when she'd moved her head, the ink had left stains all over her new white blouse. She was so angry she could have killed Charlie North—and she knew how angry her mother would be when she saw the stains on her school blouse. From long experience, she knew that telling the teacher would brand her as a tattletale—which was worse than being a "vackie" or a "townie."

"Better make sure you know where your pigtails are," Charlie teased as they filed out of the class for lunch.

Pat and Jean ate lunch together in the room next to their classroom.

"Charlie's all right, once you get to know him," Jean said, "He's just a trickster and is always clowning around."

"I don't think he's funny," Pat said hotly.

"His mother's the school caretaker. That's their house attached to the end of the school building," Jean said. "She's really nice, and a great cook. She sometimes fills in for Mrs. Harfield, the regular school lunch cook. On special occasions, when she's got enough sugar set aside, she makes a chocolate pudding with chocolate sauce that will melt in your mouth."

"This is better than the Marmite sandwiches I used to get for lunch at Bramdean," Pat said as she ate the hot stew Mrs. Harfield had prepared for their lunch.

"How could you eat that stuff?" Jean asked, wrinkling her nose in disgust.

"I didn't. I pitched it over the hedge every day," Pat said, laughing. It felt so good to have a friend again.

Out on the playground, Jean introduced Pat to other Portsmouth evacuees.

"This is Ivan Williams," Jean said, introducing a tall boy with glasses. "You should see him draw. Everyone says what a keen artist he is."

Ivan's face flushed. "I just doodle," he said shyly.

Then Jean introduced her to Kenny and Peggy Ship, who lived with the Cousens family on a watercress farm on the other side of Cheriton.

"That boy over there with the iron leg braces on is Brian Banks. He lives with Mr. and Mrs. Charlie Munday," Jean said in a confidential tone. "He walks better now than when he first came. Mr. Munday is a retired marine and nearly six feet tall. I think he was a medic or something. They are determined Brian will walk without those braces. They have him doing special exercises to strengthen his legs. He's so much stronger than when we first came out from Pompey.

"And this is Dorothy Banham," Jean said, as a plump girl with sandy blond hair approached them. "Dorothy's whole family came out to their grandparents' farm at Beauworth Crossroads."

"It's not the same as being evacuated, really," Dorothy said. "At least we all stayed together. We used to come out here for holidays, so as soon as the war started, Mum brought us out here to get away from the bombing. Dad's still back working at the dockyards, though."

"My dad's in the marines," Pat said. "My grandmother, two aunts, and a cousin from London are staying at our house in Pompey."

"Margaret Joyce came out to her grandparents' farm as soon as the war started, but she's from Pompey, too," Jean said.

Jean walked Pat around the playground introducing her to everyone. Pat said hello to her new classmates, trying to remember all of their names. Soon the bell rang and it was time to return to class.

Though the village children were friendly, the evacuees had their own little social group. Whenever she could, Pat walked or rode her bike the mile or so to the village to see Jean. First, to Pat's extreme annoyance, Nora had to make sure her new friends were all "suitable." Luckily, Nora liked Jean Ray, and the two girls became best friends.

Charlie North, however, seemed to take particular pleasure in teasing Pat. She did not take it quietly or just ignore him, as her mother, and even Jean, suggested. "He's just trying to get a rise out of you," her mother would say if she complained about it at home. It was not in Pat's nature to endure this treatment silently.

"That stubborn streak of yours has become very well developed since living with the Barters," her mother said. "It will get you into a lot of trouble one of these days."

This was not the sort of support Pat was looking for, so she stopped bothering to tell her mother about the pranks Charlie and his gang played on her. Whenever she'd try to get back at them, it was just her rotten luck that the school's headmistress would appear and she'd be the one caught and punished. Soon enough, she discovered how handy the headmistress was with the school's disciplinary cane. Whatever punishment she got at school, she got doubled at home. Her mother was clearly getting frustrated with her.

"I just don't know what to do with you," she shouted one day.

Pat's hands were still red from the school cane. She didn't say anything more to her mother about why she had done what she did, as it would only make things worse. The punishment that really stung was not being allowed to go back to the Common to visit Bert and her friends.

"You'll never go back to visit those people," Nora said. "You're quite out of control."

As Christmas approached, the weather turned cold and damp. One Thursday night, it was getting dark as Pat walked up the church path and through the cemetery to choir practice. Suddenly, a white figure leapt out from behind a gravestone, letting loose a blood-curdling howl. Pat screamed and nearly jumped out of her shoes. She turned in panic and fled back down the path, almost forgetting her bike at the end of the path. As she ran, she heard the laughing voices of Charlie North and his gang. She turned and saw him waving the white sheet triumphantly over his head. He looked at her angry face and doubled over with laughter. Furious and humiliated at being tricked, Pat got on her bike and went straight back home. She walked into the house and slammed the door.

Her mother, surprised to see her, was about to reprimand her for slamming the door, but stopped herself when she saw Pat's face.

"I am not, under any circumstances, going to sing in that choir again!" Pat declared, and without another word, she turned and walked to her room.

* * * *

The New Year of 1943 brought better news from the war front. The tide of war seemed to finally be turning in favor of the Allies, led by the British and Americans. The area around Cheriton was filling up with military camps and soldiers. The war had come to the countryside.

These days, Pat had very little time to herself. Her list of chores had grown as she took over things that John had done. She also had to amuse her younger brother and sister so her mother could get her other housework done. When she was allowed out, if she was even a moment late, her mother would be there at the door, demanding to know why she was late and handing down some punishment.

Pat was not allowed to just go out to play after getting her jobs done, as she had with the Barters. She had to stand for her mother's questioning first: "Where are you going and with whom?" Pat deeply resented her mother's attempts to change her into a "nice girl." She wanted her freedom. The more her mother tried to control her, the more she devised ways to get around the rules, stretch the truth, and cover up. She felt as though she was growing a hard shell over her skin, so the more her mother criticized, the more that disapproval simply rolled off of her. She lived her own life, inside her head, and got away from her mother's stern watchfulness as often as she could.

Nothing she did ever seemed to please her mother; nothing was ever "right." She had to do chores over again when they didn't meet her mother's standards. She always tried, for she really did love her mother, but she soon grew discouraged.

Winter dragged, and at school she continued to struggle with math and spelling. Miss Carpenter was a very patient teacher and helped her as often as she could spare the time from her many students. Pat still loved reading, and she read every book on the shelves at school, some several times. Her favorite was *Black Beauty*.

Having Miss Carpenter at Cheriton Village School was a great comfort. As often as possible, Miss Carpenter gave special attention to the evacuees. She tried on several occasions to stand up for Pat to the school's headmistress, but to no avail. One day when the headmistress made Pat stay after school, Miss Carpenter let her organize the books in the classroom. She encouraged Pat's love of reading, regularly supplementing the school's meager offerings by sharing her own books with her.

"These were my favorites when I was your age," Miss Carpenter said as she handed the books to Pat. "Louisa May Alcott was an American writer, and these stories take place around the time of the American Civil War. *Little Women* is the most famous, but I've got all the others, if you like them."

Pat loved the Alcott books and read every one that Miss Carpenter had brought with her from Portsmouth. Every minute she could spare, she had a book in her hands. She read while she was supposed to be minding Diane and Michael, and when her mother caught her, she was scolded.

"You can't watch them with your nose buried in a book!" Nora would say, snatching the book from her hands, taking it indoors and hiding it. But Pat always found it again. She even read while walking or riding her bike.

One day, riding up Harnham Hill for home, a car suddenly came over the hill toward her. There were so few cars on the road, Pat never thought about traffic. As usual, she was weaving back and forth across the hill so she wouldn't have to get off her bike and push it, reading her book propped on the handlebars, when the car was suddenly upon her. She was knocked clean off her bike, which landed on top of her in the ditch.

Badly shaken, bruised, and scraped, Pat tried to stand, but her knees were shaking too badly. Her book had been knocked into the road. The driver got out and rushed to her.

"Are you hurt? What were you doing in the middle of the road? Where do you live?" The poor old man was almost as shaken as Pat was. Despite her protests, he insisted on taking her safely to her mother.

Pat knew her mother would be furious. There was no hiding the fact that she'd been reading a book in the middle of the road and the accident had been her fault. Her bicycle was too badly bent to ride.

"You could have been killed!" her mother shouted after the driver of the car had left. Nora was nearly hysterical, and her hands shook as she cleaned the deep scrapes on Pat's legs and arms. Pat was shaking, too. There was a large lump forming on the back of her head where she'd fallen on her back, and she was developing a bad headache. When Nora examined her daughter's back and saw the huge bruises and scrapes, she ceased her scolding and sent Pat to lie down with a blanket over her.

"Obviously, you will not be riding your bike again until I say so. If I ever catch you reading while on a bike, or while walking along the road again, you will be heartily sorry you were ever born. You have given me enough fright to last a lifetime!"

All Pat could think of as she fell asleep on her bed was how to find where her mother had hidden her book.

On Ash Wednesday, Pat walked to school, reading a book as soon as she was out of sight of her house. She had new shoes for the first time in ages, but she wasn't very excited about wearing them because they had wooden soles and were extremely uncomfortable. When she complained, her mother said she should be grateful to have them.

"I used the last of our ration coupons and what was saved in the jar to buy those shoes. Your feet were growing right out of your other ones," Nora said.

"But I can't walk in them," Pat protested.

"Leather is scarce. It's being used for soldiers' boots. It's that or barefoot. Besides, you'll not be the only one wearing wooden-soled shoes. They were the last pair in your size in the shop."

That had ended the argument, so Pat was walking stiffly toward school in the uncomfortable shoes. Her bicycle was still not repaired, and she missed it terribly. As she came over the little footbridge toward the school, she was totally engrossed in her book. As soon as she stepped onto the schoolyard, Charlie and his gang jumped on her, literally. They all jumped on her feet, stomping dirt and dust all over her new shoes.

"Where's your ash? Where's your ash?" they chanted.

Hearing the commotion, the headmistress called them into the school hall, but she did not scold the boys.

"It's a local school custom," the headmistress told Pat brusquely. "I think you boys were a little rough with that," was all she said to them. She never even looked at the mess they had made of Pat's brand-new shoes as she told them to go to their classroom.

Charlie and his friends smirked at her as they walked into class.

Unfortunately, Pat knew exactly what her mother would say when she got home, and she'd be in trouble as usual.

When she went into her classroom, Charlie was sitting with his hands folded on his desk, smiling smugly. If Miss Carpenter had not been sitting right there, Pat knew she would have drawn off and whacked that smile off his smug face with the book she gripped tightly in her hand.

Miss Carpenter could see how upset she was; she had not been concentrating on her schoolwork all morning.

"Why don't you go home for lunch today," Miss Carpenter suggested kindly. "Get yourself cleaned up a bit. I think you might feel better."

Pat knew Miss Carpenter meant well, but the last thing she wanted to do was go home to face her mother. It was either that, however, or face off with Charlie North on the playground. She knew she'd do something that would only land her in even more trouble.

So she walked home, and just as her mother started to question what she was doing home in the middle of the day, she noticed Pat's shoes.

"What on earth have you done to those new shoes?" she demanded.

"Well, half of Cheriton's jumped on my feet," Pat replied hotly.

"Why did they jump on your feet? And why didn't you tell the teacher?"

"The headmistress said she couldn't do anything because it's a 'local custom.' I hate Charlie North," Pat said. Tears of humiliation streamed down her face. She also hated to cry, especially in front of her mother.

Nora heaved a great sigh, and with her voice a little more calm said, "Right. So, what's this you've got to have?"

Pat told her about the "ash" as Nora wiped her tears with the tea towel she had in her hand. Then they went out to the back garden, where Nora cut a thin branch from a small ash tree for Pat to take back to school. Her mother cleaned the footprints and scuff marks off her new shoes as best she could with a rag and some water, but made Pat put on her old wooden-soled shoes. Then she made a jam sandwich and a cup of Oxo broth for Pat's lunch before sending her back to school.

Reluctantly, Pat trudged back to school with her piece of ash. She had no idea what it was supposed to be for, but she felt like hitting someone with it. The same group of kids was waiting behind the school fence, and they jumped out and did the same thing they had done in the morning, despite her waving the branch in front of them.

"It ends at dinnertime, Townie!" Charlie shouted, laughing.

"Kids will be kids," Pat heard the headmistress say to Miss Carpenter as she rang the bell to end lunch recess.

It had been a terrible day as far as Pat was concerned. At the end of the day, she said goodbye to Jean, who was very sympathetic.

"They never did that to me," Jean said, "or I would have warned you. Tomorrow will be a better day."

"Charlie will just make up some other 'custom' or some other taunt," Pat said. "One way or the other, I'll have to have it out with Charlie North."

Maybe it was time to get John's help, she thought as she walked stiffly in her wooden-soled shoes toward home. When she walked through the door, all the troubles of the day suddenly vanished. Her dad was home!

"Hey there, Pat. You've grown a foot taller since I last saw you!" Arthur said.

He was still in uniform, his rucksack beside the door. She ran to hug him, and he picked her up and swung her around. When she looked over her father's shoulder, Nora had the biggest smile on her face that Pat had seen in a long time. She couldn't wait to tell her father all about the Barters and her friends at the Common and her new friends in Cheriton, and she talked nonstop to him while they peeled vegetables for supper.

Soon, John was home from work and they had supper as a family—for the first time in more than two years.

Arthur had brought all of them treats, as he always used to do. There was chocolate he'd saved from his rations and a few toys and trinkets he'd made. He had much less time to make things these days, he explained.

For the few days Arthur was home, Pat didn't want to go to school, nor John to work, but of course they went. Arthur did jobs for Nora that needed doing around the cottage and also repaired Pat's bicycle. Her parents spent a lot of time talking alone together after the children went to bed. Little Michael hadn't seen his father since he was a few months old. Now he was more than a year old, and Arthur was trying to teach him to say "Da-da." Diane was two and it was two days before Arthur could pick her up without her crying.

Even though it was too early to plant, Pat's father dug over a patch behind the cottage for a vegetable garden.

"You'll have to help John keep this garden going," he told Pat.

"Of course I will, Dad. I know all about gardening now," she said proudly, telling him what Bert Barter had taught her and all about Bert's bees and Rosie's cows.

For the four evenings Arthur was home, the family played their old favorite games and listened to his stories before they went to bed. He didn't talk of the war, but he did say that Iceland was an interesting place, but he wouldn't want to live there. His stories were of the old days, of the places he'd been before the war. John was allowed to stay up later than Pat, and Arthur asked his son all about his job as caretaker at Beauworth Manor.

Pat noticed that Nora laughed much more with Dad around. Her mother seemed more at ease, more like she was when they lived at Pompey. But as suddenly as he had come, it was time for him to leave again.

"When will the war ever be over?" Pat asked as they walked him to Cheriton to meet the bus to Petersfield. From Petersfield, he'd catch the train to Portsmouth, back to his base.

"Things are better now," her dad said. "With the Americans in the war, we'll win this sooner than we would have on our own. I won't lie to you and tell you it will be anytime soon. But we're going to win, I'm sure of that.

"I'll get out and see you again as soon as I can," he told Nora as they stood waiting for the bus in Cheriton. "I might not know when I'll be able to get away, but if I can, I'll let you know I'm coming. I've been posted to the *King George V* for now. I'll write with news when I can."

Chapter Eleven

"Got Any Gum, Chum?"

In April, Arthur was posted to HMS *Duke of York*. He was not able to get home at all during the summer of 1943. The family only knew he was part of the protection for shipping convoys in the North Atlantic. His letters home were sporadic. In August, the Allies marched into Rome and declared it a free city. The Italian dictator, Mussolini, had been arrested the month before, and by September the Italians were no longer the "enemy" and the new Italian government had declared war on Germany. Pat wondered if the Italian prisoners of war over at Bramdean Common would be able to go home now to their families. She was unable to visit Bramdean for some time after this, so she had no way of knowing. And she still missed Bert very much.

Pat started the fall term at Cheriton School again because she would not turn 11 until after the school term started. She would have to stay at Cheriton until Christmas. Jean Ray had moved up to the senior school, Perin's Grammar School in Alresford, and Pat missed her terribly. Charlie North had also gone on to the senior school, but Pat didn't miss *him* at all. Jean told her that Charlie was not as cheeky now that he wasn't one of the big boys at school.

The fall term passed fairly quickly. Miss Carpenter wasn't her teacher anymore, but she still helped Pat with some of her lessons after school so she would be able to go to the senior school in the January term. Pat still read while riding her bike, but was careful never to let her mother catch her doing it. These days, the time between home and school was about the only chance she had to read.

Monday was washday, and Nora washed everything by hand, boiling it all on top of the kitchen stove. Everything from the bedding to the clothes had to be washed, wrung out, and hung on lines—outside if it was fair, inside on racks if it was raining. All the water had to be hauled in buckets from the cistern out back and boiled in large pots. It was hard work. Tuesday was ironing day. Flat irons had to be heated on the stove, and every item in the wash basket had to be ironed—and Patricia had to look after Diane and Michael so her mother could do all of this work uninterrupted. Between school, chores, and seeing to her little sister and brother, Pat had little time to herself.

There was no electricity in the cottage, so the wireless ran on batteries. There were three sets of these batteries, called "accumulators." One accumulator would be in the wireless, one would be charged and ready as a spare, and the third had to be taken out to be charged. It was one of Pat's most important jobs to drop the accumulator at the motorcar garage in the village for charging on her way to school, and pick it up again on her way home. And it was her fault if the family was listening to a favorite program when the wireless died. "Who forgot to pick up the accumulator?" her annoyed mother would ask, though she already knew the answer.

Nora decided that since they had the space, she would keep some chickens to supply fresh eggs. At the farmers' auction in the village, she bought a rooster, 10 hens, and a coop to keep them in. None of the Phillipses knew a thing about keeping chickens, but the first problem was getting everything home. In the end, Pat and John made several trips with their bikes to bring home the birds, in boxes propped on their handlebars. They had to make a separate trip on foot to carry home the coop.

After much trial and error, Nora mastered the art of raising chickens, and brought the first fresh egg they produced into the house with great ceremony to show her children. She held it in her hand with wonder, as though she'd found a precious gem in the yard.

"What can we do with this egg?" she asked, for it obviously could not be wasted on anything ordinary. She decided to make a cake, even though it took all the remainder of their other rationed ingredients to do so. For all her success at raising the hens, however, Nora never did get along with the rooster. He was an ornery fowl and pecked her legs every time she stepped into the chicken yard to feed them. One day, the old bird mounted a particularly savage attack on her legs. That was the last straw. Pat watched as her mother stormed to the shed and returned with a hatchet. That night the family had roast chicken for supper.

Fall brought the harvest, and Pat was now old enough to work on a farm stacking sheaves of corn cut by the binder. Then she helped with the gleaning, picking up what the harvesting machine left behind. During October, schools closed for the potato harvest, and when she got home from the fields, Pat still had her usual chores to do.

"A girl your age needs to be helping, and keeping busy will keep you out of trouble," Nora told her.

In early November, Arthur got home for an unexpected two-day leave. He had taken the train to Petersfield and bicycled from there to Cheriton. The driver of the milk lorry at the dairy saw him on his bike, and since he was in uniform, the man asked where he was heading. When Arthur told him "Home," the man said, "Come on, toss your bike up on top and I'll give you a lift," and drove him right to their gate.

There he was, at the door, a welcome surprise. When he left again, he told Nora he'd be on the *St. George* and probably wouldn't get another shore leave for a long while.

In January 1944, the family listened to the wireless as the announcement came that America's General Eisenhower would be Supreme Commander of the Allied Expeditionary Force. John explained to Pat that Britain and her Allies were preparing to take Europe back from the Nazis.

Also in January, Pat was promoted in school and took the bus from Cheriton to Alresford to the Perin's School with all the other village children aged 11 to 14. It was the same school John had attended while they were at the Barters' in Bramdean. Not only did she get to see Jean Ray and the other friends she'd made at Cheriton, but she also saw some of her old friends from Bramdean.

Pat loved Perin's School and all of the activities that were offered there. She excelled at sewing and cookery classes because her mother had taught her so well at home, and she especially loved sports. She enjoyed track and field games, did very well in the hundred-yard dash, relay races, and hurdles jumping, and competed in the long jump.

She also became quite a good rounders player, which finally won her the respect of her former nemesis at Cheriton School, none other than Charlie North. He actually came up to her after school and congratulated her on her performance at one of the games. She was so surprised by his compliment she barely managed to utter "Thanks."

By spring, Pat and John were finally allowed to ride their bikes back to Bramdean to see the Barters. Bert was especially glad to see them. They stopped in to see Rosie and Mrs. Batten, and called in on Mrs. Silk. John visited briefly and then came back later to fetch his sister. Not much had changed at the Common. Stella and Brenda were good fun, and later in the spring, Nora actually let Pat stay a couple of weekends with the Barters.

In May, just after John turned 17, Arthur was able to get home for another visit. This time, Nora knew he was coming, and the family was drawn into a flurry of activity to get ready for his arrival so they would "pass inspection." It was such a quick visit, it was over almost as soon as he got there.

By this time, Pat was beginning to understand more about the war. The teachers at school marked the progress of the Allies on the wall maps as part of their geography lessons. The tide of the war in Europe had turned against the Germans. Fighting in Japan was still fierce, and the family in Portsmouth had not heard from Uncle Steve in some time. John worked long days at Beauworth Manor, and took on extra jobs at local farms. He also still helped his mother at home. He closely followed the news of the war, listening to the wireless and reading the newspaper whenever he could get his hands on one. He couldn't wait to turn 18 so that he could enlist in the army.

By the spring of 1944, the Cheriton area had become one huge encampment of men and equipment. In fact, people in the village began to say Britain had been invaded after all—by the Americans! American soldiers were everywhere. People couldn't stop talking about how friendly the "Yanks" were, and especially how generously they shared their plentiful rations with the locals. They were certainly more smartly dressed than the British and Canadians, Pat noticed. Some local people complained that the Americans had waited too long to join the war, but Nora and most of the others in the village welcomed the Americans with open arms.

Whenever Pat and John rode their bikes to Bramdean to visit the Barters, they saw carefully camouflaged tanks, lorries, and tents under every hedge, in every field, and under every clump of trees. There didn't seem to be a spot anywhere in the vicinity that didn't have a piece of military equipment or an encampment of soldiers on it. Nora wouldn't let Pat go to the Barters' alone, so John had to go, too, when he wasn't working at his various jobs. He was always glad to see Bert. Pat was glad to see Bert, too, and glad to be away from her mother, but now Nora only allowed short visits on Sunday afternoons.

The Americans fascinated Pat. They spoke English, but with an assortment of strange accents, and they seemed full of life, very outgoing and friendly. Pat and the other village children eagerly awaited the passing of every American convoy. "The Yanks are coming!" someone would shout, and the children would gather on the sides of the road in Cheriton or Alresford and wave like mad. The soldiers waved back and tossed candy and gum to the children as they marched or rode by.

"Got any gum, chum?" was the favorite phrase when the American soldiers were around. Sometimes groups of soldiers would stop along the road near the Phillipses' home to ask for fresh water, or for directions. The Phillips cottage was outside the village at the junction of two roads, but the signposts had been taken down early in the war to confuse the Germans in case of invasion. Pat had heard someone joke that the Germans would probably still find their way to London, even without signposts. But sometimes, American troop convoys got confused on these winding rural roads, so Nora would give the American drivers directions and let them fill their canteens from the well.

Occasionally, if there was a smaller group of Americans, Nora would make them tea. The soldiers, in return, would give her oranges or tins of food such as peaches—real luxuries for a ration-weary family. Sometimes they would leave old American comic books, which John especially appreciated. Once in a while, the Americans would talk and show pictures of their own families back home. They laughed and joked, and in their off-duty hours, they organized games of baseball, which was a sort of blend of rounders and cricket. One time, Pat summoned up the nerve to ask a young American soldier why they were called "GIs," and he laughed and said, "That's because we are genuine U.S. Government Issue soldiers."

With the steady influx of American and Canadian soldiers, people talked about the "second front" and finally pushing the Germans back. Even as the Germans once again intensified the bombing of cities like London, Hull, and Bristol, people still dared to believe that the war might be won.

As soon as she heard a convoy coming, Pat would run to the fence at the edge of the road, hoping it was the Americans. Even if they didn't stop, at least one might throw her some gum or a Tootsie Roll.

One day, there came a loud knock at the Phillipses' door. Nora opened it to find an American soldier standing on the front step with three-year-old Michael in his arms. He tipped his helmet and said in a slow, southern American drawl, "Found this in the road, ma'am. Does he belong to you?'

For the first time in her life, Pat saw her mother caught speechless, as she took the smiling toddler from the soldier's arms.

"Thank you," was all the flustered Nora could say.

Pat stood with her mother and watched the soldier stride back to his jeep at the head of a long convoy. A large cloud of dust hung over the road even after the vehicles had moved out of sight. Pat was glad she hadn't been blamed this time for her little brother being in the road. Had her mother asked her to keep an eye on him? She couldn't remember.

In early June, the Phillips family and the other people of the village woke to find that all the soldiers had suddenly gone. The massive Allied force had moved out in the predawn hours for Southampton and other embarkation points along the south coast.

On the evening of the sixth of June, the family sat silently by the wireless and listened as John Savage of the British Broadcasting Corporation Home Service read the official announcement:

> "D-Day has come. Early this morning, the Allies began the assault on the northwestern face of Hitler's European fortress…Under the command of General Eisenhower, Allied naval forces, supported by strong air forces, began landing Allied armies this morning on the northern coast of France."

Later, American General Dwight Eisenhower himself came on the wireless and addressed the people of Europe, who had suffered terrible hardships during the long years of Nazi occupation. He told them: "The hour of your liberation is approaching."

Pat wondered if the young soldier who had brought Michael to the door would ever make it back home to his family. She wondered, too, where her own father was at that moment, and felt herself shiver a little.

Nora switched off the wireless. "Maybe we can finally hope that this long war will be over soon," she said.

In the following days, news reports from the "second front" were not all hopeful. The Allied casualties in the first days of the invasion were heavy, and already the dead and wounded were being shipped back to England. Optimism that the war might soon be over was short-lived.

Within a week of the D-Day invasion, the Germans unleashed a new weapon with which to terrorize the British civilian population. On the night of June 12th and on into the next day, the first "V1" flying bombs landed in Britain. These aircraft had no pilots and were winged like small planes, with flames shooting from their tails. They quickly earned the nickname "doodlebugs" because of the *putt-putt* noise they made. People quickly learned that when the noise suddenly stopped it was time to run for cover.

"Why are they called 'V1' bombs?" Pat asked her brother.

"Hitler's calling them his 'vengeance weapons,'" John said. "I guess the German word for vengeance begins with a V, too."

"What is it vengeance for? Didn't Hitler start this war in the first place?" Pat asked.

"I can't figure out the mind of a madman any more than you can. I just know that the Americans and the RAF have been hitting German cities pretty hard, too, and Hitler is using any way he can to fight back."

Over that summer of 1944, the doodlebugs wreaked havoc over Britain. London was taking the hardest hits, but even the countryside wasn't safe. By the end of June alone, nearly two thousand people had been killed and close to six thousand injured. Nearly a hundred of the V1s attacked Britain every day, launched from sites in Nazi-occupied France. About half of these bombs were direct hits on London. The others caused destruction and casualties between London and the coastal areas of Kent, which became known as "bomb alley."

Nora said it was a good thing Grandma Phillips and the rest of the family had left London and gone to Portsmouth. Things weren't as bad there.

"Everyone who can is getting out of London now. It's horrible," she said.

By the twenty-fifth of August came the news that the British Second Army had liberated Paris. Within that month, the Allies had disabled the V1 launching pads in the Pas de Calais. The people of London and the south coast breathed a collective sigh of relief. But this reprieve was short-lived, and by early September, it was clear that the Germans had even worse in store—the V2 rockets.

"I heard that the government at first tried to say the V2 rockets that hit London last week were explosions at the gas works," John said at supper one night.

"Why would they tell people that?" Pat asked.

"Because they didn't want people to panic," John said. "But no one believed them, and people panicked anyway. A guy I know who was up in London when it started said the government had to tell people what they were."

"What are they?" Nora asked.

"They are rockets without pilots, like the doodlebugs, but they fly faster than the speed of sound so they are on top of you before you even hear them. No use in air-raid sirens or shelters, and the Ack-Acks can't shoot them down. There is so much explosive in these things that if they land anywhere near you, you've got no chance. They are forty-five feet long and weigh fourteen tons," he said. "No one's seen anything like them before."

"I'm glad you're not old enough to be called up yet," Pat said.

"I can't wait," he said. "I'd rather fight than be a target for the V2s or whatever horrors the Nazis think up next. This probably isn't even the worst."

With the V2 attacks, the news from London was grim. Hundreds were being killed or injured every day.

"Is this ever going to end?" Pat said one night after switching off the wireless. "Just when things begin to look up, something else comes along."

"We've got to keep doing our best, one day at a time," Nora sighed.

It had been a long time since Pat and her mother had actually had a conversation that didn't end in an argument, and realizing this made Pat even sadder. Her mother's efforts to reform her into a "good girl" were an ongoing battle. Pat was now 12 and desperately wanted more freedom, but her mother seemed to put even tighter restrictions on her. She hadn't allowed Pat far from home for months because of the threat even in the country of the new German rockets.

"The Germans are just as likely to hit us here as over at Bramdean while I'm visiting the Barters," Pat protested one day.

"For arguing, you can now forget seeing Jean after school tomorrow. You'll come directly home," Nora said.

It was only with the utmost self-control—and out of fear of what her mother might take away from her next—that Pat said no more to her mother about visiting the Barters or her other friends at Bramdean.

When John was home, he tried to keep the peace between his sister and his mother, but he was frequently as frustrated by Pat's behavior as his mother was.

"Why do you have to defy her so, when you know how it's going to end?" he asked Pat one evening while they were feeding the chickens.

"I can't stand her criticizing me all the time, over everything I do. Nothing is ever good enough. I can't do anything right, so I might as well have my say."

"It would be easier if you'd just keep your tongue and do what she says," John replied.

"I just can't, John. I wish I could just go back to the Barters'. I'm not really wanted here, except as someone to watch the little ones and do chores," Pat said.

"That's not fair. Mum cares for you same as the little ones, same as me," John said. "She's always telling me how worried she is that you'll get into trouble and get a bad reputation."

"Not much chance of that! You and the babies are all she cares about, no matter what you say," she retorted.

John said no more. He was working long hours most of the time anyway, so he had little time to run interference between his mother and sister.

Christmas 1944 was quiet at the Phillips cottage. No one seemed to feel much like celebrating, and they didn't know when Arthur would be home again. The New Year of 1945 began with one of the coldest Januaries on record, and they had to very carefully conserve all fuels from coal to lamp oil to wood. Everything was in short supply.

As the year wore on, the news from the war front was beginning to look a little more hopeful, and people began to talk again about the war being won by spring—in Europe at least. As winter gave way to spring, the wireless reported that the American president, Franklin D. Roosevelt, had died. The new president was named Harry S. Truman.

"People in the village are really sad about President Roosevelt," Nora said to John as they ate supper the night of the announcement. "He was liked here because he helped us even before the Americans came into the war."

"Well, the news is finally turning now," John said. "The Germans are crumbling on every front."

"I just hope it ends before you are old enough to enlist," Nora said.

On April 30th came the stunning news that Adolph Hitler, the German leader everyone in Britain despised, had shot himself in his underground bunker in Berlin. Then, on May 7th, the German high command surrendered all German forces to the Allies in Rheims, France.

"The war is over, in Europe at least!" Nora said when Pat came into the house that night. The next day was declared a national holiday—Victory in Europe, or VE, Day. There would be a huge celebration in every town and village. Since it was so near to John's eighteenth birthday, Nora allowed him to take Pat to Portsmouth to stay at their old home with their grandmother Phillips, and attend the street party there. Pat couldn't believe her mother was letting her go, and she was on her best behavior before they left in case Nora changed her mind. She was almost 13 years old.

Pat and John took the bus to Petersfield, and then the train to Portsmouth. Neither of them had been back to the city of their birth since they had been evacuated nearly five years before. After the bus ride, the rest of the trip was one Pat knew she would never forget. Pompey was totally changed, and many of the landmarks they looked for as they came through the city were gone. Even though they had heard the news, seeing the damage with their own eyes was a different matter. It was strange not to see the old Guild Hall in the center of town.

At least Highgate Road had not changed much. They would stay that night in Pat's old bedroom, as it was just for the one night. She and John visited whatever friends were still around their old neighborhood, and the entire street was turned into a party. There were tables and chairs set out in the street, and party lights were strung from the light poles. Several bonfires lit up the night sky as afternoon turned to evening. The blackout curtains had been taken down and there were lights on everywhere. Tea and cakes, jellies and candy were served, treats no one had seen for most of the war. People were singing. It was a magical day and night, at least for those whose loved ones were safe or accounted for.

Aunt Katie would not come out to the party. Her husband and many others were still in the Pacific, fighting or captured or unaccounted for, and she was angry that the country was celebrating so soon.

"The war's not over for everyone. They shouldn't be celebrating until it's all over and everyone comes home," she said.

Pat felt sad for her aunt and others like her. She also felt glad that at least her father would be coming home soon, and that the worst was over before her brother could enlist. Being away from her mother for a bit, celebrating anything happy, was a good thing as far as she was concerned.

She stood on the front steps of their old house, watching her brother talk to old friends. Someone had a wireless in an open window. Vera Lynn's voice wafted across the street scene as Pat looked on and listened.

When the lights go on again, all over the world…

Pat knew she would never forget this night. So much in her life had changed forever. The house on Highgate Road belonged to her grandmother now, and it no longer felt like home. She hoped her parents would decide to say in Cheriton. There was no longer anything for them in Portsmouth, now that her dad would be retiring from the marines. Her life and her friends were in the country. Now, at long last, her father would come home each night. That someday, far-off time everyone had talked about for half of her life—"after the war"—had finally begun.

EPILOGUE:
How It All Ended

As the war in Europe ended in May, church bells across Britain pealed joyously after six long years of silence. On August 15, 1945, several days after the United States dropped atomic bombs on the cities of Hiroshima and Nagasaki, the Japanese officially surrendered. The dark days of World War II were over at last.

On October 15, 1945, Arthur Phillips came home to his family in New Cheriton, wearing the dark brown, pinstriped "de-mob" suit the government issued to servicemen and women as they were demobilized and returned to civilian life. The Phillips family, like countless others in Britain and the world, turned to the task of rebuilding their lives. But life would never be the same. Time and the war had changed everything.

Evacuee children who had not already done so began returning to their families. Jean Ray, Kenny and Peggy Ship, and all of Pat's fellow evacuees all returned to their homes. Pat missed Jean terribly. The Mundays succeeded in helping Brian Banks walk without leg braces. They wanted very much to adopt Brian, but his family wanted him back.

Though their house in New Cheriton was tight quarters for a family of six, the Phillips family felt fortunate to have a home at all. Nearly four million houses had been damaged in the war, about one-third of the total available housing. Over 475,000 houses were completely destroyed, along with countless churches, factories, schools, hospitals, and commercial buildings. For some years after the war, building materials were in short supply. Prefabricated military buildings were remade into civilian housing, as the old corrugated tin supply huts from World War I had been. Because of the shortage of housing in the major cities, many evacuees had to wait to be reunited with their families. It was not until March of 1946 that the resettlement of evacuees was completed, and the rationing of many items of food, clothing, and fuel continued through 1954.

Pat's grandmother kept the Portsmouth house and did not return to London to live. Her Uncle Steve, Aunt Katie's husband, had spent years in one of Japan's most infamous prisoner of war camps. Even after months in a military hospital after the camp was liberated, he returned home gaunt and silent, never again the spirited and good-humored man he'd been before the war.

Though Pat and her family visited their family in Portsmouth on occasion, Cheriton remained their home. Arthur and Nora had put the decision to stay or go back to Portsmouth to a family vote, and everyone voted to stay in Cheriton. Arthur retired after 27 years in the marines, and took over John's caretaking job at the Dr. Barnardo's Home when John went into the service.

Right after the war, John entered the Army Tank Corps, serving in Allied-occupied Germany for his two years of national service. After he completed his service, he returned to the Cheriton area and married Joan Francis, who was from the neighboring village of Beauworth, where John's first job out of school had been. They had three daughters, Dawn, Hazel, and June. John had learned to drive while in the tank corps, and once back to civilian life he drove delivery lorries for several companies. He later became a long-distance lorry driver and remained active in the British Legion. He and Joan lived with their family in Alresford. He passed away in 1993.

In 1947, at the age of 14, Pat contracted food poisoning at a banquet honoring the Perin's School championship rounders team. She was months recovering and never went back to finish school. As soon as she was well enough, she began a series of farm jobs and did a brief stint in domestic service in the local manor house in Cheriton. She also worked in a local shop and on a dairy farm.

In 1953, at the age of 20, Pat married and began her own family. She told my daughter the unusual story of how she met her husband:

"I was working in the fields picking up potatoes after the tractor and saw him up on the tractor and thought 'Oh, I like the look of him,' so I picked up a spud and threw it at him…hit him right on the back of the head."

"Why did you throw a potato at him?!"

"I wanted him to notice me."

"OK…then what happened?"

"There was a dance in the village and I was allowed to go if my brother went. Well, I walked in, and he was there and I was there and that was it."

Peter North was the elder brother of none other than Charlie North, the boy who had made her first year in Cheriton so miserable. Charlie did not recall the pranks he played on Pat when they were children, and as adults, Pat and her brother-in-law were good friends. Shortly after they were married, Peter and Pat North moved to Portsmouth, where Peter served on the city's police force. After ten years in Portsmouth, they moved with their young family to Winchester. Pat has four children, Jane, Paul, Susan, and Patrick, along with several grandchildren and great-grandchildren.

As adults, Pat and John never discussed the evacuation, even though it had changed the entire course of their lives. There were so many painful family issues, from Pat's continued attachment to the Barters, to her ever-rocky relationship with her own mother. Looking back, Pat suggests it also might have been because after the long years of war everyone was anxious to move on and put the painful war years behind them. She never told anyone about being abused while she was an evacuee until she was being interviewed for this book.

Once the stories from survivors of the concentration camps, prisoner of war camps, and those who suffered under the brutal occupation of the Nazis throughout Europe came to light, the trauma of their evacuation experience seemed to pale in comparison, Pat says. Fifty-five million people died in the war, including 20 million civilians. Millions of Jews, gypsies, and other people Hitler considered "undesirables" were murdered by the Nazis in the concentration camps. So many families around the world had suffered the loss of loved ones, the Phillips family felt fortunate to have survived at all.

Pat continued to visit the Barters for some years after she returned to live with her mother. Just before the war ended, Bert Barter took a job at another farm, but Pat does not recall where it was. The couple later moved to Barton-on-Sea, and she visited them there on one of her summer holidays. Nora Phillips was not pleased about these reunions, as she had wanted a clean break from the Barters. However, she realized the depth of Pat's attachment to Nel and Bert and allowed the visits, hoping they would eventually become fewer and farther between. Pat says Bert seemed lonely, and he always wrote how much he missed them.

Sure enough, though they kept in touch with Pat through Christmas cards for many years, her relationship with her former foster parents grew distant, and after a few years, she didn't see them again. One year, Bert wrote to tell her that Nel had died, and some time after that, the Christmas cards from Bert stopped coming, so she assumed he had also passed away.

Pat's relationship with her mother remained distant and at times strained. The teen and preteen years can be a difficult time between parents and children, even under normal circumstances. For Pat and Nora, that time was made more confusing by their long separation during the evacuation.

> "I'd got taken away from where I wanted to be," she recalled. "So I was going to be rebellious. I gave my mother a hard time. Really, we were never, ever close. It really ruined what would have been my mothering because I saw it in my sister. I could see what she had and what I never had. And I never had it. There was always a difference between us, the way she treated us. And the way I treated her. It wasn't just one way. It was both of us."

With this broken parent–child bond, the Phillipses' experience was typical of many evacuees who spent precious formative years separated from their parents, never regaining the closeness they once shared. Sadly, Pat and John were not the only evacuee children to suffer abuse or neglect at the hands of people who were supposed to protect them. These brave former evacuees like Pat have come forward as adults to share their stories.

Professional help or family therapy to encourage parents and former evacuee children to talk about their experiences and feelings was not available, nor even much thought of at the time. The lack of understanding between Pat and her mother left them both frustrated and unable to bridge the divide that, with the years, only grew wider between them. Pat did, however, reconnect with her father, and the two remained close, especially in the years between her mother's death in 1973 and Arthur's own death in 1983.

Largely because of the evacuation, Pat and John learned to be independent, to adapt to change, and to endure whatever life sent them without complaint. They also developed a close bond with their foster father, Bert Barter, whose kindness and patient teaching left a lasting impression on both of their lives.

> "My life would have completely changed. I would never have met my husband, so that would have been different. My father was a marine, and it would be nothing for him to be gone two years. To have a man there, the whole time, like he [Bert] was, we had a bond with him that we should have had with our own father but didn't. My love of gardening I'm sure I learned from him. Whatever he saw, whatever he did, he always drew you along with it."

Thinking back over more than 70 years, it is clear that for Patricia Phillips North, the evacuation experience had benefits as well as traumas. "If we had grown up in the town, we would have been different people. Really, there are so many angles to it," she says.

It's also possible that, without the evacuation, Pat and John might not have survived the war at all. More than 60,000 British civilians died in the bombing and fires of the Blitz. According to figures from the Imperial War Museum in London, 7,736 British children were killed in the bombings, and 7,662 were wounded.

Still, Pat says that if she had to choose today whether or not to send her own children away to live with strangers, she would never do so. As a mother, now a grandmother and great-grandmother, she understands how difficult it must have been for her own mother to make that decision under such terrible circumstances. She still emphatically declares that she would take her chances and keep her family together. In this, she is like most former evacuees.

* * * *

Historians and social scientists have studied the evacuation in depth. They agree that it succeeded in saving lives, and that moving millions of people efficiently to safety was a major logistical achievement. However, even most of these scholars have concluded that it would have been healthier emotionally for children to have stayed with their families, especially if the poor living conditions of children and families in the inner cities, especially London, had been addressed before the war.

It is important for those of us who did not experience the war to remember one seemingly obvious fact we often take for granted. We know how the war ended, with the Allies victorious. But victory was never certain, and the war was in fact very close to being lost at several critical junctures. Despite Churchill's courageous "V for Victory" wave, victory was not assured. Remembering this helps keep in perspective the choices individual people made during the dark days of the Second World War.

In 1995, people the world over celebrated the 50th anniversary of the end of World War II. In London, on May 8, Queen Elizabeth II, who had been a young princess during the war, flipped the switch to the beacon light of the famed Post Office Tower. It was the climax of extensive V-E Day festivities. As the beacon light pierced the night sky, Dame Vera Lynn, still possessed of her rich, clear voice, once again sang the song that gave hope to so many during the darkest years of the war, "When the Lights Go On Again." Millions sang along with her, from the crowds in London to those watching their televisions at home. Younger generations stood in awe of the national unity and sacrifice for a common purpose that had enabled their parents, grandparents, and great-grandparents to survive the most devastating conflict the world has ever known.

While evacuation experiences varied from child to child, most evacuee children learned important survival skills that would serve them well for the rest of their lives. Children like Pat and John Phillips learned to make the best of a tough situation, to be resourceful and adaptable, and to make the most of opportunities they might otherwise never have had to create new lives. Like Pat, many evacuees still carry scars from their experiences. Telling their stories brings healing and sheds the light of truth on a very dark time in human history.

I'm glad that in the telling Pat has at last found healing from the trauma of the evacuation. Our friendship grew even deeper through the journey together going back across those war years. It set the stage for what was to come next: Pat's next life journey.

PHOTOGRAPHS

At the age of 16 Pat was allowed to attend a special dance with Peter at the Guildhall in Winchester. The famous Harry Davidson Orchestra played an "old time dance" with quadrilles and other dances such as the "military two-step." Pat recalls that she had worn this dress before and her mother made it over with the black netting skirt and matching gloves.

Before the war, Pat took ballet and tap dancing lessons at Miss Cannoway's School of Dance, which used the Naval Barracks hall for their recitals. Pat's mother insisted that she continue her lessons after she was evacuated to Bramdean, and sent her host family money to pay for them.

Pat on her three-wheeled bicycle just about the time war broke out. She recalls that the metal rails seen here on the garden walls in front of the houses on her street were taken and melted down for the war effort.

John turned 15 a few months before the Phillips family was reunited, and he was overjoyed to have his family together again. Pat and John stayed close, but John could never understand why Pat remained so attached to the Barters.

This photo, probably taken by John, shows Nora with Pat and the two younger children at about the time the family was reunited.

Nora Phillips was anxious to bring her family back together after the long time of separation, but this photo, taken in the summer of 1942, shows how difficult that would prove to be in Pat's case. Here the family stands on the footbridge in Cheriton Village, known as "Admiral's Arch," with Nora holding Diane, John holding Michael, and Pat, nearly 10 years old, standing at a distance.

Once she was back with her mother, Pat was no longer the baby of the family, but instead was the older sister to two siblings she hardly knew. Her mother depended on Pat to help keep Diane and Michael occupied, and she resented the loss of the freedom to go wherever she wanted that she had enjoyed with the Barters.

Diane, here about 2, was born in February of 1940, just before Pat and John were evacuated to Bramdean. Michael, just over a year old, was born in March of 1941, a few months after Pat and John were sent away. Here, the two younger siblings stand in the doorway to the cottage on Harnham Hill. This was probably taken about the same time as the photos of the family on the bridge, in summer of 1942.

The cottage on Harnham Hill in New Cheriton, where Pat and John were reunited with their family after being evacuees in the nearby village of Bramdean.

Pat left school at around age 14, as was customary for working-class youths of the time. She held a succession of jobs from working in a shop to working as a kitchen maid in one of the nearby manor houses. At the age of 16, she started working in a dairy in nearby Tichborne, where she worked until after she was married to Peter and their first child was born.

Pat's younger siblings, Diane (here about 9) and Michael (about 8), were born during the war. Pat recalls that the vest her sister is wearing in this photo was made from wool "picked out" and re-knit from wool socks and vests issued to their father by the marines for his mission to Iceland. When he returned, wool being scarce, it was not wasted.

Peter and Pat were "courting" when he gladly took the job of giving the family dog, "Chum," a bath. The henhouse is in the background.

When Pat was 16, she and Peter North, age 21, took a bus trip to London to buy an engagement ring. While there, they did a little sight- seeing in the city, and here is Pat outside the Houses of Parliament.

In 1953, many items in Britain were still rationed, including cloth. But Pat was able to obtain silk for her dress, and it was designed and sewn by the lady's maid at one of the houses in which Pat was "in service."

Pat and Peter North were married at St. Michael and All Angels Church in Cheriton on February 7, 1953. Here she is walking up the church path with her father, Arthur Phillips.

After Pat and Peter were married, Peter had an opportunity to attend Police College, and while he was training, the couple lived with his parents in the house attached to the Cheriton village school. This photo was taken in 1953 in the schoolyard. Peter's first post was in the City of Portsmouth, where the Norths lived for ten years. Though it was the city in which she had been born, Pat was very happy to leave when Peter was assigned to the police force in Winchester.

Pat took this photo of her mother, Nora Thompson Phillips, (left) and Peter's mother, Lillian Isobel Daisy North, (right) while on a trip to London in about 1958.

Afterword

Mother-Daughter-Sister-Friend: The Journey Continues

In the winter of 1999, Pat was with us in Maine when Peter suddenly took ill and she had to hurry home. His recovery was slow and she was unable to visit, but we made a plan for my daughter Melody and me to visit them in June of 2000, at the close of Mel's freshman year of high school. Melody and Aaron had become very close to Pat over the years, referring to her as their "English grandmother."

By the time we arrived, Peter had been ill for a year and it was apparent to me that he was not getting better, though his whole family, and Pat especially, of course, held out hope that the doctors would find out what was wrong with him and he would still recover. Their eldest daughter, Jane, picked us up at the airport with Peter. Even though the family had been keeping me informed on how poorly he'd been doing, seeing how ravaged he had been by his illness was a huge shock. I was glad we had come. Pat needed the support and Peter needed the diversion that my teenaged daughter full of energy and life could provide.

One warm, sunny day, Peter and I were sitting alone in their beautiful garden. I thought he was looking a bit brighter and said so.

"I have good days and bad days, but it's nice having you and Melody here. Good for Pat. I know exactly where she'll go when I'm gone. And I know you'll be there for her."

"If that helps you to worry less, I assure you I will. But I think you're going to get better," I said.

"We'll see," he said, and changed the subject as we looked up to watch some planes overhead.

"My biggest regret is not coming over and seeing America for my-self. I have enjoyed it all through Pat, but I wish now I'd gone myself."

"Maybe you will still get that chance," I said.

That visit turned out to be the last time I saw Peter. In a last-ditch effort to find out what was wrong, the doctors did exploratory surgery that fall. Though he came back home from the hospital, he never fully recovered. Peter died December 25, 2000, just after the family had fin-ished Christmas dinner at their daughter Susan's house. As one ambu-lance came for Peter, Pat had a heart attack and was rushed to the hos-pital in a second ambulance. She nearly died herself.

It took weeks for her to recover her strength, so Peter's memorial service wasn't held until January 25, 2001. I wasn't able to get back to Winchester until April, when all of their family and close friends gath-ered to install Peter's ashes in a favorite place in their garden. Pat was still struggling physically as well as emotionally, but I was impressed with her courage and her resolve to get back on her feet again, and we planned a visit for her to America, as soon as she was strong enough to travel.

It was 2002 before she got back here, and just as Peter had pre-dicted, Pat decided she wanted to live in America. In August 2003, Su-san and her husband, Ian, sold their home, and together with their two adult daughters, moved into the family home on Woodfield Drive in Winchester so that she would have a home base to always return to. That winter she came for a seven-month visit, and Ron and I, along with Pat, worked with our contractor and friend Tom Valley to design an addition to our home to give Pat her own suite. Our original intention was that she would spend most of the year here and "visit" her home in Winchester. The addition became known as "the Pat Flat,'" and Peter's prophecy came to fruition.

When Pat and I showed our friend Linda Dunmon through the soon-to-be-finished Pat Flat, Linda was still trying to figure out this unique friendship.

"Let me get this straight. Pat's your friend, but more like a sister, or sort of like a mother to you?" Linda suggested.

"Well, sometimes I'm actually like a 'mother' to her," I quipped.

"Yes, and sometimes even two mothers aren't enough to keep Gay in line," Pat said. We all laughed in agreement with that one.

"I've got it!" said Linda. "You're Mother-Daughter-Sister-

Friends!"

Pat and I have referred to each other that way ever since.

I think my journal entry for Saturday, December 18, 2004, pretty much summed it all up:

Everyone's home and it feels wonderful. Aaron got home around 7:30 and we had a nice dinner waiting. I had made a pork roast, mashed potatoes, green beans almondine, applesauce, and an apple pie for dessert. Aaron brought us a bottle of Jameson's Irish whiskey, so we sat for a libation before dinner and toasted being together for the holidays. We sat around and told some stories and had some laughs.

Pat arrived last night and is having her first soak in her whirlpool tub. She absolutely loves her new space. She teared up when she walked in and saw it all finished. She was up this morning fairly early and was sipping tea sitting on her new sofa gazing out the windows at the river.

"I woke up and thought I must have died and gone to heaven," she said.

Having a place just for her, done her way, and she is so pleased with it, is just so amazing and wonderful for her. It's made all the work and mess and upheaval all this summer and fall worthwhile. She had her hair done this morning and Mel and I met her when she was all beautified and we three girls went out for lunch at Applebee's and then up to Michael's to see if we could get Pat a little tree. But there weren't any, so we came home, too tired and put off by the crowds to shop. Had a cuppa in Pat's new place. Great day!

She stayed until June of 2004, and we helped her settle her English things into her new American home, including boxes of china and precious bits that arrived in layers of bubble wrap in huge boxes over that winter and spring. By May, the place was the coziest nook in the house, the place everyone automatically gravitated to, where the kettle was always ready to switch on and the tea always flowed. Naturally, Pat also planted a garden, and with me as the grunt labor, the "under-gardener," our little home along the Kennebec began to resemble an English country cottage.

However, things don't always work out exactly as we hope in life, and it didn't take long to find out that in all of our planning we had failed to consider the all-important United States immigration rules. Pat's diary entry for June 16, 2004, just days after she had returned to England, put the situation into stark reality:

Sue rang the American embassy and I can't go back to Gay until next year. You can't spend more than six months in one year there. I thought things were going too well. It's going to spoil everything. What's the use of having one's own place if you can't stay in it more than six months? So I am going to do some travelling. Maybe go somewhere with someone, or on my own. Gay will be upset. But what's to do?

How many people in the space of five sentences can go from anger and despair that their carefully laid plans have started to unravel to a plan to just go out there and see the world? Having walked back through her war experiences with her, and watched her piece her life together after her husband died, after seeing her battle cancer and recover from a heart attack, I should not have been surprised.

Going back together over the traumatic days of her childhood war memories, I came to a deeper appreciation of her strength, her courage, her spirit of adventure, and her ability to take life's most difficult blows and bounce back. Resilience, it's called. Pat has time after time faced and healed her deepest wounds, grieved deep losses, and moved on, determined not to remain a victim of circumstance.

With her own courageous spirit, the support of her family in England, and her American family, Pat created a new life for herself—though not the life she always wanted; she says often that she would give it all back for just one more day with her beloved Peter. But it's a life that is rich and full and a true example for the rest of us of how to take what life sends us and make the best of it. Had she not been an evacuee, she would never have met Peter. In her own words, as we went over the lessons of the war years, she admits that her life would have been completely different had the evacuation never happened.

Similarly, had she been allowed to stay in the States as long as she wished, the next chapter of her life would also have been completely different. Instead of moaning endlessly about what she couldn't do, Pat decided to do the next best thing. She became an intrepid world traveler, and has seen more of the globe than almost anyone I know. I believe now that her spirit of adventure and her sense of independence were awakened on that first day she arrived as a child evacuee in the verdant Hampshire countryside in the village of Bramdean.

When people first meet Pat, they are pretty much universally charmed by her unique combination of open friendliness that despite her years in America still has a hint of that ubiquitous British reserve.

She is quick-witted and deeply interested in other people's stories and curious to learn new things. In large groups, she is often quiet, but in smaller groups and one-to-one she is unguarded, quite witty, and loves to laugh. These traits make her a wonderful traveling companion, and she and I, sometimes on our own and sometimes with my family or friends, have gone many places together, both here in America and in England. She has also struck off for distant places all on her own —and people are astounded by the list of places this tiny gray-haired English lady has been.

Having already traveled with her granddaughter Ginette Rooke to Ireland in May of 2003, she and Ginny in September 2004 took a coach trip to Scotland, something Pat and Peter always planned to do but never did. She went down to Devon and visited her dear friend Allison, and regrouped. By December she was back with us for Christmas and a quick trip in January 2005 with our friend Becky Arbour and me to Charleston, South Carolina. In March she and Ginny went to Paris for the weekend. From April to August, she was back in the States. In September she and Ginny took a weeklong tour of Italy, and Pat even climbed Mt. Vesuvius—at the age of 74. She returned to us in November for the holidays and stayed through January 2006, returning for a longer stay during the better weather from May to August.

In September, she and Ginny were on the road again traveling to Poland. In October, Ron and I visited Pat and her family with two dear mutual friends, Al and Gail Parker, then she was back to us in November for the holidays again. In the New Year 2007, Pat took a trip to New York City with my daughter Melody to visit our friend Collette Sosnowy and to see the holiday decorations in the city.

Pat had a "bucket list" long before the movie of that name came out! There were places she wanted to go that were hard to find traveling companions for, so she went to her travel agent and booked another big excursion with a tour group. In April of that year, since she already planned to be in the States for Melody's college graduation in May, she booked herself a train trip across the Rocky Mountains in Canada from Toronto to Vancouver, from whence she took a cruise to Alaska, flying over a glacier in a helicopter and landing to walk around on it! She stayed with us through August for the wedding of another dear friend, Heidi Marsella, and returned again in November for the holidays.

In April and May of 2008, at the age of 75, Pat took a Hawaiian cruise that included climbing around a volcano. From San Francisco, she took a coach tour all around the American Southwest, from the Badlands to Yellowstone National Park and dozens of stops and hundreds of miles along the way back to Los Angeles, before flying back across the country to meet me in Boston. She stayed with us until September 4th that year, the day after we threw her a huge 76th birthday bash—since I could think of no one else who exhibited the "Spirit of 76" any better!

At this point it would be tempting to just summarize Pat's adventures and keep listing the wonderful places she has seen. That would be only partly the truth, however, and since we are into the story so deep now, why stop on the surface? During her time with us that late summer that turned to fall 2008, Pat began to notice that her eyesight had changed rather dramatically. She said nothing to me, but when she got home, she went to her optician to see about changing her glasses. It was clearly more serious than a change of prescription, and she saw a specialist on October 6, 2008, who diagnosed her with macular degeneration in the left eye. She would from this point on require monthly examinations and injections into the eye to try to hold back the deterioration of her central vision. Her right eye at this point was stable, but there was macular there as well.

Anyone would be devastated by such a diagnosis. Certainly someone who counts on her eyesight for everything she loves to do—from gardening to knitting to cross-stitching—would be frightened at the prospect of going blind. When she came to us for the holidays that year, her trip had to be sandwiched between her injections in December and January. Our visits were now limited to one month, a far cry from the six months the U.S. government would allow.

She was not in a celebratory mood that year, and who could blame her? But sympathy was not what she needed from me. We had been through too much together and our honesty with one another was complete. I told her she needed to "buck up" and face this challenge as she had faced so many other challenges before, with courage and with resiliency. In her diary for January 7th she wrote that I had "given her a good talking to," and not only had it cleared the air between us, but she "felt better afterwards." She knew what she had to do. In the face of circumstances she could not control, she used her energy to control whatever was left to her.

The year 2009 did not progress well on the eyesight front. Some months, things were stable; in others there was deterioration. Now her right eye was also affected. In her diary for April 4, 2009, in her usual succinct style, she wrote, "Not looking good for going to Gay's." However, the daughter of our dear friend Becky was getting married in June, and Pat was determined to be here. And she *was* here, from May 28th to June 21st, and on June 22nd, just hours after arriving back in England, she had an injection in her right eye.

As Pat faced the likely loss of her eyesight, she began to accelerate her plans to see the last places on her bucket list. She and Peter had often talked about seeing the amazing animals of Africa—one of the few places her non-traveler husband had really wanted to see. On September 21, 2009, Pat joined a tour group in Johannesburg, South Africa, for a Safari trip. She saw the animals, visited Zimbabwe, and stood on top of Table Mountain and gazed out over the Horn of Africa.

In December 2009, she was back for Christmas, but things were not the same at our house, either. While Pat's life was changing to respond to her new situation, so things on my side also changed. Both of our children had left home. Aaron was out in Milwaukee attending graduate school after a two-year stint in the Peace Corps. Melody was living and working in Manchester, New Hampshire. I had started my own writing business and it was flourishing, but I worked at home. I needed my office to be downstairs again. As hard as it was for Pat to adjust to the changes in our old plans, so it was for me. Now I had a "Pat Flat" with no Pat, and a large garden to tend on my own.

Everywhere I looked in our home, there was a memory of life the way it used to be, or never quite was, and spaces that went unused for most of the year. It was time to make some changes. Though I had prepared Pat for this on her previous visit, and even had talked with her about what pieces of furniture might move where, when she arrived that Christmas to see that I had moved her furniture around and added some of ours to make her flat more of a family room, the physical manifestation of our changed circumstances hit her hard. It felt to her as if we no longer wanted her, that we no longer had "room" for her in our lives. No amount of explaining that she would always have her special "room" in our lives no matter what the physical space looked like could help her adjust to this loss. It would take more than words; it would take time and our showing her that "old age" did not change the fact that she was part of our family, part of us. I just knew that for my own sake I had to begin to let go of the past and learn to roll with whatever came, and I would have to help her do so as well.

We also talked about the situation at home with Susan and her family, now grown to grandchildren who were frequently at the house. Lovely as they are, tiny children's toys underfoot for a person losing their eyesight can be a hazard. The situation on that side had changed as well, and in her usual style, Pat realized that it was time to move on to a new sort of life that still included her family, and as much as possible travel to America and other places, but afforded her a compact, supported environment in which to settle for the next phase of her life. She began to plan in earnest to find a small flat for herself in a senior complex where she could live independently but also get immediate help and support if she required it. With the help of her son Patrick, she found such a place, and in 2010 she moved into her cozy little flat in Eastacre, just a few miles from her old home in Winchester. She knows she still has a room back at her old home at Woodfield Drive if she ever needs it, but she settled into her new life the way she does everything. She planted a garden! And took another trip!

In 2010, at the age of 78, Pat took the Trans-Siberian Railway from St. Petersburg, Russia, across the steppes of Mongolia, sailed on Lake Baikal, and got to China. She stayed in a yurt, marveled at the huge steel statue of Genghis Khan out in the middle of virtually nowhere, and was nearly trampled to death in the Moscow subway, but she made it, and stood on the Great Wall of China in Bejing. She says she never would have survived this arduous trip without the help of the tour group she traveled with, who, charmed by her as everyone always is, and amazed at her courage to strike off on such a trip at the age of 78, took her under their wing and saw that she made it with the group. When she was back with us that Christmas, Ron took out the National Geographic Atlas and showed her on two pages spread out on the table how far she had traveled.

"Do you realize that at that latitude you traveled a third of the way around the globe?" he asked her.

"Really? I never thought about it. I just knew I wanted to see those things and that was the way to do it. I just bought the ticket and went. It was an amazing journey. If I had known beforehand how difficult it would be, I never would have done it. But I am glad I didn't know. I wouldn't have missed it for the world."

In 2011, Pat planned her trips to America around Aaron's graduation in May from Marquette, where he had earned his master's degree, and Melody's wedding to Tim Santos in October. She was here for both events, and again for the holidays. In 2012 she wasn't able to get to us until November, so we celebrated Thanksgiving and Christmas— "Thanksgiving-Mas," Melody dubbed it—together as a family. In 2013, since she was not able to come to us, we went to her. Ron and I returned from a visit to her just last week, as I sit here at the Hermitage putting the finishing touches on this book about Pat and our unique friendship. We hope she will come to us in 2014, and that our story will continue. For my part, I was grateful to catch up with her family in England, who are like family to us, see her new place, meet the new friends who have become so important to her, and see her new garden. For wherever Pat goes, she plants something.

After 29 years, she has a permanent place in our family. She is still my children's "English grandmother," and my mother calls Pat her "English sister." Her youngest son, Patrick, and I are as close as brother and sister, and we talk, text, and e-mail regularly. Pat is so beloved here among our family and friends that everyone looks forward to her visits. When she's here, I joke that I become her social secretary as the invitations pour in! Who would ever have thought such a thing could happen way back in 1979? Who knew that September third would become such a prominent date in both of our lives?

There is an old saying that goes, "If you want to make God laugh, tell her your plans." The way I see it now, the very best parts of life happen when you have planned something else. I have no doubt that Pat will navigate the new territory of her life as she has all the others. And I expect to hear soon where her next voyage will be.

Pat standing on the Great Wall of China, Beijing, June 2, 2010. After the tour group finished in Beijing, Pat had arranged to stay on her own for a few more days. She hired a local guide and a driver, and was able to see the major sights of the city, including a visit to a Chinese home and a ride in a rickshaw.

Glossary of British Words and Phrases

Air raid wardens—were volunteers who worked to ensure the black-outs were observed and shelters were constructed, and helped in cases of emergencies.

Balaklava hat—covered the face with holes for eyes and sometimes the mouth.

Biscuits—cookies

Bomb shelters—included Anderson Shelters (named after the Home Secretary of the time), tables that could be used for cover, under the stairs in houses, and street shelters where people could run if they had no other place during an bombing raid.

Boiler suits—one-piece workers' coveralls

Boxing Day—the day after Christmas is still celebrated as a holiday in Britain. It comes from the tradition of having a box at the back of the church in which to put offerings for the poor. Priests opened the boxes on the 26th of December—St. Stephen's Day—and distributed the contents to those in need. This was sometimes called the "dole of the Christmas Box" or "box money," so the day came to be called Boxing Day. In more recent times, it is the day that tradesmen and workers would expect tips from customers or employers in a Christmas box.

Christmas pantomime—a theater show for children always held around Christmastime that traditionally featured a prince, a princess, and a wolf!

Cornish pasty—a delicious meat-and-potato-filled folded-over pastry that traditionally was carried by the tin miners of Cornwall into the mines so they would have a midday meal they could eat like a sandwich without coming back up out of the mines. Now they can be purchased in bakeries, pubs, and cafés and still make a hearty lunch or picnic.

Cot—baby's crib or bed; also refers to folding camp-type beds.

Cricket/cricket pitch/wickets—a popular game similar to American baseball. The "pitch" is the field and wickets are used as markers.

Doctor Bernardo's Homes—a charitable organization providing shelter for disabled or other hard-to-place children.

Dressing gown—bathrobe

Flannel—facecloth

Fortnight—two weeks

Jumper—sweater that goes over the head, a pullover (with buttons or zipper, it's a cardigan).

Land Army/Land Girls—civilians who came out to the farms to help with planting and harvests. Many were young women who took the places of men who were drafted or had enlisted in the military.

Local Defense Volunteers—a voluntary service organized to be the last line of defense in case of an enemy invasion. It consisted mainly of men who were either too old to serve in the regular forces (in some cases, veterans of the First World War) or who were disqualified from military service for health or employment reasons. (Men who worked in areas necessary to the war effort, such as farming, or factories that produced war materials, were exempt from the draft.) Prime Minister Winston

Churchill later renamed it the Home Guard.

Loft—attic space under the roof of a house

Lorry—truck

Nappy—diaper

Oxo—a brand name but used generally to describe all bouillon cubes that dissolve in boiling water to make broth

Pavement—sidewalk

Pegging out the wash—hanging clothes on a clothesline

Pegs—clothespins

Pinafore—apron

Pompey—nickname for Portsmouth

Pram—baby or doll's carriage

Privy—an outside non-flush toilet

Pushchair—a baby stroller

Removal van—moving van

Rock cakes—delicious dropped scones with dried fruit such as raisins or dates.

Rounders—a popular game similar to American softball played in Pat's day mostly by girls. Pat was very good at it!

Rucksack—backpack

Running boards—the step-like footboards of cars and trucks

Tea—for working-class families, refers not just to the beverage but to the evening meal. In upper-class homes, "tea" would be what we Americans think of as the British custom of cakes, cookies, and little sandwiches with the crusts cut off, served with a cup of tea at about four o'clock, followed by an evening meal, dinner, served around 7 or 8 p.m. In ordinary homes, "tea" would be followed by "supper" of a light snack sometime before bedtime.

Tins—cans

Torch—flashlight

Wireless—radio

Women's Institute—a national charitable organization of women who perform community service.

WRNS—Women's Royal Naval Service

Workhouse—a place where people were sent when they couldn't pay their debts or were homeless. They were often dreary old factory-like shelters that required people to work for their keep.

Bibliography

Interviews

• Patricia Phillips North, interviews with the author: tape recordings 26 Feb. 1996, Gardiner, Maine; 24 Sept. 1997, Winchester; notes 18 Oct. 1996, Bramdean, Cheriton and Winchester; 21 Oct. 1996, Portsmouth; Oct. 1997, Winchester. **Note:** We also had her father's service records, found among John's papers by his wife.

• Ray Bolwell, interview with the author, tape recording, 24 Oct. 1996, Abberley, Worcestershire. Mr. Bolwell was evacuated from Kentish-town, in Northwest London to Great Chissell in Hampshire, about 40 miles away, in November of 1939.

• Warren Grimes, interview with the author, notes, 25 Oct. 1996, in Arley Kings, Worcestershire. Mr. Grimes was evacuated from Birmingham to a small family farm near the village of Abberley, early in 1939.

• George Rovai, interview with the author, notes, 25 Oct. 1997, Winchester. Mr. Rovai was evacuated from London with his entire school, St. Jude's, in the "first wave," August of 1939, to the village of Collarton, Devonshire.

• Mrs. George Jones, interview with the author, tape recording, 24 Oct.

1996, Abberley. Mrs. Jones hosted evacuees.

• Mrs. Beaman, interview with the author, tape recording, 26 Oct. 1996, Abberley. Mrs. Beaman hosted evacuees.

• Phillipa Stevens, Local History Librarian, interview with the author and Patricia Phillips North, 17 Oct. 1996, Hampshire County Library, Winchester.

Museums/Archives/City Records

• City of Portsmouth, Records of the Corporation, 1936–1945, compiled by G.E. Barnett and V. Blanchard.

• Imperial War Museum, London.

• Portsmouth Library, local history archives.

• Royal Marines Museum, Southsea, Portsmouth.

Audio Sources

• BBC Wireless Collection: The Second World War, Original Recordings from the BBC Sound Archives. Compiled and produced by Mark Jones, Alison Johnston, and William Grierson, 1985.

• "Goodnight Children Everywhere," by Gaby Rogers and Harry Phillips (published by Edward Kassner Music Company Limited) from Vera Lynn's "Yours: A Collection of Sentimental Favorites," 1995, Pickwick Group, Limited.

• Music and comedy of the war period, 1995, 50th anniversary celebrations, by BBC Television, from videotapes by Peter North.

Books

Bilson, Geoffrey. *The Guest Children.* Saskatoon, Saskatchewan, Canada: Fifth House, 1988.

Britain, Vera. *Testament of Experience.* London: Victor Gollancz, 1957.

————. *England's Hour.* London: Futura Books, 1981.

Brown, Mike. *Evacuees: Evacuation in Wartime Britain 1939–1945.* Gloucestershire, England: Sutton Publishing Ltd., 2005.

Cavendish, Marshall. *The War Years 1939–1945: Eyewitness Accounts.* London: Marshall Cavendish Books, 1994.

Churchill, Winston S. *Memoirs of the Second World War.* (An abridgement of the six volumes of *The Second World War.*) Boston: Houghton Mifflin, 1959.

Collier, Richard. *1940: The World in Flames.* Harmondsworth: Penguin Books, 1980.

Crosby, Travis L. *The Impact of Civilian Evacuation in the Second World War.* London: Croom Helm, 1986.

Doughty, Martin, Ed. *Hampshire and D-Day.* Hampshire, England: Hampshire Books, for Hampshire County Council, 1994.

Felton, Monica. *Civilian Supplies in Wartime Britain.* London: Department of Printed Books, Imperial War Museum, 1997; reprinted from British Ministry of Information Series, *British Achievements of the War Years.*

Goodman, Susan. *Children of War.* London: John Murray Publishers, 2005.

Harris, Carol. *Women at War 1939–1945: The Home Front.* Gloucestershire: Sutton Publishing Ltd., 2000.

Inglis, Ruth. *The Children's War, Evacuation 1939–1945*. London: William Collins and Sons Company Limited. 1989.

Isaacs, Susan, ed. *The Cambridge Evacuation Survey: A Wartime Study in Social Welfare and Education*. London: Methuen and Company, 1941.

Jackson, Carlton. *Who Will Take Our Children?* London: Methuen, 1985.

Johnson, B. S., ed. *The Evacuees*. London: Victor Gollancz, 1968.

Massey, Virginia. *One Child's War*. London: Ariel Books, 1978.

Millgate, Helen D. *Got Any Gum, Chum? GIs in Wartime Britain, 1942–1945*.
Gloucestershire: Sutton Publishing Ltd, 2001.

Minns, Raynes. *Bombers and Mash: The Domestic Front 1939–45*. London: Virago Press, 1999.

Peake, Nigel. *City at War*. Portsmouth, England: Milestone Publications, in conjunction with *The News*, Hilsea, Portsmouth, 1986.

Robins, Phil. *War Children: The Second World War in Their Own Words*. London: Scholastic Ltd., in association with the Imperial War Museum, 2005.

Stevenson, John. *British Society, 1914–1945*. Harmondsworth: Penguin Books, 1984.

Titmus, Richard A. *Problems of Social Planning: History of the Second World War*. London: Her Majesty's Stationery Office, 1950.

Wicks, Ben. *No Time To Wave Goodbye: The True Story of Britain's Wartime Evacuees*. New York: St. Martin's Press, 1988.

———. *The Day They Took the Children*. Toronto: Stoddart Publishing Company Limited, 1989.

Books for Young People

Marx, Trish. *Echoes of World War II*. Minneapolis: Lerner Publications, 1984.

Reynoldson, Fiona. *The Home Front, 1939–1945: Evacuation*. East Sussex. Wayland Publishers Limited, 1980.

Westall, Robert. *Children of the Blitz: Memories of Wartime Childhood*. Harmondsworth: Penguin Books, 1985.

The author, Gay Grant, with Pat in 2007. Photo by Gail Parker

About the Author

GAY M. GRANT owns and operates The Write Way consulting service, through which she has secured millions of dollars in grants for Maine nonprofits, and helped clients tell their own stories. She is the author of *Along the Kennebec: The Herman Bryant Collection* (Arcadia Publishers), and her articles have appeared in local newspapers and historical publications. Inspired by her participation in the University of Southern Maine's exchange program with King Alfred's College in England in 1979, she has traveled frequently to that country to visit friends and to research this book. Grant is serving her first term in the Maine House of Representatives and lives with her husband, Ron, in South Gardiner, Maine.